How the World Became Rich

Mark: For Desiree.

Jared: To my father, Thom, and the memory of my mother, Linda.

How the World Became Rich

The Historical Origins of Economic Growth

Mark Koyama
Jared Rubin

polity

First published in 2022 by Polity Press

13

Polity Press
65 Bridge Street
Cambridge CB2 1UR, UK

Polity Press
101 Station Landing
Suite 300
Medford, MA 02155, USA

ISBN-13: 978-1-5095-4022-8
ISBN-13: 978-1-5095-4023-5 (pb)

A catalogue record for this book is available from the British Library.

Library of Congress Control Number: 2021944393

Typeset in 10.5 on 13pt Swift
by Cheshire Typesetting Ltd, Cuddington, Cheshire
Printed and bound in Great Britain by CPI Group (UK) Ltd, Croydon

The publisher has used its best endeavours to ensure that the URLs for external websites referred to in this book are correct and active at the time of going to press. However, the publisher has no responsibility for the websites and can make no guarantee that a site will remain live or that the content is or will remain appropriate.

For further information on Polity, visit our website:
politybooks.com

Contents

Tables and Figures   vi
Preface   ix

 1 Why, When, and How Did the World Become Rich?   1

Part I Theories of How the World Became Rich

 2 Did Some Societies Win the Geography Lottery?   19
 3 Is It All Just Institutions?   37
 4 Did Culture Make Some Rich and Others Poor?   66
 5 Fewer Babies?   88
 6 Was It Just a Matter of Colonization and Exploitation?   104

**Part II Why Some Parts of the World Became Rich First,
       Why Other Parts Followed, and Why Some Are Not There Yet**

 7 Why Did Northwestern Europe Become Rich First?   129
 8 Britain's Industrial Revolution   149
 9 The Rise of the Modern Economy   176
10 Industrialization and the World It Created   198
11 The World Is Rich   222

References   226
Index   250

Tables and Figures

Tables

4.1	Most populous cities in Western Eurasia, 800 CE	76
5.1	Black Death mortality by country	94
6.1	English crop yields, 18th century	107
7.1	British borrowing and interest rates, 1693–1739	145
8.1	Most populous English cities excluding London (with populations of at least 10,000)	157
9.1	Major inventions of the Second Industrial Revolution	181

Figures

1.1	Countries that were richer in 2018 (annual per capita income) than the US in 1900	1
1.2	Countries that were richer in 2018 (annual per capita income) than Great Britain in 1800	2
1.3	People living in extreme poverty, 1820–2015	3
1.4	Year that per capita GDP exceeded $10 per day (2018 USD)	4
1.5	Yearly per capita income for selected regions, 1 CE–present	5
1.6	US GDP per capita, 1720–2018 (2018 USD)	7
1.7	Ruggedness and income in African and non-African countries	12
1.8	The reversal of fortunes within formerly colonized nations, 1500–1995	13
2.1	Coastlines of African countries	20
2.2	Africa's "malaria belt"	21
2.3	Verticality and horizontality of the continents	23
2.4	Technology adoption levels in 1500 (% of frontier technologies adopted)	24
2.5	Temperature deviations across Europe, 1100–1800	26
2.6	The Roman road network	28
2.7	The increase in turnpikes in England and Wales: 1680–1830	30
2.8	Changes in US market access, 1870–90	31

2.9	Location of cities in England and France in the Roman and medieval periods	33
2.10	The price of energy in the early 1700s	34
3.1	Rule of law vs. per capita GDP	39
3.2	Night lights on the Korean Peninsula	40
3.3	Rule of law index, 2017	42
3.4	The first(?) formal legal system: the Code of Hammurabi	44
3.5	Legal origins throughout the world	47
3.6	Polity score, 2017	48
3.7	Democracy score, 2017	48
3.8	Parliamentary activity in Europe, 1100–1800	59
3.9	Tax revenues per capita for six European powers, 1500–1900	61
3.10	Interest rates in city-states and territorial states, 1200–1800	63
4.1	Subcultures of the US	67
4.2	Percentage Protestant, Catholic, and Muslim vs. per capita GDP	72
4.3	Percentage of Protestants vs. school enrollment rate in early 19th-century Prussia	74
4.4	Ruler duration in Western Europe and the Islamic world	79
4.5	The north–south Italy divide: cousin marriage, trust, and judicial efficiency	81
4.6	The relationship between trust and per capita GDP	84
4.7	Traditional plow use, female labor force participation, and female firm ownership	86
5.1	Life expectancy around the world, 2015	89
5.2	The Malthusian model	90
5.3	The Malthusian model: illustrating the effects of reducing the birth rate	91
5.4	Black Death mortality rates (%) in 1347–52	93
5.5	Population and wages in England, 1209–1750	97
5.6	Fertility and female age of marriage in England, 1590s–1830s	98
6.1	Countries colonized by Great Britain, France, Spain, Portugal, the Netherlands, or Belgium, 1500–1950	107
6.2	Number of slaves in the transatlantic slave trade by carrier	109
6.3	Number of slaves taken in the slave trades	110
6.4	The relationship between slaves exported and economic indicators	112
6.5	Africa's ethnic boundaries prior to colonization	113
6.6	Settler mortality, institutions, and long-run development	115
6.7	Agricultural investment in India	118
6.8	Ethnic partitioning and the "scramble for Africa"	119
6.9	The Indian railroad network, 1930	121
6.10	Modern literacy and proximity to Jesuit missions in Argentina, Brazil, and Paraguay	124
7.1	The steppe and state formation in China and Europe	133

7.2   Real per capita GDP, 1450–1700, select countries   142
8.1   GDP, GDP per capita, and population in England/Britain,
      1270–1870 (1700 = 100)   150
8.2   England and its largest cities, 1520–1801   157
8.3   The spinning jenny   165
8.4   Arkwright's water frame   167
8.5   Crompton's spinning mule   167
8.6   Schematic of the Newcomen steam engine   169
8.7   The Watt steam engine   170
8.8   Number of letters in Voltaire's correspondence in the Republic
      of Letters, 1755–76   172
9.1   GDP per capita and real wages in England/Great Britain,
      1270–1870 (1700 = 100)   178
9.2   Fertility and mortality in England, 1541–1839   183
9.3   Children born per woman in Western Europe and the US,
      1800–2000   184
9.4   Human capital and the demographic transition in England,
      1730–1890   186
9.5   Shares of world industrial output, 1750–1938   191
9.6   US population and immigrant share, 1850–2010   195
10.1 Per capita GDP in select Asian countries, 1960–2019   199
10.2 Percentage of Indians living in extreme poverty, 1977–2011   202
10.3 Per capita GDP in England/Great Britain and Japan, 1280–1850   203
10.4 Per capita GDP in South Korea and Nigeria, 1960–2019   207
10.5 Per capita GDP in various parts of the world, 1960–2019   208
10.6 Chinese per capita GDP, 1960–2019   212

Preface

The world is rich, although it may not always seem like it. Poverty is still all too prevalent. Approximately one billion people around the world barely have enough to survive. The fate of millions of people living in poverty and violence in places like Venezuela, Syria, Burundi, or the Democratic Republic of Congo is deplorable. Even in the developed world, poverty is far, far too common.

Yet, by historical standards, the world is very rich. Most people are much better off than their ancestors were. In fact, most people living right now are better off than almost every person who ever lived prior to two centuries ago (save a very small fraction of elites who lived in luxury ... or what was considered luxury at the time). As the world has become richer in the 20th and 21st centuries, more and more people have been lifted out of poverty. And there is good reason to hope that, within our lifetimes, a significant fraction of the remaining poverty around the world will be eliminated.

How did the world become rich? This is the question this book attempts to answer. It is by no means easy to do so. In fact, there is almost certainly no one correct answer! Yet, it remains perhaps the biggest question in the social sciences. A proper understanding of why certain parts of the world have become rich – and others have not (yet) – can help us tackle some of the biggest problems facing us in the present. As you read this book, it will soon become clear that there is no panacea to lift a country into riches. However, there are many factors that historically tend to be present alongside sustained economic growth. It is our goal to both highlight these factors and provide insight into when they do and do not contribute to growth.

Throughout this book, we draw on an immense and fast-growing scholarship in global economic history. The first half of our book is mostly meant to be an overview of what we consider to be the leading theories for how the world became rich. Our debts to this scholarship are evident throughout. Naturally, as this book is addressed to a broad audience, we have not been able to cite every piece of specialist research. We apologize in advance for any omissions. We do, however, direct the reader towards the relevant literature wherever possible.

Many people helped us along the way. We cannot possibly thank everyone without this Preface taking up half the book. Sascha Becker, Desiree Desierto, Anton Howes, Nathan Nunn, Tuan-Hwee Sng, Felipe Valencia Caicedo, and John

Wallis read parts (or all!) of the book. Their insightful comments helped us significantly improve the manuscript. Our editor at Polity, George Owers, gave excellent guidance at each step of the process. Dan Bogart, Dave Donaldson, Erik Hornung, Noel Johnson, and Jonathan Schulz shared their data files so that we could produce some of the figures in this book. Mark thanks his many coauthors, from whom he has learned a tremendous amount over the years. Jared will always be indebted to Avner Greif, Timur Kuran, Larry Iannaccone, and Ran Abramitzky – the best mentors, coauthors, and friends he could hope for.

Much of this book was written while we were quarantined on opposite coasts of the US due to COVID-19. We would like to thank the people who helped us get through that time – without them, this book would not be possible. For Mark, these include his wife and frequent collaborator Desiree, his parents Ninette and Noboru, and his brother Jonathan. For Jared, these include his family – Thom, Debbie, and Tyler Rubin and Samantha and Ryan Sully – and friends Rob Ainsley, Ted Chang, Doug Haney, Matt Menefee, Travis Menefee, Scott Shumate, and JJ Singh. Most of all, Jared is indebted to his amazing wife Tina and their two beautiful children, Nadia and Sasha.

1

Why, When, and How Did the World Become Rich?

The world is rich. Certainly, some parts of the world are richer than others, and many millions still live in poverty. But the world is richer than it has ever been, and it continues to grow richer with each passing day.

Don't believe us? Let's compare income around the world today to some of the wealthiest countries in the past. Figure 1.1 maps all of the countries with greater per capita income in 2018 than the *wealthiest country in the world* in 1900: the United States. The average income in much of the world is now greater than the average income in the world's richest country just over a century ago. The startling level of modern wealth comes into even clearer focus when compared to the wealthiest country in 1800: Great Britain (see Figure 1.2). Almost every nation in the world, with some exceptions, mostly in sub-Saharan Africa, has a greater average income than the world's leading economy just two centuries ago.

Modern wealth of course extends well beyond average incomes. Even in many of the poorest parts of the world, we have luxuries that our ancestors could

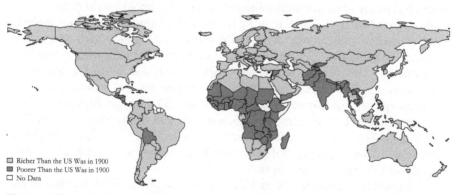

Figure 1.1 Countries that were richer in 2018 (annual per capita income) than the US in 1900

Data source: Bolt and van Zanden (2020). Average income in the US in 1900 was $8,970 in 2011 USD.

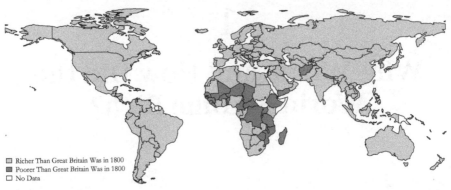

Figure 1.2 Countries that were richer in 2018 (annual per capita income) than Great Britain in 1800

Data source: Bolt and van Zanden (2020). Average income in Great Britain in 1800 was $3,731 in 2011 USD.

have only dreamed of. Forget about smartphones and flat-screen TVs – even our richest ancestors would have been jealous of our indoor plumbing, electricity, vaccinations, low child mortality, and long life expectancy.

Think about it: would you trade your current life for the life of a wealthy English baron in, say, 1200? Sure, you would have servants, and you'd have the social and political benefits that come with being a member of the upper crust. But you would also live in a drafty, uncomfortable castle, and you would likely have multiple children die in infancy. And let's hope you didn't get a bad bout of diarrhea (you probably wouldn't survive). If you didn't die young on the battlefield, odds are you would die of some now-curable disease such as dysentery (which killed English kings John [r. 1199–1216] and Henry V [r. 1413–22]), smallpox (which killed French king Louis XV [r. 1715–74] and English queen Mary II [r. 1689–94]), or plague. Some of us might trade our current lot for that of the baron, but many of us (including the authors of this book) would not.

We are not heartless. There is still a tremendous amount of extreme poverty in the world. We appreciate that the *entire* world is not actually "rich" by current or historical standards. But the fact of the matter is that extreme poverty is in rapid decline. This decline began two centuries ago and it has accelerated in recent decades. The trends, summarized in Figure 1.3, are striking. Just two centuries ago, 94% of the world lived on less than $2 a day (in 2016 prices), and 84% lived on less than $1 a day. By 2015, less than 10% of the world lived on less than $1.90 a day, and that number continues to decline. To be clear, 10% of the world is still a lot of people. But as the world continues to become richer, that number will dwindle all the more.

It's not just that there has been a reduction in absolute poverty as the world has grown wealthier. More and more of the world has moved further from the edge of subsistence in the last century. Take, for instance, the relatively arbitrary milestone of $10 per day in 2018 USD. This is not much: $3,650 per year is

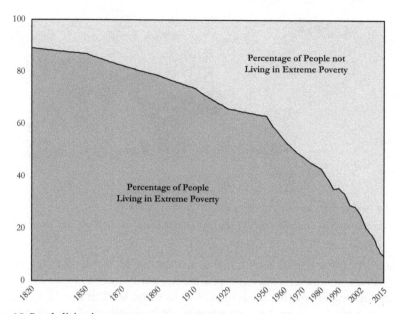

Figure 1.3 People living in extreme poverty, 1820–2015

Data source: Roser (2021c). For the sake of this figure, extreme poverty is defined as less than $1.90 per day.

hardly a king's ransom. However, in most economies it is more than enough to afford the basics of life (food, shelter, clothing, etc.). This is even more true in relatively poor countries, where modest housing and food can be had cheaply. Figure 1.4 shows when each country reached this milestone. It represents a level of security unknown throughout most of human history.

How did the world become rich? Why are some so rich and others so poor? This book provides some answers to these questions. The answers are by no means obvious, and they are the subject of much debate among economists, historians, and other academics. This is reflective of just how important the questions are. To alleviate poverty, we must understand wealth. We still do not have all the answers, but enough strides have been made that we can dedicate a book to answering the question: "What do we know about how the world became rich?"

What Is Economic Growth?

Throughout most of world history, a vast majority of the world's population – well above 90% – was poor. Whether your ancestors are from China, India, Africa, Europe, the Middle East, or elsewhere, the odds are very high that most of them lived on little more than a few dollars a day. That is clearly no longer

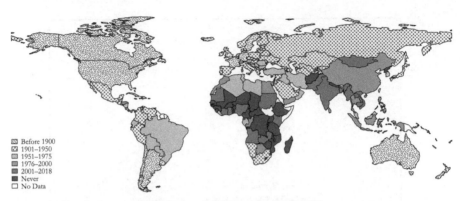

Before 1900
1901–1950
1951–1975
1976–2000
2001–2018
Never
No Data

Figure 1.4 Year that per capita GDP exceeded $10 per day (2018 USD)

Data source: Bolt and van Zanden (2020). Italy reached $10/day sporadically in the 15th century.

the case. As shown in Figure 1.3, the proportion of the world's population living in extreme poverty has dropped precipitously in the last two centuries. Most of the readers of this book likely live in some level of comfort, and even our poorest readers would be the envy of their ancestors. After all, they can read! How did the world get to this point?

On the surface, the answer to this question is simple: the last two centuries have seen more *economic growth* than the rest of human history combined. Economic growth refers to a sustained increase in economic prosperity as measured by the total goods and services produced in the economy (commonly referred to as gross domestic product, or GDP). We care about economic growth not because it is an end in itself, but because it is the key to alleviating the type of poverty experienced by almost everyone who lived prior to 1800, and that still plagues way too large of a share of the world's population today.

Our focus on economic growth does not mean that we don't value other aspects of human development. Leisure time, long life, good health, literacy, education, female empowerment, and rights and protections for the vulnerable are all central to having a happy and fair society. That said, we hope to convince you by the end of this book that all of these features *are made possible by economic growth*. It is no coincidence that the last 200 years have seen dramatic strides in those very aspects of human development. Even though there is clearly a long way to go to achieve the type of society that most of us want, economic growth will be a key part of the solution.

Economic growth on its own is not necessarily a panacea. It can be accompanied by environmental degradation, increased inequality, or worsening health outcomes. For instance, air quality declined and life expectancy fell during the British Industrial Revolution. Today, issues such as climate change and social polarization are among the most important challenges that policy-makers face. The point that deserves emphasis here is that economic growth makes available the resources and the new technologies needed to tackle these important challenges. Of course, humanity actually needs to employ these resources to address these challenges. But in the absence of economic growth, we may not have such an opportunity.

It is a mistake to think that we *necessarily* have to choose between economic growth and other values (such as preserving the environment). For example, a more unstable climate poses potentially catastrophic risks to our society. Yet, we've seen in recent years that measures to reduce carbon emissions can be accompanied by economic growth. The UK, for example, saw carbon emissions fall by 38% between 1990 and 2017, from 600 million tonnes to 367 million tonnes (Hausfather, 2019). Meanwhile, total GDP (adjusted for inflation) increased by over 60% in the same period.

Nor do we necessarily have to choose between economic growth and a fairer society. In fact, a *lack* of economic growth has serious moral downsides. Historically, it is in stagnant or declining economies that one observes the worst episodes of violence, intolerance, and political polarization. On the other hand, social mobility and greater equality of opportunity are much more likely in an economy that is growing. As Friedman (2005, p. 86) puts it, stagnant economies "do not breed support for economic mobility, or for openness of opportunity more generally."

So, how has the world economy grown over time? Figure 1.5 gives some rough estimates of per capita GDP in the world's most populous regions since

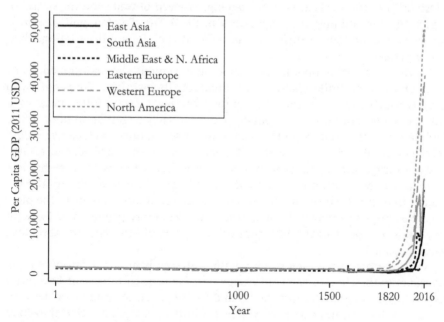

Figure 1.5 Yearly per capita income for selected regions, 1 CE–present
Data source: Bolt, Inklaar, de Jong, and van Zanden (2018).

the birth of Christ. While these numbers are admittedly speculative – and likely more volatile prior to the 18th century than the figure suggests – the pattern is clear (and uncontroversial). Prior to the 19th century, the *wealthiest* region in the world never reached more than $4 a day average (in 2011 USD). Throughout most of world history, $2–3 a day was the norm. Yes, there were fabulously wealthy people, and these societies produced some of the greatest art, architecture, and literature the world has known (pursuits not generally associated with people on the brink of starvation). These artists and authors are the people from the past you may be the most familiar with, since they are the ones who generally fill our history books. But this was not the lot of almost the entirety of humanity prior to the 19th century. The fact is that most people who ever lived – at least, prior to the 20th century – lived in conditions very similar to those of the very poorest in the world today. The economic growth of the last two centuries has alleviated a vast majority of this poverty, although the job is clearly not finished.

To be clear, there were spurts of economic improvement here and there in the past. Goldstone (2002) calls these "growth efflorescences." One such period of economic improvement occurred in classical Greece, where there was both population growth and an increase in living standards as measured by the size and quality of homes (Morris, 2005). Other episodes were due to political pacification, such as the "Pax Islamica" over large parts of the Middle East, North Africa, and the Iberian Peninsula in the centuries following the spread of Islam. The "Islamic Peace" permitted higher levels of trade and the spread of agricultural techniques and crops (Watson, 1983). The "Pax Mongolica," which allowed parts of Asia to thrive in the wake of the Mongol devastations, had similar effects.

Another cause of temporary economic improvement was widespread death through disease. While plagues were undoubtedly awful for the people who lived through them – in the 14th century, the Black Death killed between a third and a half of Europe's population and probably a similar amount in the Middle East – they did mean that there were fewer mouths to feed. Per capita income tended to rise for at least a few generations in the wake of these events. The most important cause of economic improvement, however, was technolog-ical change. New varieties of disease-resistant grains, new agricultural tech-niques that improved soil quality or irrigation, and improvements to the plow are all examples of new technologies that allowed more people to be fed with less labor. Yet, prior to the 18th century, all spurts of economic improvement were *temporary*.

What matters in the long run is whether growth is *sustained*. Sustained eco-nomic growth refers to the continuous positive growth rates that have been experienced by countries like the US and the UK since the middle of the 19th century. What is unique about developed countries today is not that they have experienced a rapid acceleration of economic growth (Hausmann, Pritchett, and Rodrik, 2005). Many countries that are poor today have experienced temporary

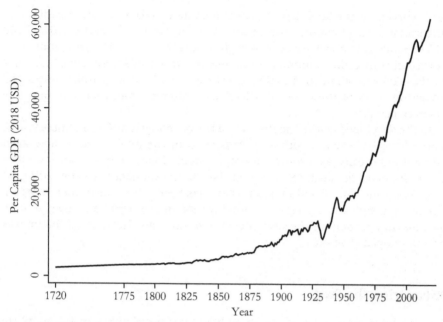

Figure 1.6 US GDP per capita, 1720–2018 (2018 USD)

Data source: Bolt and van Zanden (2020).

growth accelerations in the past as well. What distinguishes rich countries is that they have not experienced *growth reversals*. For instance, US GDP has grown fairly constantly since 1870 (Figure 1.6). Even the Great Depression – the one shock that does register in Figure 1.6 – only had a temporary impact on economic growth. The point is that prior to the first few decades of the 19th century, the continuous economic growth experienced by the UK, the US, and other developed economies in the past two centuries was all but unheard of. What was more common was periods of growth offset by periods of contraction, like that experienced by Venezuela between 2011 and 2021. Broadberry and Wallis (2017) call this "shrinkage". From this perspective, the main difference between rich and poor countries is not that rich countries grow fast during their periods of growth. Rich countries are those that have experienced fewer periods in which the economy has gotten smaller.

Sustained economic growth has been accompanied by a dramatic reorganization of society and production. This is what we refer to as *economic development*. By this we mean a fundamental and transformative restructuring of the economy associated with urbanization and the growth of non-agricultural sectors of the economy such as manufacturing and the service sector. This process of development was also associated with the emergence of new ways of organizing economic activity: factories, corporations, and stock markets. In contrast, before 1800, the majority of the population lived in the countryside and worked on the land. Sure, there was some variation in urbanization and the prominence of manufacturing or service sectors. In Italy between 0 and 200 CE, urbanization may have been as high as 30% (Wilson, 2011). Iron production soared in Song China. Commerce and long-distance trade were important parts of the economy of late medieval Venice, Bruges, and Antwerp. Nonetheless, the structure of all of these societies was vastly simpler than that of almost any modern economy.

In the developed world, the *structure* of the economy is different. Importantly, agriculture has shrunk both as a proportion of the total economy and, even more dramatically, as a source of employment. Today, only 1.3% of the labor force works on the farm in the US. In the UK, the number is smaller still (just 1%). Alongside this structural shift, there has been a transformation in organizational complexity. This is most notably seen in the rise of long-lived organizations independent of the state such as corporations. These are all hallmarks of a developed economy.

Measuring the Past

You might wonder: how do we know how poor people were in the past? No country had an office of national statistics collecting information and compiling GDP estimates until the mid-20th century. Instead, social scientists and historians have had to reconstruct the past. The first exercise of this kind was the pioneering work of Angus Maddison. He spent decades creating high-quality estimates of per capita GDP back to 1820 (Maddison, 1983, 1991, 2001). Maddison also produced a set of highly influential estimates for earlier periods, including estimates of per capita income at the regional level for the Roman Empire (Maddison, 2007). But these estimates were of much more questionable veracity. More recent work, including the Maddison project (Bolt and van Zanden, 2020) and the work of numerous scholars such as van Zanden and van Leeuwen (2012), Fouquet and Broadberry (2015), Broadberry, Guan, and Li (2018), and Palma and Reis (2019), has produced updated estimates of per capita GDP that are on a much firmer footing.

But GDP estimates are far from the only source of information we have on past economies. Since the 19th century, economic historians have been collecting information on wages and prices in order to produce estimates of how much an unskilled worker would have been able to purchase in the past. Owing to the work of Robert Allen, Jean-Pascal Bassino, Greg Clark, Charles Feinstein, Peter Lindert, Debin Ma, Jeffrey Williamson, and others, there now exist comprehensive estimates of the purchasing power of workers for a host of European and Asian cities. Allen's method is based on the construction of a consumption basket for a representative worker. These baskets are constructed by consulting numerous diaries and the budgets of poor houses and orphanages. A benefit of constructing consumption baskets is that it allows us to compare living standards across time and space, while remaining cognizant that people's preferences were different in different regions at different times. Whereas rice would have made up a large portion of the East Asian diet, grains or bread would take its place in Western Europe.

There are other measures we can use to assess living standards in the past. One common measure is height. Economic historians such as Jorg Baten, Robert Floud, Robert Fogel, and Richard Steckel have put together estimates of heights for many countries across many centuries (for an overview, see Steckel, 2009). Height is determined by several factors, including genetic endowments. Height is also influenced by in vitro conditions and the nutrition available to the mother during pregnancy and as a child. We observe a strong positive relationship between gains in height and per capita GDP in the past 200 years. People in the past were short. The mean height of an 18 year old in the English army between 1763 and 1767 was 160.76 cm (around 5'3") (Floud, Fogel, Harris, and Hong, 2011, p. 27). The increase in average height partly reflects the improvements in nutritional standards achieved since the onset of modern economic growth.

A final measure of the standard of living is life expectancy. Modern economic growth is associated with large increases in life expectancy (Pritchett and Summers, 1996; Fogel, 2004; Acemoglu and Johnson, 2007). This matters for two reasons. First, increased life expectancy represents a significant component of the additional welfare brought about by economic growth (Becker, Philipson, and Soares, 2005). Second, increased life expectancy is a possible cause of economic development itself. An increase in life expectancy increases the value of investment in human capital (Cervellati and Sunde, 2005), the term economists use to encompass education and other investments in an individual's productive capacity.

The answer to the question "How did the world become rich?" must explain where, when, and how human societies were able to achieve sustained economic growth. The where and the when we know the answer to: northwestern Europe and North America, in the early to mid-19th century. All of the metrics we discussed above agree on this point. It is the third question – *how* did the escape from stagnation happen – that is so vexing.

Understanding the origins of wealth is one of the most important pursuits of the social sciences, and for this reason it has been the center of much debate. The purpose of this book is to present and distill this debate. Ultimately, any credible hypothesis must be able to account for a number of facts. First, modern, sustained economic growth is the result of sustained technological innovation. Britain in the late 18th century experienced such a spate of innovations during the period known as the Industrial Revolution. Initially, economic growth was slow to follow. But unlike earlier episodes of economic growth, it did not peter out. By the mid-19th century, the rate of both innovation and economic growth accelerated as industrialization and structural economic change spread to other parts of the world. Why did this process first take hold in Britain? Why in the 18th century? Why not in some other part of the world? Second, Europe was an economic, technological, and cultural backwater around 1000 CE. What changed in that continent that allowed it to pull ahead of China, India, and the Middle East, all of which at one point had societies well ahead of even the most advanced societies in Western Europe?

What Will You Learn from This Book?

The goal of this book is to bring together the many social scientific theories on the origins of modern, sustained economic growth. This is a big issue with important implications, and unsurprisingly it has been the focus of many great minds. Almost all of these theories focus on one aspect of the origins of growth, such as geography, culture, institutions, colonialism, or demography. By construction, these arguments tend to ignore each other. We hardly fault the authors of the arguments for this. Building and substantiating a theory can take hundreds of pages. Delving into other, far-removed causes of long-run growth can make for a tough read. Most researchers understand this, and they understand the limits of their explanations. Many a successful career has been made by exploring just one aspect of the origins of modern wealth.

Yet, the emphasis on specific theories of "how the world became rich" has left two gaps in our knowledge. This book hopes to fill these. First, no existing work summarizes all of the advances that have been made by social scientists in the last few decades in a dispassionate, objective fashion. While we do have opinions on what we view as the most convincing hypotheses regarding the origins of sustained economic growth – we have both written on this topic in our own academic work – the goal of this book is not to privilege our preferred theories at the expense of others. The first half of this book simply presents, as objectively as possible, the major hypotheses and debates on the origins of sustained economic growth. If it were not for our book, a reader who wants to get an idea of the current state of the literature would have to read countless books and articles, each putting forth their own hypotheses. This is still a useful exercise, as there is much nuance that we will have to skip over. But presumably most of our readers have lives outside of reading academic tracts. If you want to get an idea of where the debates stand, we've done the time-consuming part for you.

The first half of the book classifies and surveys the major strands of literature related to the origins of sustained economic growth: geography, politics, institutions, markets and states, culture, human capital, demography, and colonization. Many explanations fall into multiple categories. Likewise, some are well suited for one time and place but not for others. For instance, coal deposits likely played a role in Britain's rise but not Japan's, religion may have played a role in the Middle East's economic growth but not in China's, and so on. In some cases, factors that hamper economic growth under some conditions favor it in others. Take, for instance, the ruggedness of the African terrain. In general, ruggedness is bad for prosperity. Rugged terrain is difficult to traverse (thus hampering trade) and difficult to farm. However, in Africa, Nunn and Puga (2012) find that ruggedness had a *positive* effect on income. This was because it mitigated the impact of the slave trade: rugged terrain was more difficult for raiders to traverse and easier for those pursued to hide within. Long-run economic growth, on which the slave trade had such a large negative effect (a fact we will cover in Chapter 6), was thus indirectly promoted (see Figure 1.7).

Most theories on the origins of economic growth are concerned with pushing one side of the debate. As a result, less attention has been given to how the various theories are *connected*. A phenomenon as important and widespread as the origin of modern economic growth is almost certainly not monocausal. For example, many theories attempt to account for the role that institutions played in economic growth. Institutions are those legal, political, and religious features of a society that determine the "rules of the game" which dictate the costs and benefits of taking certain actions. Some institutions are viewed as being good for economic growth, such as those that protect property rights, encourage investment in public goods, and apply laws equally to all people. Yet, where "good institutions" come from is a difficult question to answer. Sometimes, they come from geographic conditions. For instance, where geographic conditions were not suitable for exploitation, colonial powers tended to invest in institutional development that, perhaps for unintended reasons, had positive effects on long-run growth (Acemoglu, Johnson, and Robinson, 2001, 2002). In fact, Acemoglu, Johnson, and Robinson (2002) argue that this resulted in a "reversal of fortunes": those places that were flush with natural endowments at the end of the medieval period were also the places that were most easily exploited. As a result, those places tended to get worse (colonial) institutions, and are largely poorer today. The reversal is seen in Figure 1.8, which plots urbanization rates (an indicator of economic potential) against modern per capita GDP. Past urbanization rates are negatively correlated with modern income, while modern urbanization rates are positively correlated with income. Geography alone cannot explain this pattern, although geography may have *worked through* institutions to create the reversal of fortunes.

In other cases, institutions may operate through their impact on culture to affect economic growth. For instance, in a study of the long-term developments of trust, Nunn and Wantchekon (2011) find that places in Africa that were more prone to slave raids in the past are less trusting in the *present day*. It is understandable why people in the past who were subject to slave raids would be mistrusting of others, even neighbors, who may have wanted to enslave them. The fact that a culture of mistrust persists to the present suggests that culture is "sticky," and thus helps determine long-run economic fortunes.

Throughout the book, we draw on the most up-to-date social scientific research and data in the context of recent debates among economic historians,

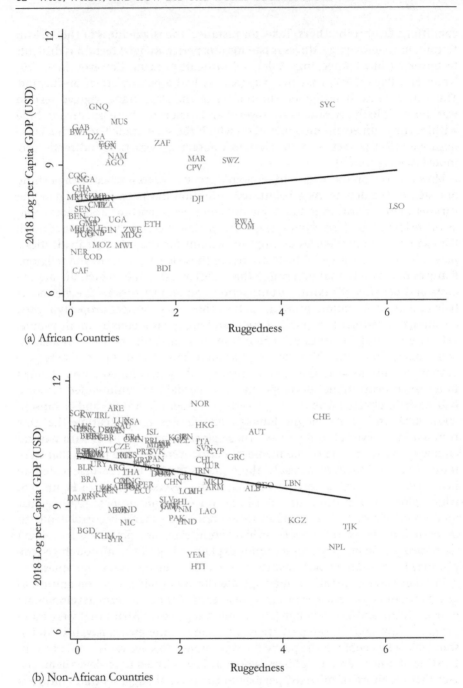

Figure 1.7 Ruggedness and income in African and non-African countries

Data sources: Nunn and Puga (2012) for ruggedness, Bolt and van Zanden (2020) for GDP per capita.

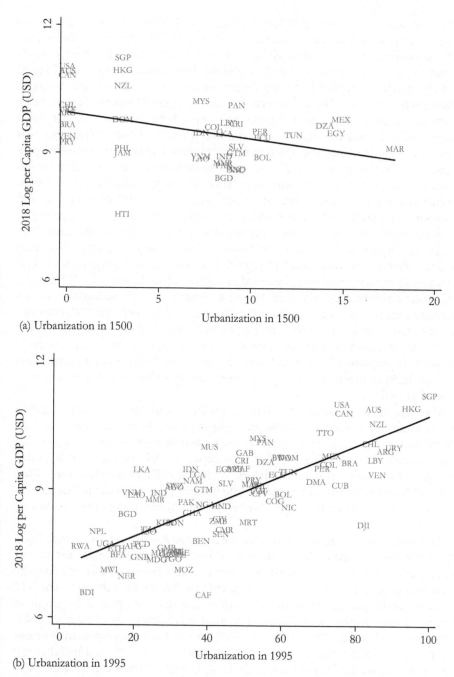

(a) Urbanization in 1500

(b) Urbanization in 1995

Figure 1.8 The reversal of fortunes within formerly colonized nations, 1500–1995

Data sources: Acemoglu, Johnson, and Robinson (2002) for urbanization, Bolt and van Zanden (2020) for GDP per capita.

development economists, political scientists, and historical sociologists. One important development in the past twenty years is that discussions of the origins of economic growth have gone global. It is no longer sufficient to narrow one's attention to Great Britain or Western Europe. For instance, one of the biggest debates in the literature is on the origins of the "Great Divergence" between Western Europe and China. The term "Great Divergence" was made famous by Pomeranz (2000), who argued that the divergence between China and the West happened relatively late (after 1750) and was a result of the existence of coal reserves in England and the opening up of the New World, which relieved population pressures and provided new and abundant raw materials. This view has been subject to much debate, with new data suggesting the divergence may have occurred prior to industrialization (Allen, Bassino, Ma, Moll-Murata, and van Zanden, 2011; Brandt, Ma, and Rawski, 2014; Broadberry, Guan, and Li, 2018).

In the final chapters, we assess the relative strengths and weaknesses of the major arguments and lay out the ones we find the most convincing. Our focus shifts to Britain, the home of the Industrial Revolution, and ultimately the first country to achieve modern, sustained economic growth. We ask, "What were the preconditions that made sustained economic growth possible in northwestern Europe?" We then address the flip-side of this question: "Why did sustained economic growth not first happen elsewhere?" Next we delve into the Industrial Revolution itself, as well as its connection to sustained economic growth. We explore what we find to be the most convincing explanations of its causes, linking these back to the broader sources of sustained, long-run economic growth.

The first set of explanations that we prefer – both for the onset of industrialization and for modern economic growth – emphasize the link between economic and *political* development. Such explanations touch on topics like institutional change, the growth of state capacity, and the rule of law. In our reading of the literature and of history, we find it difficult to tell a compelling story of long-run economic growth while ignoring the role that political institutions played in encouraging or (more often than not) dampening economic growth.

The second set of explanations that we find convincing are those that highlight the role of culture. To be clear, we do not mean the type of Eurocentric explanations popular in the early 20th century that made claims regarding the supremacy of some aspect of European culture. We mean culture in the way cultural anthropologists use the term: those heuristics employed by people to interpret the complex world around them (Cavalli-Sforza and Feldman, 1981; Boyd and Richerson, 1985; Henrich, 2015). Recent scholarship demonstrates that culture is amenable to serious social scientific study. Several insights can be gleaned from this line of research. First, cultural values can be extremely persistent (Guiso, Sapienza, and Zingales, 2006; Nunn, 2012). Second, cultural values interact with institutional development (Greif, 1994, 2006; Alesina and Giuliano, 2015; Bisin and Verdier, 2017).

In the penultimate chapter, we consider the "Great Convergence" between the many parts of the rest of the world and the West. One of the great stories of the last half-century is the *billions* of people pulled out of abject poverty. China has been a huge source of this economic progress, but so have many parts of South Asia, Southeast Asia, and Latin America. As we write this book, another half a billion or so people in India seem on the brink of escaping absolute poverty. In fact, the last twenty years have been characterized by faster economic growth in poor countries than in rich countries (Patel, Sandefur, and Subramanian, 2021). The time horizon might be a little longer for sub-Saharan Africa and the poorest countries in Latin America and Central Asia, but there is reason to be optimistic that we will experience a further dramatic eradication of poverty in those regions in our lifetime. All of this would be impossible without economic growth.

Just because we find some explanations for how the world became rich more compelling than others does not mean that the other theories have little merit. In fact, we believe there are important insights in all of the theories outlined in this book. In the end, we need to remember that an issue as wide-ranging as "how the world became rich" almost certainly has many causes. Intelligent people can and will disagree on what weight to put on each of these causes. What matters most is understanding the conditions under which certain causes are important and the conditions under which they are not. It is our hope that this book will provide a better understanding of these conditions.

What This Book Does Not Do

For all we are attempting to accomplish with this book, we want to be clear about a few things we will not do. First, our goal is to present all of the major arguments on "how the world got rich" in a fair-minded fashion. This means that, when initially presenting the theories, we will do our best to not let our own biases creep in. We certainly have views on the various issues presented in the book, and we do think that some views are more convincing than others. The later chapters of the book lay out the reasons we believe some of the proposed causes in the literature have greater explanatory power than others. However, we aim to give each of the main explanations a fair shake and present them, to the best of our ability, the way that the authors of the theories would want them presented.

This book is thematic and conceptual. We elucidate the major themes running through the academic literature and contextualize them in a digestible manner. As such, we won't present a comprehensive economic history of specific countries. Such histories can be extremely valuable. In some cases, they shed light on important aspects of the origins of economic growth. We pay particular attention to developments in Great Britain in the 18th and 19th centuries. But this is simply due to the fact that we are seeking to understand the origins of modern, sustained growth, and Great Britain was the locus of the first modern economy. We also pay attention to places that failed to be the center of the first modern economy – despite a head start relative to Western Europe – such as China and the Middle East. We do not provide a deep dive into the specifics of the economic histories of these regions. Instead, we selectively choose various aspects of their histories to help substantiate theories espoused in the literature.

Finally, we do not spend much time discussing the drawbacks to economic growth such as pollution, climate change, and the capacity to create deadly weapons. We are by no means denying the importance of these topics, but these issues are simply outside the scope of this book. We have written a book on the *origins* of modern economic growth. While we believe economic growth in general to be a good thing, the focus here is on what caused economic growth, not its consequences.

Part I

Theories of How the World Became Rich

2

Did Some Societies Win the Geography Lottery?

Does geography determine the fate of nations? Is the key to unlocking riches preordained by factors like climate, natural resources, soil quality, and access to the ocean? Geographic explanations have long been a favorite of thinkers looking for reasons why their society pulled ahead. According to the Muslim Andalusian thinker Abū al-Qāsim Sā'id (1068): "The exceeding distance [of Northern Europeans] from the sun thickens the air making their dispositions cold, their natures rude, their skin color white and their hair straight. Thus . . . dullness and ignorance overpower them" (quoted in Chaney, 2008, p. 2). On the other hand, in Book XIV of *The Spirit of the Laws*, the French philosopher Montesquieu made a similar argument but drew an opposite conclusion:

> People are . . . more vigorous in cold climates. . . . The inhabitants of warm countries are, like old men, timorous; the people in cold countries are, like young men, brave. If we reflect on the late wars . . . we shall find that the northern people, transplanted into southern regions, did not perform such exploits as their countrymen who, fighting in their own climate, possessed their full vigor and courage. (Montesquieu, 1748/1989, p. 317)

Modern scholars have also argued that geography and climate play a crucial role in explaining patterns of economic development. Perhaps the most well-known insights are those of Diamond (1997), who argues that factors like the relative length of continental axis, the disease environment, proximity to the equator, and access to coasts and rivers had a tremendous influence on long-run economic prosperity. We discuss Diamond's influential hypothesis in depth in this chapter.

But is geography fate? Are locations with "good" characteristics destined to be more developed? Davis and Weinstein's (2002) seminal study of Japanese urban development in the aftermath of World War II provides evidence for the importance of geographic fundamentals. The authors examined what happened to the distribution of urban centers after the destruction of Hiroshima and Nagasaki by the atomic bomb. They show that after experiencing complete destruction, both Hiroshima and Nagasaki returned to the same relative positions in Japan's distribution of cities within twenty years. This suggests that a major shock to the distribution of population was insufficient to overcome the intrinsic geographic advantages of these two locations. Whether such findings are generalizable is something we will discuss throughout the book.

What about the Industrial Revolution? Britain's position as a large island off the coast of Europe, endowed with a moderate climate, numerous rivers, and a long coastline, helped shape the formation of its political institutions. Abundant coal resources played an important role in its early industrialization. It is worth asking: could this be why Britain industrialized first?

Geography and Modern Development

Geography matters for economic development today, especially in the poorest parts of the world. For instance, many countries in sub-Saharan Africa are landlocked, and most others have only a small amount of coast (see Figure 2.1). Without coastlines, they are unable to directly ship goods to other countries. They also have to rely on expensive and hard-to-maintain road and rail networks which can easily be blocked or cut off by their neighbors.

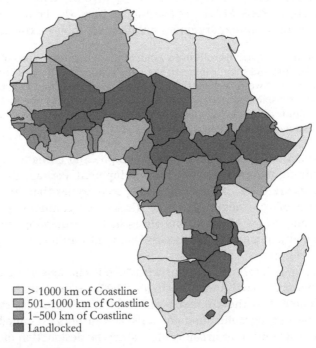

☐ > 1000 km of Coastline
▨ 501–1000 km of Coastline
▨ 1–500 km of Coastline
■ Landlocked

Figure 2.1 Coastlines of African countries
Coast length data from: CIA (2019).

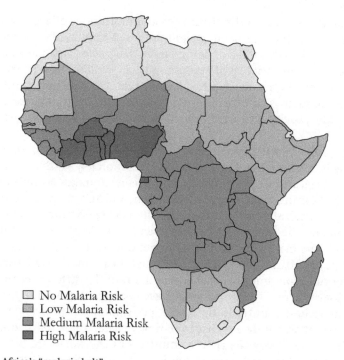

No Malaria Risk
Low Malaria Risk
Medium Malaria Risk
High Malaria Risk

Figure 2.2 Africa's "malaria belt"

Data source: Hay, Guerra, Gething, Patil, Tatem, Noor, et al. (2009).

Another important geographic factor is disease burden. Countries in the "malaria belt" in sub-Saharan Africa continue to be underdeveloped (see Figure 2.2). Malaria has probably killed more human beings over the course of human history than any other disease. But the burden of malaria is also economic. All else being equal, countries where a high proportion of the population are infected with malaria had growth rates that were around 1.3% lower than other countries (Sachs and Malaney, 2002). They also have higher infant mortality and lower investment in physical and human capital.

Other diseases are also endemic in sub-Saharan Africa. One particularly potent disease is sleeping sickness, which the tsetse fly transmits via parasites. The effects of the tsetse fly are not limited to humans. The same parasite causes nagnana, which is deadly to livestock. Livestock played a crucial role in agricultural development in other parts of the world. People in regions affected by the tsetse fly were historically much less likely to domesticate livestock. Alsan (2015) documents how in these parts of sub-Saharan Africa, intensive agriculture was less likely to develop, the plow was less likely to be employed, and large domesticated animals were rarer. These patterns of economic underdevelopment also had political consequences, as they made it less likely for centralized states to develop.

These examples point to the attractions and limitations of arguments based on geography. On the one hand, geography-based arguments are simple and geography has the advantage of being largely *exogenous*. This means that it is not affected by other variables of interest. As such, we don't have to worry about geography being the result of other factors that are also important for economic growth, such as culture or institutions. Hence, geographic explanations can potentially provide a straightforward explanation of economic growth and poverty.

The big problem with geographic explanations, however, is that geography is largely unchanging. Geography is not completely static, of course. For instance, fisheries can be over-fished, and this encourages societies to adapt accordingly (Ostrom, 1990; Dalgaard, Knudsen, and Selaya, 2020). And natural resources are generally not just there for the taking – finding them requires exploration and the capacity to extract (David and Wright, 1997). But geography is much less malleable than other societal features such as demography, institutions, or culture. This can be a problem for explanations linking geography to long-run economic growth, because many of the differences in incomes that we observe across the world today have changed dramatically over time. In 1750, the richest country in the world (per capita) was probably the Dutch Republic. Yet, it was only at most four times richer than the poorest countries in the world. Today the richest countries in the world are between one hundred and two hundred times richer in terms of measured GDP per capita. More perplexing still, geography has a difficult time explaining economic reversals. As it is mostly fixed, it cannot easily explain why the Middle East was much more developed in 1000 than Western Europe yet by 1800 Western Europe was far ahead of the Middle East.

Guns, Germs, and Steel

In his Pulitzer Prize-winning book *Guns, Germs, and Steel*, Diamond (1997) asked why it was that Europeans were able to conquer the New World so easily. How was it that they had not only superior weapons and technology but also more deadly germs than the native inhabitants of the Americas? His answer was geography. To explain why Eurasian societies were more technologically advanced, he drew on the work of Crosby (1986), who argued that the relative height and length of the Eurasian, African, and American continents had a deep impact on long-run development. Vertically aligned continents contain numerous microclimates, which limit the spread of crops, domesticated animals, and people. After all, crops suitable for rain forests are unlikely to grow in the savannah or mountains. So, the domesticated plants and animals of Mesoamerica did not spread to Peru or the Amazon basin. Perhaps more importantly, technology and knowledge spread more easily horizontally than vertically, since climatic characteristics vary less. The "verticality" of the Americas and Africa south of

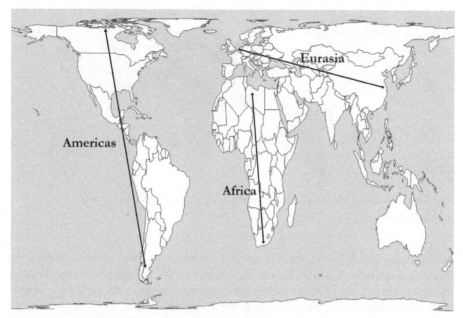

Figure 2.3 Verticality and horizontality of the continents
Reproduced using map in Diamond (1997). Gall-Peters map projection.

the Sahara (see Figure 2.3) may have therefore imposed huge hurdles to long-run economic growth.

This, according to Diamond, was why the Near East was the birthplace of human civilization. It was in the Near East that wheat, barley, and the pea were first cultivated. The rich fertile plains between the Tigris and Euphrates rivers were surrounded on several sides by so-called "hilly flanks." Goats and sheep were first domesticated 11,000 years ago in the hills of northern Syria and northern Mesopotamia. Pigs and cattle followed soon afterwards and spread throughout the Fertile Crescent. In total, thirty-three of the world's fifty-six heaviest wild grasses originated in either Europe, the Near East, or North Africa. The majority of these crops were first domesticated in the Fertile Crescent. Moderate climatic differences between Europe and the Middle East ensured that agricultural techniques could spread between the two.

Of the fourteen species of large domesticable animals, only one, and perhaps the least useful – the llama – originated in the New World. Nine of the world's fourteen large domesticable herbivores originated in Eurasia. This left inhabitants of the New World at a decided economic disadvantage. Livestock are a tremendous source of both animal power and protein. But domesticated animals are also a source of epidemic disease. The absence of large domesticable animals left New Worlders particularly vulnerable to new diseases. Because interactions between humans and animals are a major source of epidemic disease, human

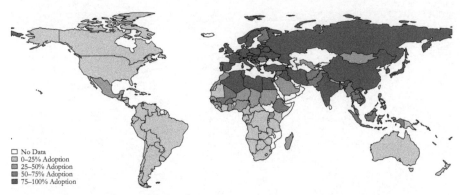

Figure 2.4 Technology adoption levels in 1500 (% of frontier technologies adopted)

Data source: Pavlik and Young (2019).

populations which have a long history of exposure to these diseases are more likely to acquire immunity. This is why contact with Europeans was so deadly for Native Americans. Recent estimates suggest there was a 95–98% drop in the Native American population between its pre-1492 peak and 1900 (Mann, 2005).

Diamond's arguments about the diffusion of technologies across regions have received empirical support. Pavlik and Young (2019) find that technologies moved more easily between east–west neighbors than between north–south neighbors. This is plainly seen in Figure 2.4, which maps how close to the technological frontier different parts of the world were in 1500. On the eve of the European discovery of the Americas, the technology of the Eurasian east–west axis was clearly more advanced than that of the American north–south axis or that of the sub-Saharan Africa north–south axis. These differences would only become exacerbated with the onset of colonization (see Chapter 6).

Mountains, Coasts, and Climate

Markets are unlikely to exist where it is difficult to transport goods and people. Geography is thus an important determinant of market size today (Redding and Venables, 2004). It mattered even more in the pre-industrial period. Prior to the spread of the railroad in the mid-19th century, water transport was by far the most cost-effective way to transport goods from one place to another. It was often twenty times cheaper to transport a good by sea than by land. So, it is reasonable to suspect that access to navigable waterways was historically an important component of economic growth.

Venice and the Low Countries provide instructive examples. Both were among the centers of commerce in late medieval Europe. Neither were ideal places to set up cities. Both were established on marshlands that required heroic feats of hydraulic engineering just to be viable (and, for this reason, both are in danger if sea levels rise too much in the 21st century). Why did people not only inhabit these regions but thrive while doing so? Access to water is one clear answer. The Low Countries have numerous ports that spilled out into the lucrative North Sea trade. Venice is on the Adriatic Sea, giving it prime access to the Mediterranean. But access to water is likely not the only reason people settled there. Montesquieu speculated that trade first developed in marginal lands where the land was unproductive and where individuals only settled because they were fleeing violence and predation. Indeed, it is these factors that are often emphasized in tales of the founding of Venice.

Another important geographic factor is ruggedness – how mountainous a particular territory is. Rugged terrain impedes trade and communication. This barrier was especially severe in pre-industrial times prior to the invention of the automobile, steam engine, and airplane. Japan, for example, is highly mountainous. Only a tiny fraction of the Japanese islands are suitable for rice cultivation or are possible locations for cities. Mountain ranges form a spine running through the country. This very well may have held Japan back. Yet, as we discussed in Chapter 1, although rugged terrain is usually seen as a major impediment to economic development, Nunn and Puga (2012) highlight the blessing of bad geography in sub-Saharan Africa. Historically, rugged territories were less likely to suffer the predation of slavers. Hence areas with "bad" geography in sub-Saharan Africa are richer rather than poorer today.

The quotes cited at the beginning of the chapter from Abū al-Qāsim Sā'id and Montesquieu argued that one reason why geography mattered was climate. Climate, unlike other geographic characteristics, is not fixed, however. For example, the climate of the Mediterranean was both warmer and wetter around 0 CE. Solar activity was high and stable. Evidence from tree rings and ice cores suggests that the 1st century CE was warmer than even the last century and a half (since 1850) (Manning, 2013). Consequently, the land available for agriculture expanded. Ancient historians like Harper (2017) link this Roman Climatic Optimum to the rise of the Roman Empire.

Wheat agriculture is highly sensitive to temperature. Warm growing-season temperatures are especially critical. The downside to higher temperatures is aridity and the risk of drought. The Roman warm period, however, was also wetter. This environment made it possible for Romans to expand the cultivation of Mediterranean crops inland into mountainous terrain. According to Harper (2017, p. 53) this warmth "was the enabling background of the Roman miracle. . . . If we *only* count the marginal land rendered susceptible to arable farming in Italy by higher temperatures, on the most conservative estimates, it could account for more than all of the growth achieved between Augustus and Marcus Aurelius" (that is, between c. 0 and c. 150 CE).

The passing of the Roman Climatic Optimum was associated with political crises. Periods of lower rainfall, especially in the 3rd century CE, were associated with military mutinies and imperial assassinations (Christian and Elbourne, 2018). Similarly, colder and more volatile weather together with the spread of epidemic disease helped to account for the failed attempts to rebuild the Roman Empire. Volcanic eruptions possibly led to what is known as the "Year without Sun" (536 CE). The century that followed has been called the Late Antique Little Ice Age. Although historians no longer use the term "the Dark Ages" to describe the early Middle Ages, the phrase *does* capture something vivid about how possibilities narrowed after 550 CE (Ward-Perkins, 2005).

Climatic change also played a role in the revival of the European economy after 1000. Cultivated land expanded. Vineyards proliferated in England. Iceland and Greenland were settled by Vikings. In Chapter 3, we discuss the period of economic expansion – known as the Commercial Revolution – that occurred between 1000 and 1300, during a period of unusually warm weather (Lamb, 1982). Institutional innovations were critical. But the climate was an important enabling condition. Similarly, populations and cities expanded in Southeast Asia and in North America in this period before collapsing in the late 13th and 14th centuries (Richter 2011, pp. 11–36; Reid 2015, pp. 50–6).

In the late 13th century, the climate began to become more unstable and cooler. The 15th century was especially cold due to low levels of solar activity. Although there were warmer conditions in the 16th century, the climate worsened again in the 17th century. Consequently, the entire period is often labeled the Little Ice Age. Figure 2.5 plots estimates of temperature deviations from 1100 to 1800. The Little Ice Age was both colder and more volatile.

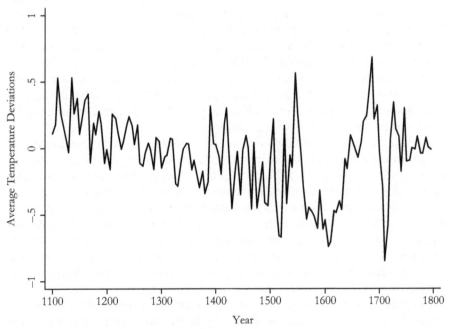

Figure 2.5 Temperature deviations across Europe, 1100–1800
Data source: Anderson, Johnson, and Koyama (2017).

The downturn in the climate that occurred in the late Middle Ages had real economic consequences. For one, it impacted city growth rates (Waldinger, 2019). Worsening climatic conditions generated political instability across Eurasia (Parker, 2014). The climate downturn also made minority communities like Jews more vulnerable to persecution. As entrenched antisemitic attitudes were common across Europe, Jews were frequently scapegoated for economic ills and political crises. Unusually cold weather increased the probability that a city would persecute its Jewish community by as much as 50% (Anderson, Johnson, and Koyama, 2017).

Colder weather associated with the Little Ice Age affected war and conflict more generally. Using geo-coded battle locations, Iyigun, Nunn, and Qian (2017) find that colder weather was associated with more conflict between 1400 and 1900. These effects were stronger in areas with worse-quality soil and regions that were already cold in 1400. Nevertheless, despite colder weather, it was in these centuries that the seeds of modern economic growth were sown. This raises the question: how can geographic and climatic constraints be overcome?

Geography and Transport Infrastructure

Can investment in transport infrastructure overcome the curse of geography? It seems possible. The Trans-Siberian Railway brought harsh terrain in contact with markets and goods to a degree previously unimaginable. But can transport infrastructure fully overcome the curse of bad geography or just ameliorate it?

Infrastructure projects can be financed by private individuals or by the state. But why do some institutional arrangements facilitate private investment in infrastructure while others deter it? Why do some states invest and others do not? When are states even capable of undertaking such projects in the first place? These questions suggest that overcoming "bad" geography may require institutions capable of diverting resources to infrastructure. Although we will return to this issue in Chapter 7, we outline here some of the ways that investments in transport infrastructure affected historical economic development.

The Roman Empire invested in a road system. By the reign of the Emperor Trajan (r. 97–117 CE), the road network comprised 80,000 km (see Figure 2.6). It was complemented by massive inland waterways that crisscrossed the empire and connected landlocked cities with the Roman lake that was the Mediterranean Sea. The Roman road system was built for military reasons. But once established, it played a crucial role in knitting the empire together economically and culturally. The suppression of Mediterranean piracy and the establishment of safe sea-lanes was also critical in lowering transport costs, which enabled inter-regional trade and specialization. Archaeological evidence attests to the fact that manufactured goods such as amphorae (pottery) were mass produced and transported over long distances.

Figure 2.6 The Roman road network

Map provided by Erik Hornung from Flückiger, Hornung, Larch, Ludwig, and Mees (forthcoming). Grey lines symbolize roads, solid black lines navigable river sections, and dashed lines coastal shipping routes.

Following the conquest of the Mediterranean region, the Roman economy experienced a period of economic growth driven by market expansion. Adam Smith (1776/1976) observed that the greater the extent of the market, the greater the scope for specialization and the division of labor. This suggests that an increase in market size can itself be a source of productivity improvements and economic growth. This type of growth is often called Smithian growth. Over time, Smithian growth encourages capital investment. Individuals invest in longer and more complex production processes. This investment, in turn, increases the productivity of labor and the returns to trade, thereby setting in motion a virtuous cycle of economic development. Favorable geography or improvements in infrastructure can be a source of Smithian growth. Smithian growth can be derailed by war or natural disasters that upend markets and disrupt patterns of specialization. It runs into limits and ultimately into diminishing returns in the absence of sustained innovation.

In the case of Rome, the process of Smithian growth was aided by the benign climatic and geopolitical conditions discussed above. Investment in transport infrastructure, nonetheless, played a critical proximate role in Roman economic growth. Studying the distribution of terra sigillata, a red-gloss tableware made out of clay, Flückiger, Hornung, Larch, Ludwig, and Mees (forthcoming) find evidence that the intensity of Roman trade in this product reflected transportation costs. Places with lower transportation costs due to Roman infrastructure had greater inter-regional specialization, while better-connected areas traded more. As the Roman Empire declined, the road network remained in place. Until the 18th century, there was little new transport infrastructure. Flückiger et al. find that the effects of the Roman transportation network outlived the Roman Empire and were associated with much greater trade intensity up to the invention of the steam engine.

Transport infrastructure also mattered for Chinese economic development. Economic growth in the Middle Kingdom was greatly aided by the creation of the Grand Canal by the Sui (581–618 CE) and Tang (618–907 CE) dynasties and improved by their successors. The Grand Canal, said to be 40 meters wide, connected the Yangzi to the Yellow River. Its construction needed thousands of laborers and the vast expenditures involved caused the collapse of the Sui. The canal transported grain to the capital city, Luoyang, and played a critical role in supplying the army guarding the northern frontier. In the Tang dynasty, 130,000 tons of grain were transported north each year (Ball, 2017, p. 120).

Though the primary purposes of the Grand Canal were political and military, its creation brought economic benefits. According to Scheidel (2019, p. 263), between the Yangzi and Yellow Rivers, "the Grand Canal and multiple smaller rivers and feeder canals created . . . a huge fertile crescent united by cheap and safe transport. . . . No inland waterway system in world history approaches this one as a device for integrating large and productive spaces." As we discuss in Chapter 3, market integration in China was comparable to that in many parts of Europe until the latter part of the 18th century. One reason for this was the massive investments made by several dynasties in the Grand Canal.

A final example of the importance of transport infrastructure comes from industrializing Britain. Before 1700, Britain (like other pre-industrial economies) was afflicted by extremely high transport costs. By 1870, this situation had been transformed. As Dan Bogart and his collaborators document (Bogart, 2014; Bogart, Alvarez-Palau, Dunn, Satchell, and Taylor, 2017; Bogart, Satchell, Alvarez-Palau, You, and Taylor, 2017), this transformation was partly due to steam power and the introduction of the railways. It was also due to investment in the road and canal network beginning in the 18th century.

The story of these investments in transport infrastructure is partly technological and partly institutional. The institutional part of the story will be discussed in Chapter 3. Here, we focus on the consequences of these improvements. Stagecoach speeds increased from 1.96 journey miles per hour in 1700 to 7.96 journey miles per hour in 1820. This was due to improvements in the road network, stagecoach design, and the number of way-stations. By 1840, Britain had twice the road density of France or Spain. Figure 2.7 depicts the expansion of the road network in England and Wales. The greatest improvement in land transportation came with the railway: rail travel in 1870 was ten times faster than coach travel had been in 1700. Goods, ideas, and people could move across Britain in a way and at a speed that had previously been impossible.

Another major area of improvement in industrializing Britain was the canal network. Waterborne transport was much more cost-efficient than road transport. Canals played an important role in linking together Britain's growing industrial heartland in the northwest with coal.

This transportation revolution had a dramatic impact on the British economy. Bogart, Satchell, Alvarez-Palau, You, and Taylor (2017) find that improvements

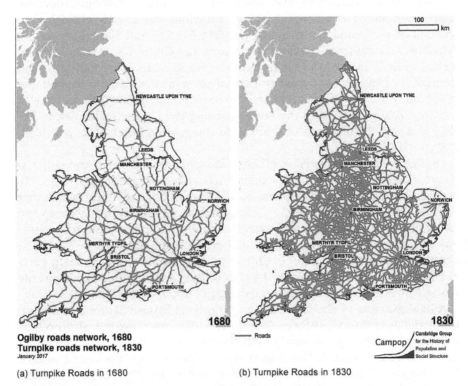

(a) Turnpike Roads in 1680   (b) Turnpike Roads in 1830

Figure 2.7 The increase in turnpikes in England and Wales: 1680–1830

Map provided by Dan Bogart from Bogart, Satchell, Alvarez-Palau, You, and Taylor (2017). Lines represent turnpike roads in 1680 (panel a) and 1830 (panel b).

in turnpike roads and inland waterways played a key role in driving population growth and structural change. Locations further away from turnpikes and canals grew more slowly. They also remained more agricultural than those closer to the improving transport network.

One of the challenges in measuring the benefits of infrastructure investment is that beyond the *direct* effects of lowering transport costs, there are numerous (potentially important) but difficult to measure *indirect* effects. We can think about these improvements through the concept of market access, which summarizes all the ways both goods and factor markets – that is, markets for labor, land, and capital – change in response to a change in transport technology or infrastructure.

In an influential book, Fogel (1964) argued that the benefits of the railroad to American growth were modest because in its absence other transportation techniques such as waterways and canals would have been used. However, Donaldson and Hornbeck (2016) show that once the improvements to market access are taken into account, the railroad did have a more sizable impact on economic growth, especially during the rapid period of railroad expansion in the late 19th century. This was most pronounced in the Western states, which became more closely connected with the larger markets on the Eastern seaboard (see Figure 2.8). Donaldson and Hornbeck find that removing all railroads in 1890 would have decreased the value of agricultural land by 60.2%, which translates to 3.22% of GNP.

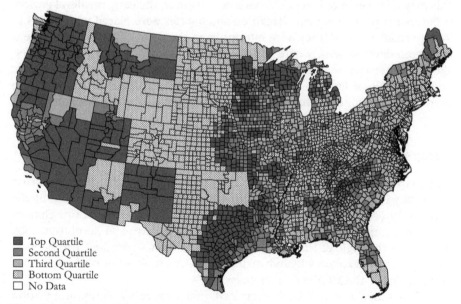

Top Quartile
Second Quartile
Third Quartile
Bottom Quartile
No Data

Figure 2.8 Changes in US market access, 1870–90
Data source: Donaldson and Hornbeck (2016).

Moreover, Hornbeck and Rotemberg (2021) show that railroad access greatly increased US manufacturing output. They estimate that US aggregate productivity would have been 25% lower in 1890 in the absence of railroads. In the context of Industrial Revolution Britain, Bogart, Alvarez-Palau, Dunn, Satchell, and Taylor (2017, p. 23) find that improved market access had a direct effect on population growth. Had there been no improvements in transportation, there would have been 25 percentage points less urban growth between 1680 and 1831 and 97 percentage points less growth from 1831 to 1851. These are enormous numbers. They indicate just how important transport improvements were for the growth of the British and US economies.

Donaldson (2018) employed a similar methodology to examine the building of railroads in India under the British Raj. Transport investments made it possible to transport bulky goods such as wheat and rice over land as much as twenty times faster than had been possible with pre-industrial technologies. The railroad network thus brought regions of India out of near autarky, integrating them with the rest of the country and the world.

Infrastructure investments can help overcome the "curse of geography." But they can also have unforeseeable, counter-productive effects in the long run. For instance, prior investments in transport can lock countries into particular, and potentially inefficient, economic configurations. A fascinating example of such lock-in comes from the western part of the Roman Empire. Michaels and Rauch (2018) contrast England with France. In France, Roman city locations remained settled throughout the early Middle Ages. Michaels and Rauch show that while this may have benefited French economic growth in the early medieval period, it harmed it in the long run. Because French cities were placed with access to Roman roads in mind, they were inferior from the point of view of subsequent economic development, where water travel dominated. In England, however, the urban network was reset following the collapse of the Roman Empire. This allowed medieval English cities to relocate along coasts and rivers that were more beneficial for economic activity in subsequent centuries (see Figure 2.9).

Geography and Industrialization

This chapter opened with the question: is geography fate? We have shown that geography is not fate, but there are important instances where it undoubtedly matters for economic outcomes. The final question we address in this chapter is: can geography help explain why and where the Industrial Revolution took place? Can the logic of Diamond's argument in *Guns, Germs, and Steel* be used *within Eurasia* to explain why industrialization first took off in Western Europe and not China, the Middle East, or elsewhere?

Within Eurasia, it has been suggested that Europe's geographic position made it more likely to discover the Americas and benefit from Atlantic trade (Fernández-Armesto, 2006). Within Europe itself, however, access to the Atlantic

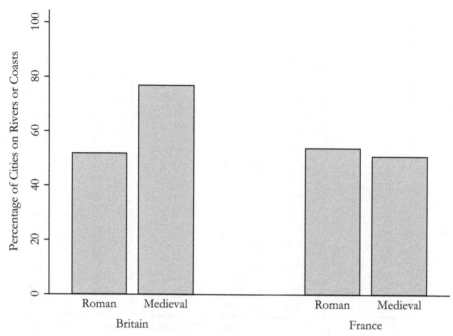

Figure 2.9 Location of cities in England and France in the Roman and medieval periods
Data source: Michaels and Rauch (2018).

was a mixed blessing. Acemoglu, Johnson, and Robinson (2005*b*) studied the impact of Atlantic trade on European economic development. They found that the discovery of the Americas and the development of new trade routes had varying effects on economic growth, depending on the society's political institutions. In other words, geography played a role in determining economic outcomes via its effect on institutions. Where long-distance commerce was already controlled by the crown, access to the Atlantic strengthened royal power. Two prominent examples of this are Charles V and Phillip II, who ruled Spain for most of the 16th century. Access to the Atlantic – and all of the wealth flowing from South American mines – allowed them to dispense with representative institutions. Thus, while Spain was initially enriched by the Americas, the long-run impact on economic growth was negative, since it resulted in more extractive institutions. In contrast, where monarchs lacked the ability to control or monopolize long-distance trade (such as in England or the Dutch Republic), the discovery of the Americas strengthened the merchant class and enabled them to constrain royal power. We discuss this point in more detail in Chapter 7.

Perhaps the most direct impact of geography on economic growth is through the availability of natural resources. Nef (1932) demonstrated that 16th-century England faced an energy crisis as the charcoal supplied by local forests could not meet the demands of a growing urban population. Coal relaxed this

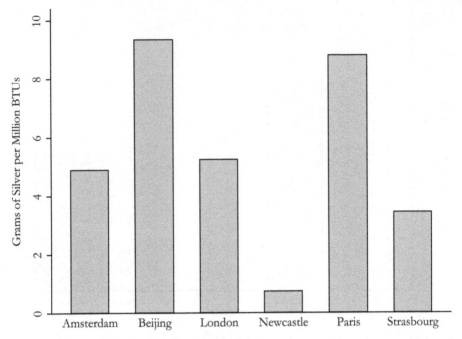

Figure 2.10 The price of energy in the early 1700s
Data source: Allen (2011*b*). (BTUs = British Thermal Units.)

constraint. Sure, English coal had been there long before the 16th and 17th centuries. But the demand for it was not. Once the steam engine was vastly improved in the late 18th century, cheap coal from the north of England (see Figure 2.10) allowed the British economy to harness vastly more energy than had previously been possible (Allen, 2009*a*, 2011*b*).

Building on this argument, Wrigley (1989, 2010) argues that without coal there would have been no Industrial Revolution. Specifically, he distinguishes between an organic economy (in which energy is extracted from human or animal muscle or from wood) from a mineral economy (in which energy stored up over millions of years becomes available for human use). Productivity is always bound to be low in an organic economy. Coal permitted Britain to escape from the constraints of an organic economy. Wrigley acknowledges that the presence of coal alone did not guarantee that it would be exploited. But without coal, industrialization would have been impossible.

In his now famous contribution to the Great Divergence debate, Pomeranz (2000) argued that British industrialization relied crucially on the proximity of coal deposits to the new industrial centers and on resources from the Americas. Traditional forms of energy such as timber were land-intensive. In comparison, coal yielded more power per unit of land. New crops from the Americas, notably the potato, increased the productivity of land in northwestern Europe. Natural resources shifted Britain and northwestern Europe from a labor-intensive path of economic development into an energy-intensive and innovative development path. For Pomeranz, access to the New World (and slavery)

> offered what an expanding home market could not have: ways in which manufactured goods created without much use of British labour could be turned into ever-increasing amounts of land-intensive food and fiber (and later timber) at reasonable and even falling prices. Precious metals enabled Europeans to trade with Asia. Without silver it is difficult to imagine another European good being exported as much.

This argument has been challenged. After all, China had abundant coal deposits. So did the Ruhr Valley in Germany. The question of whether they were located close to industrial centers is perhaps the wrong one to ask. In Britain, industrial towns grew where coal was plentiful and energy cheap. It was also possible to transport coal cheaply by sea from Newcastle to fuel London's demand for energy.

Mokyr (1990) argues that coal was unlikely to have been decisive, for a variety of reasons. First, the Industrial Revolution was broader than steam power, and even steam power did not absolutely require coal. Water power was an important substitute. Had coal been more expensive, innovators would have had an incentive to economize on it and develop alternative energy sources. The supply of coal was highly elastic (Clark and Jacks, 2007). This implies that coal production expanded as demand for coal increased with industrialization. By this account, the expansion of coal output could have occurred in earlier decades had there been demand. In other words, had Britain had no coal, this would not have prevented industrialization. Coal would simply have been imported from Ireland, France, or elsewhere in Northern Europe. This would have been costly, but the additional costs were unlikely to have been decisive for Britain's industrialization. This speaks against Pomeranz's claim that the supply of coal was a binding constraint for industrialization to take place.

Chapter Summary

One can hardly deny the power of geography in explaining many patterns in the pre-industrial world. Geographic characteristics were critical in the emergence of agricultural and urban life in the Fertile Crescent. Geographic features such as access to rivers and coasts and high-quality agricultural land also help explain many patterns of comparative development prior to industrialization.

But this does not mean that geography can provide a full answer for the puzzle of comparative economic development. Before 1800, better-endowed lands were not much richer in per capita terms than were less well-endowed lands. They just tended to be more densely populated. Moreover, while geographic characteristics can explain much of the variation in the location of economic activity, they do not provide the full story. Firms benefit from being near each other. So do workers. Economies of scale and the network effects associated with close proximity (known in economics as agglomeration effects), rather than geographic fundamentals, often explain why certain cities outperform others. Most importantly, geography on its own cannot account for the *timing* of the Industrial Revolution, the onset of modern, sustained economic growth in the 19th century, or the various reversals of fortune that we observe in the historical record.

Where does this leave us? Is there a role for geography in explaining why the world became rich? Hopefully, this chapter has convinced you that geography has played an important role in determining certain outcomes that differ between societies, but that it cannot explain everything. If it could explain everything, our fate would have been written thousands of years ago with little room for human agency. In the remaining chapters, we will show that human actions have played a significant role in determining the economic trajectories of societies. These decisions range from the most intimate (how many babies to have) to the type of legal and political systems societies have. Yet, even though human actions have played a key role in determining the world's economic distribution, geography likely played some role in these decisions. To some degree, geography has helped shape societies' institutions (the subject of Chapter 3), culture (the subject of Chapter 4), demography (the subject of Chapter 5), and colonization (the subject of Chapter 6). We will keep these interactions in mind as we proceed through the first half of the book.

3

Is It All Just Institutions?

In Afghanistan, justice is mostly provided at the tribal level. Whether you win your case or not depends in part on its merit. But it also depends on who you are, which tribe you belong to, and who is overseeing your case (Murtazashvili, 2016). In the Ottoman Empire, a well-functioning court system existed. But it was biased: it favored men, Muslims, and elites, regardless of the merits of their cases (Kuran and Rubin, 2018). These systems of justice differ considerably from those found in the wealthier parts of the contemporary world. True, the rich can buy better lawyers, and justice is hardly color-blind, especially in the US. But the fact is that the disadvantaged can, and frequently do, win cases when the facts are in their favor. The relative impartiality of courts, in turn, encourages economic activity. When people know they have legal recourse should their partner cheat them, they are more likely to engage in exchange. Might these differences in legal systems have played some role in determining which parts of the world have become rich?

Differences across societies are hardly relegated to the legal sphere. At a higher level, differences in political systems can play an important role in economic decision-making. Where autocrats rule, violence often follows. In North Korea, those on the wrong side of the regime tend not to last long. In Stalin's Soviet Union, anyone remotely expected of having anti-regime sentiments ended up in a gulag or executed (as well as many who had no such sentiments).

Political systems affect more than just violence. They affect whether you have to pay bribes to do business, whether you have the right to sell and use your property as you please, and whether you have the freedom to move when the economic opportunity presents itself. The degree to which a society enables – or restricts – people in this fashion is of first-order importance in determining its economic potential.

These political, legal, religious, and economic organizations are a society's *institutions*. In this chapter, we examine the literature on institutions. We begin by explaining what institutions are and why they impact economic development. We then show why different institutions in different parts of the world have placed societies on different economic trajectories.

What Are Institutions?

Until recently, textbook accounts of economic growth focused on investment in physical capital and technological change as the key determinants of growth. Such an approach is natural for economists interested in creating mathematical models of economic growth. However, it is of limited value in understanding the historical origins of economic growth. There are simply too many examples of societies *not* investing in capital or technology to boil it down to investment decisions. This is as true of the past as it is today. Investment is relatively sparse in places like Afghanistan, Haiti, and Niger. The marginal return to capital in these countries is likely very high. Why, then, do individuals in these societies forgo what is more or less a free lunch? What are the constraints people face in these societies? And how do these constraints evolve over time?

These questions were posed by North and Thomas (1973). They argued that the factors on which economists focused – investment in capital machinery, factories, and schooling – were not independent causes of economic growth. They *were* economic growth. To understand the causes of growth, one has to study the incentives that led individuals in some societies to build factories and invest, to go to school, and to acquire new skills. One must also study why individuals in other societies were not incentivized to do these things. North and his co-authors called the aspects of society that formed these incentives *institutions* and they proposed reorienting the study of economic growth around the study of them.

For North, institutions are the rules of the game. For example, in a game of football (soccer), the rules determine the nature of the game and thus structure the incentives facing the players. If we want to explain the different behavior of players in football compared to a game of rugby, the best explanation may reside not in differences in the individuals playing the two games but in the different rules, and hence incentives, they face.

North's thinking about institutions evolved over the course of his career. Initially, North and Thomas (1973) supposed that institutions had a tendency to evolve towards efficiency. Over time, inefficient institutions would be weeded out and more efficient institutions would be promoted in the same manner as market competition weeds out less efficient firms in favor of their more efficient competitors.

Later, North (1981) came to the view that there is no process analogous to the competitive market process to "select" the most efficient institutions. The incentives in the political sphere differ from those in the marketplace. Hence, inefficient institutions can persist for decades or even centuries. Such inefficient institutions can be a source of lasting poverty. They may even be a leading cause of why some countries are rich and others are poor.

Building on North's insights, Greif (2006) developed an alternative definition of institutions. His framework incorporates the critical role cultural beliefs play in enforcing, and indeed constituting, institutions. For Greif, institutions are not only the "rules of the game," but also comprise the beliefs and social norms that uphold these rules. Beliefs and social norms, like institutions, can be hard to change. This is true even when there are clear economic benefits from doing so. One of Greif's key insights is that cultural beliefs and institutions can reinforce each other. When one strengthens the other, both are all the harder to change. Greif proposes this as a key reason why some economies fail to grow while others prosper. We discuss these insights further in Chapter 4.

One key component of institutions is the degree to which they permit *economic freedom*. The more economic freedom a society has, the more individuals are free to allocate their resources as they see fit. Economic freedom is closely associated with the rule of law. When a society follows the rule of law, laws are applied equally and all types of rights are protected. This of course includes economic rights. Economic freedom is strongly correlated with per capita income (Gwartney, Lawson, and Holcombe, 1999; Gwartney, Lawson, Hall, and Murphy, 2019). Rodrik, Subramanian, and Trebbi (2004) show that raising the degree to which a society follows the rule of law one standard deviation – roughly corresponding to the difference in institutions between Bolivia and South Korea – is associated with a 6.4-fold difference in per capita income (see Figure 3.1). Incidentally, this is about the income gap between Bolivia and South Korea. This finding should not be taken as gospel, however. There are major challenges

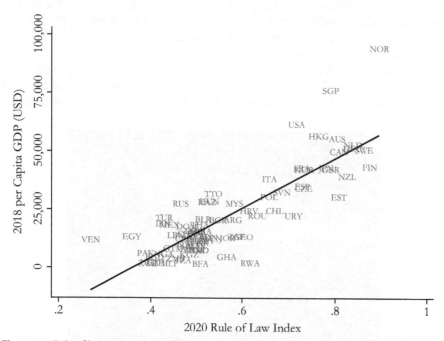

Figure 3.1 Rule of law vs. per capita GDP

Data sources: World Justice Project (2020) for rule of law, Bolt and van Zanden (2020) for per capita GDP.

in estimating the importance of institutions when relying solely on variation across countries. This is because countries differ across so many dimensions it is hard to isolate the specific effects of institutional quality.

For this reason, one of the most persuasive examples illustrating the importance of institutions is the comparison between North and South Korea (Acemoglu, Johnson, and Robinson, 2005a). For centuries, North and South Korea were part of a single country, with the same language, culture, and religious traditions. To the extent that there were major regional differences, the north of the country was more industrialized and developed. Then, in 1948, the Communists took over the North. Ever since the war that followed, the economic story between the two nations has been one of divergence. The contrast between the prosperity of the South and the poverty of the North reveals the importance of their different institutions: market-based in the South versus Communist in the North. These differences are immediately visible in Figure 3.2, which is a photograph taken from space of the two countries at night. Night lights are a measure of economic prosperity because they reveal economic activity and electrification. One can clearly see the South Korean border and its many economic hubs. North Korea is almost entirely pitch black.

We rarely have examples as clean-cut as North and South Korea, however. In their absence, institutional arguments can be difficult to test. One critique is that "good institutions" is simply a label for all things a particular author approves of (Clark, 2007, pp. 145–65). The problem is that a label of approbation has little explanatory value. It cannot be operationalized or used to discriminate between points of view.

There are two ways around this problem. One is that pioneered by Greif and his co-authors. Greif developed carefully specified theoretical models of how specific economic institutions functioned. These models have two virtues:

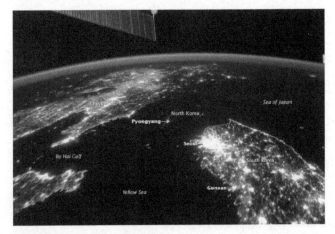

Figure 3.2 Night lights on the Korean Peninsula
Source: https://visibleearth.nasa.gov/view.php?id=83182.

the assumptions are transparent and they are capable of generating novel predictions.

Another approach relies on studying so-called "natural experiments." The comparison of North and South Korea made by Acemoglu, Johnson, and Robinson (2005a) is one such natural experiment. In comparing the two Koreas, factors like culture and history are held constant. Borders often provide a nice way to test the effects of institutions. When borders change, people are immediately subjected to a new institutional environment, although nothing changes about their culture, history, or geography. Yet, finding clean natural experiments is difficult, and there are many questions we wish to answer for which no natural experiment exists.

Property Rights

One of the lessons from England's political and economic rise is that well-functioning property rights matter for economic success. Property rights are perhaps the most basic institution studied by economists. Besley and Ghatak (2010, p. 4526) define a property right as an owner's right to use a good or asset (for either consumption or production), to transfer it, or to contract on the basis of it (for example, by mortgaging it). But why do property rights matter? Why have they intrigued economists for so long? What do they have to do with institutions?

Secure property rights ensure that individuals earn a return on their investments. One widely used measure of property rights is the World Bank Governance Indicators (WBGI). These measure a range of factors relating to rule of law, government quality, and regulation. We briefly discussed the rule of law earlier as being key to economic freedom. According to the WBGI, the rule of law index reflects the "perceptions of the extent to which agents have confidence in and abide by the rules of society, and in particular the quality of contract enforcement, property rights, the police, and the courts, as well as the likelihood of crime and violence" (Kaufmann, Kraay, and Mastruzzi, 2011). Figure 3.3 shows the variations in rule of law throughout the world in 2017. Another widely used measure for security of property is expropriation risk. This is the risk that the state will deprive, expropriate, nationalize, or confiscate the assets of private business, whether domestic or foreign. Such confiscation can be disastrous for investment. Why would one invest if doing so makes them a target for expropriation?

Restrictions on property rights were a dominant feature of pre-modern European property law. Feudal property rights, in particular, were often impediments to developing markets for land or encouraging investment in infrastructure. In England, for example, the law of entails meant that land had to be passed undivided to one male heir. The purpose of this law was to preserve the land of the nobility, who were expected to possess enough land to supply a

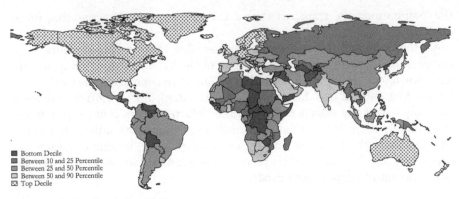

Figure 3.3 Rule of law index, 2017

Data source: Kaufmann, Kraay, and Mastruzzi (2011). Data available at https://info.worldbank.org/governance/wgi/#home.

mounted warrior to serve the king in times of war. The law traded off military security for economic productivity. Land is more valuable when users have the right to sell or divide it. Over the centuries, the military justification for the law of entails diminished, as professional armies replaced knightly hosts. Yet, the law remained the writ of land.

For property to be put to its most efficient use, there must also be a way of rearranging property rights when it is productive to do so. Different systems of property rights have different consequences for economic development. In 17th- and 18th-century England, property rights had to be reordered in order to make the best use of new investment opportunities in areas such as mining (Bogart and Richardson, 2011). For this to happen, there needs to be a way that property rights can be renegotiated and reallocated if it is beneficial to do so. This was made possible only when political institutions also changed.

As Cox (2016) points out, the crucial advantage that England had by the 18th century was that in Parliament it had a centralized forum where these claims could be adjudicated. Local veto players could be, and often were, overruled if the gains to reallocating property rights were large enough. The problem facing rulers who were not constrained by institutions like Parliament is that they could not credibly commit to not using these powers to reallocate property rights in their favor. In France, the monarchy could not be trusted to refrain from abusing this power. Landlords therefore insisted on retaining local veto power on any adjustments in land use. All of this suggests that property rights cannot be viewed in isolation from the legal system as a whole.

Van Bavel, Buringh, and Dijkman (2018) present a fascinating case of weak property rights discouraging investment. They study investments in the major labor-saving capital goods of the late medieval period: water mills, windmills, and cranes. These were expensive to build, but offered an immense return on investment. Because of their cost, they were precisely the type of capital goods that were only likely to be invested in when property rights were secure. Van Bavel, Buringh, and Dijkman find that, over the period 900–1600, their use increased over time in Western Europe but diminished over time in the Middle East. The decline in Middle Eastern capital investments coincided precisely with a decline in the security of property rights.

It is not just the security of property rights that matters. How rights are assigned is also crucial. In particular, overlapping property rights, in which multiple parties are able to claim rights to the same good, generate holdup problems and impede investment (Lamoreaux, 2011). A holdup problem occurs when one party has an incentive to strategically delay or impede the investment in order to extract a larger share of the resulting profits (Williamson, 1985). For example, in France prior to the Revolution, complex and rigid overlapping property rights prevented landowners from investing in irrigation or in drainage projects (Rosenthal, 1992). If anything, these property rights were "too secure."

It is also possible for property rights to sow the seeds of an economy's demise. Van Bavel (2016) shows that the rise and fall of Abbasid Iraq (750–1258), medieval northern Italy, and the early modern Dutch Republic all followed a similar pattern. In each case, there was a feedback loop in which secure property rights in factor markets allowed underutilized resources to become more productively used. This led to specialization and division of labor, which led to economic growth, which resulted in greater use of factor markets, and so on. However, with factor market growth came political and economic inequality. Those who owned the factors of production gained more political power. They used it to dominate the markets for land, labor, and capital, as well as financial markets, making these markets less free in the process. These vested interests squeezed the little remaining productive power out of the economy, leaving little for the rest of society.

The Legal System

The legal system is the meta-institution that spells out the formal rules of the game and the manner in which they are enforced. Legal systems vary tremendously across societies. Many small-scale societies rely on informal and decentralized legal systems based around ostracism and feuding. These legal systems differ considerably from those of large-scale agrarian states, let alone highly commercialized, market-oriented societies.

Small-scale societies rely on repeated interactions and social sanctions to enforce order. In small-scale, closely knit societies, these mechanisms are powerful in enforcing cooperation. Individuals in these societies expect to interact with each other again in the future. They thus have an incentive to develop a reputation for fair dealing. It is the threat of missing out on future rewards that induces them to refrain from violence or theft in the present (Kandori, 1992; Dixit, 2004).

However, mechanisms dependent on the logic of repeated dealings may be unable to support cooperation in large-scale societies, where people are unlikely to interact consistently. As societies become more complex, therefore, formal legal systems tend to emerge. A formal legal system prescribes rules that outline licit and illicit behavior and specify punishments for those who disobey the law. The first such legal system that we have a record of is the Code of Hammurabi, dated to 1754 BCE (see Figure 3.4).

Legal systems structure the incentives that individuals face. For example, the Code of Hammurabi prescribed numerous harsh punishments. A son who hit his father was to have his hands chopped off, while lovers who conspired to murder a husband were to be impaled. The Code of Hammurabi specified harsher punishment for lower-status individuals and for crimes directed against one's social betters. For instance, "if a man knocks out the teeth of his equal, his teeth shall be knocked out," while knocking out the teeth of a social inferior only resulted in a fine. The Code of Hammurabi thus reinforced existing power structures and a hierarchical social system.

Figure 3.4 The first(?) formal legal system: the Code of Hammurabi

Source: https://upload.wikimedia.org/wikipedia/commons/0/06/Prologue_code_Lipit-Ishtar_AO_54 73.jpg.

In other words, the Code of Hammurabi was a set of laws based on *identity rules* rather than impersonal rules (Johnson and Koyama, 2019). The kind of punishment varied according to the social identity of the parties involved. Such identity rules tend to entrench the power of existing elites. There are many historical examples of identity rules. Medieval European Jews faced their own set of laws, including what they could wear and where they could live. Many medieval European cities had sumptuary laws, specifying which clothes individuals could wear based on their social class (Desierto and Koyama, 2020).

In contrast, a society structured around *impersonal rules* is committed to treating individuals the same regardless of their social identity. Impersonal rules are often more consistent with the protection of property than are identity rules. They enable impersonal rather than personal exchange and hence are more likely to promote investment and economic growth.

The distinction between identity rules and impersonal rules is one of the key differences between *rule by law* and the *rule of law*. In a "rule by law" society, laws exist but are not necessarily applied to everyone. The ruling elites tend to be above the law. In these societies, the dictum "rules for thee but not for me" applies. As we noted earlier in this chapter, moving away from such a society to one in which rulers are constrained by the law was key to economic growth (Greif and Rubin, 2021).

Societies that have a strong rule of law tend to be richer (see Figure 3.1). What is it about the rule of law that leads to positive economic outcomes? Fuller (1969) argued that the rule of law requires (1) a concept of legal equality – that is, all individuals from the ruler downwards are equally subject to the law; (2) that laws should be prospective, open, and clear; (3) that laws should be stable over time; (4) that the making of laws should be open and guided by impersonal rules; (5) that the judiciary should be politically independent; (6) that legal institutions such as courts should be accessible to all; and (7) that rules should be general and apply uniformly. These are all conditions that decrease uncertainty, and hence increase investment and incentivize exchange.

Importantly, the rule of law depends on a nexus of different institutions. It depends on a political system that is bound by rules that constrain the power of the executive. It also depends on a standardized legal system in which individuals know what to expect and in which there are clearly defined standards that cannot be subverted through corruption or patronage.

Many scholars have argued that the rule of law played a critical role in the rise of Western Europe. It provided a check on the power of government, guaranteed each individual their own private sphere of non-interference, and offered a platform of institutional stability conducive to long-run economic growth (Hayek, 1960; Cooter, 1997; Weingast, 1997). The idea is that rule of law, rather than rule by men, provides the stability and certainty that enables individuals to truck, barter, and exchange their way to prosperity (Dicey, 1908, pp. 198–9). The question is: how do societies develop impersonal rules? Where does the rule of law come from?

In *Law and Revolution*, Harold Berman (1983) attributed particular significance to the emergence of the Western legal tradition during the Middle Ages. This legal tradition has its origins in ancient Rome. As the Roman economy was commercialized and market-oriented, Roman legal scholars developed a theory of contracts and property (Arruñada, 2016). Roman law was largely lost in Western Europe following the collapse of the Western Roman Empire. During this period, Germanic or customary legal codes dominated. These laws were based on identity rules and better suited to governing small-scale societies rather than providing a framework for impersonal trade. Beginning in the 11th and 12th centuries, however, Roman law was rediscovered and the principles underlying the Roman law of contracts began to be studied by lawyers of canon law in universities like that of Bologna (Fernández-Villaverde, 2022). While customary laws remained in place for centuries, the principles of Roman law would eventually form the basis for both the French and Germanic legal systems.

At roughly the same time, a different legal system was emerging when Germanic and local legal systems were unified into common law during the 12th and 13th centuries. English common law was influenced by Roman law, but only indirectly via canon law. Numerous scholars, including the great legal scholars Pollack and Maitland (1895) and Dicey (1908), saw English common law as it evolved in the Middle Ages as playing a critical role in enshrining and protecting property rights. They reasoned that common law provided a set of stable but adaptive principles that in later centuries enabled more complex organizational forms to emerge.

Building on this tradition, La Porta, de Silanes, Shleifer, and Vishny (1998) argued that the English common law tradition is associated with better protection of property rights, less onerous regulations, and a more favorable environment for markets than systems based on Roman Law (such as the French or German legal systems). In particular, La Porta et al. argued that protection for investors was systematically stronger in common law countries. Common law countries tend to give both shareholders and creditors the strongest rights, regardless of GDP. This is important for financial development because it limits the extent to which corporate insiders can expropriate investors. Other research has found that within a country such as France, which had both civil and common law traditions prior to the Revolution, there is little evidence that civil law was worse for economic development (Le Bris, 2019). Particularly problematic for the legal origins argument is the finding that financial development varies greatly over time, and that in 1913 France's stock market capitalization, as a proportion of the economy, was almost twice that of the US (Rajan and Zingales, 2003).

Nevertheless, the type of law that countries have is one of the important relics of the colonial era. Countries that were colonized by Europeans – which, as we will see in Chapter 6, was much of the world – tended to get their legal institutions (see Figure 3.5). Some speculate that this is why English colonies, steeped as they were in English common law, tended to do better than other

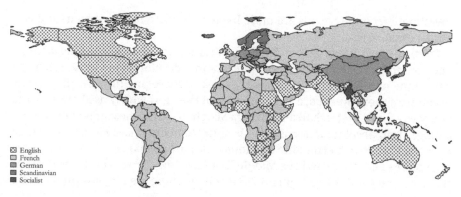

Figure 3.5 Legal origins throughout the world

Data source: Shleifer, de Silanes, and Porta (2008).

European colonies. Other scholarship suggests that what matters is how different legal traditions were transplanted to the colonies (Berkowitz, Pistor, and Richard, 2003). In particular, Oto-Peralías and Romero-Ávila (2014) argue that whether or not the British introduced common law to a colony hinged on initial levels of population density, which determined how costly it would be to enforce a new legal code. We leave the discussion of the long-run effects of colonization to Chapter 6.

What about other legal systems? Non-European systems of law dominated much of the rest of the world in the pre-colonial period. How did they affect economic growth? While there has been much less research undertaken in the social sciences on this issue, Kuran (2011) has highlighted the role that the rigidity of Islamic law played in Middle Eastern economies falling behind those of Europe. We delve into this in more detail in Chapter 4, since it is as much an issue of culture as it is of institutions.

Political Institutions

If institutions form the "rules of the game" that people play, one reason that people around the world play by different rules is the *political institutions* of their society. Political institutions shape how we act. For one, the state generally has something close to a monopoly on violence. It can therefore use force – or the threat of it – to incentivize people to act in certain ways.

The distribution of a society's resources is also highly dependent on political institutions. Resource distribution often reflects the desires of those with political power as well as the desires of those who can keep them in power. In a democracy, this might be "the people." Elsewhere, this may be a select group of warlords. Political institutions are also crucial for encouraging economic activity. Institutions designed to protect rights, limit confiscation, and encourage investment in public goods are more likely to incentivize investment and economic exchange.

Political institutions vary widely. This variation is one of the leading causes – and consequences – of differences in economic development. Social scientists have come up with numerous ways to measure these institutions, allowing us to compare them over space and time. One of the most widely used metrics, the polity score index (Marshall and Elzinga-Marshall, 2017), measures countries on a range from absolute autocracy to absolute democracy (see Figure 3.6). These data track well with economic development. Europe and North America have high scores and Africa and the Middle East have low scores. This is also true of the democracy index (see Figure 3.7). Of course, there are major outliers: India

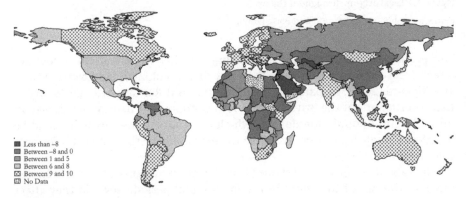

Figure 3.6 Polity score, 2017

Data source: Marshall and Elzinga-Marshall (2017). Note: polity scores range from -10 (strongly autocratic) to 10 (strongly democratic).

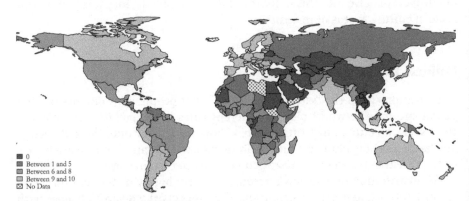

Figure 3.7 Democracy score, 2017

Data source: Marshall and Elzinga-Marshall (2017). Note: democracy scores range from 0 to 10, with higher scores indicating more competitiveness in executive recruitment, more openness of executive recruitment, more constraint on the chief executive, and more competitiveness of political participation.

and Mongolia score relatively well on these indices, despite not having close to the per capita income of OECD countries. Moreover, these indices capture the autocratic and democratic leanings of a society's institutions. This is just one aspect of how "good" or "bad" political institutions are.

But does the type of government one lives under matter for economic growth? If so, why does it matter? What can governments do – or not do – to facilitate growth?

Institutional economists argue that political institutions matter for growth because they ultimately shape the incentives that exist in society. In an unconstrained autocracy, the rule of law cannot function because it does not apply to the ruler, who can use the legal system to favor his cronies and harm his opponents. Autocratic regimes are often more corrupt than non-autocratic regimes. Liberal democracies – those which secure basic rights and liberties for their citizens – tend to have less corruption. Yet, the evidence for whether (liberal) democracy promotes economic growth, or is itself a product of economic growth, is mixed. There are examples of democracies outperforming autocracies and vice versa. As we discuss in more depth in Chapter 10, China has outperformed India since the 1980s despite similar initial levels of development. The Chinese government is autocratic while India is the world's largest democracy.

Whether a country is democratic or not is not all that matters for economic growth. Whether or not state power is limited is likely more important, as we shall discuss below. Moreover, among nondemocratic states it matters how broad the ruling coalition is and whether it represents the interests of merchants and owners of capital. In what follows, we discuss some of the additional factors that connect political institutions to economic development.

More Equal Rights for All

Which are more important for a society's long-run growth: economic institutions or political institutions? Political institutions determine who has power in society. However, political institutions tend to depend on economic resources and hence past economic institutions. Those who control political institutions can use them to increase their control of economic resources, thereby increasing their political power (Acemoglu and Robinson, 2006). This is one reason why institutions can be a source of lasting poverty. In societies where the political system is in the hands of a narrow elite, this elite can use their power to construct economic institutions that benefit themselves but impoverish the rest of society.

There is therefore a feedback between economic institutions and political institutions. The economic institutions of a society are a function of its political institutions, while political institutions help dictate the economic incentives people face. But in what ways do they do so? Are some political institutions "good" for growth and others "bad"?

Acemoglu and Robinson (2012*b*) argue that whether political institutions are good or bad for growth hinges on whether they are inclusive or extractive. Inclusive institutions create broad-based economic incentives and opportunities. They tend to be characterized by a broad distribution of political power. They bring people from varying socio-economic classes, ethnicities, and cultures to the political bargaining table. This makes it tough for one group to transgress the rights of another. Democratic institutions are often seen as relatively inclusive. In a well-functioning democracy, office holders can be challenged, anyone that meets certain qualifications (age, citizenship) can run, and unpopular officials can be voted out.

On the other end of the spectrum are extractive economic and political institutions. These institutions do not create broad-based incentives. Instead, power is held by a small group of powerful elites who are subject to few constraints from the rest of society. When power is held narrowly or the state is too weak to be effective, the conditions are ripe for some individuals or groups to extract from each other. Long-lasting economic development is rarely achieved in such an environment. One need look no further than modern-day autocracies for examples of extractive political institutions. In North Korea, Eritrea, and Turkmenistan, the political elite live in luxury while much of the population barely gets by. Funds that could be used for the public good line the pockets of the elite. There is little incentive for either domestic or foreign investment, since the proceeds of such investment are insecure. These economies tend to stagnate over time.

But what institutions count as "inclusive" as opposed to "extractive"? One problem with this taxonomy is that institutions that are inclusive for some can also be extractive for others. The Athenian democracy was a very inclusive system for adult male Athenians (Ober, 2018). Yet it behaved in a highly extractive manner to its large slave population – many of whom labored in the silver mines of Laurion in horrific conditions – and to the members of its alliance or empire who had to pay tribute in order to maintain the fleet. Was the Athenian democracy more inclusive and less extractive than later societies that did not practice democracy but also did not have slaves or an empire? A similar insight applies to Republican Florence, which granted its citizens civil and political rights but imposed extractive institutions on neighboring towns and cities (Epstein, 2000). To take a more recent example, since the 17th century, political institutions in North America have been more open and equal – for white males – than in almost any other part of the world. At the same time, even after the abolition of the slavery, the US suppressed the voting (and many other) rights of African-Americans until the 1960s.

Acemoglu and Robinson (2019) introduced the concept of a "narrow corridor to liberty" to resolve this apparent paradox. They acknowledge that political development is a process. Inclusive institutions are made possible by a functioning state – one able to repress powerful interest groups or corrupt elites. But inclusive institutions will also be upended by an overly powerful state. Civil society needs to develop alongside the growth of state power because it is civil society that is capable of limiting state power. When the state becomes too powerful relative to society, a society can be knocked out of the corridor, resulting in despotic rule and extractive institutions. But the state cannot be too weak, either. This is when we get anarchism, tribalism, and weak public good provision. For Acemoglu and Robinson, the former situation describes societies like China, while the latter situation explains the poverty and stagnation of much of sub-Saharan Africa.

A related concept is the distinction between what North, Wallis, and Weingast (2009) call the "natural state" and the "open-access order." In the natural state, which was the only form of political organization more or less anywhere prior to the 18th century, personal relationships form the basis of social organization. People are treated differently based on whom they know and where they stand in the social and economic hierarchy. The law, where it is applied at all, applies differently depending on one's standing. Although growth can happen in the natural state, it is limited. The elite can extract from the non-elite, and there is little investment in any goods that do not directly benefit the elite. Nearly every society in history was structured this way, as are many contemporary societies. Feudal Europe, Shogunate Japan, and practically every European colony had natural state political institutions. Today, many states in Africa, the Middle East, and Central Asia are in the "natural state."

Key to this argument is the concept of *rents*. Economic rents are returns above opportunity cost. Rents can be generated by government policies and restrictions on economic activity that limit entry. The insight of Tullock (1967) was that the cost of rents includes all the resources economic actors expend in pursuit of them. These costs can be very large. The concept of rent-seeking can be used to explain many institutions that were prevalent in the past, including restrictions on interest rates (Ekelund, Hebert, Tollison, Anderson, and Davidson, 1996; Koyama, 2010a), the sale of monopolies (Ekelund and Tollison, 1997), and government offices. What North, Wallis, and Weingast (2009) mean when they argue that rents hold a natural state together is that they bind together individuals with the capacity to use violence. Rents make it in their interest to adhere to the existing political order rather than challenge it by resorting to force.

According to North, Wallis, and Weingast (2009), long-run economic development requires a society to transition to the open-access order. This is a type of political system similar to what Acemoglu and Robinson (2012b) call "inclusive." But the emphasis for North, Wallis, and Weingast is on the ability of individuals and groups to form long-lasting organizations that are independent of the state. What matters for sustained economic growth is less whether or not a country is a formal democracy, but rather how easy it is to set up a rival political party or establish a large business without getting favors from political insiders. By this measure, North, Wallis, and Weingast argue that only a small number of countries today are truly open-access orders.

The question is: how do societies transition to an open-access order or inclusive institutions? How do they enter what Acemoglu and Robinson (2019) call the "narrow corridor"? This is the key question from a development standpoint. Noting which institutions are necessary is one thing. Figuring out how we get there is another. For Acemoglu and Robinson (2012b), there are "critical junctures" in a society's past that allow it to make the leap (or not). For North, Wallis, and Weingast (2009), there are a set of "doorstep conditions" a natural state society needs to achieve in order to be able to make the leap. But even then the leap is not assured.

In short, there is no general answer to how a society achieves "good" political institutions. Some societies have done it and others have not. Yet, this does not mean this literature teaches us nothing. Understanding how the societies that took off did so is important for teaching us what *can* work.

Institutions and the Commercial Revolution

Between 1000 and 1300, Europe experienced a period of sustained economic growth. The population grew, per capita income increased, urbanization rates increased dramatically, and the volume of trade expanded many times over. This was not modern economic growth, as we described in Chapter 1, because it eventually petered out. But it was growth nonetheless. For some economic historians, it was this growth that set the stage for what was to come. Southern (1970, p. 34) went so far as to suggest that "that moment of self-generating expansion, for which economists now look so anxiously in underdeveloped countries, came to Western Europe in the late eleventh century." Cipolla (1976, p. 139) described the rise of cities in Europe in the 10th through 12th centuries as one of the "turning point[s] in the history of the West – and, for that matter, of the whole world." These statements may be exaggerations. But there is no doubt that this was a period of remarkable economic growth.

The Commercial Revolution was characterized by the revival of long-distance trade. This trade spanned political borders and jurisdictions. Yet, there were no political authorities capable of enforcing contracts between merchants operating in different cities. So how did trade occur? How could a merchant punish someone who cheated him?

Medieval merchants selling in different jurisdictions faced the following problem. Say an English merchant has wool valued at £5 in England. He decides to take the wool to Flanders, where it is valued more. He meets a Flemish merchant who can sell it for £8. If goods and money can be exchanged there and then, the trade can take place at a price between £5 and £8 and both merchants will gain. Trade is mutually beneficial.

But now suppose that there is some delay between either the goods or payment arriving. Let's say the Flemish merchant has to pay on credit since hard specie is in short supply. This delay between purchase and payment gives the Flemish merchant an opportunity to renege on his promise. The English merchant cannot therefore know whether the Flemish merchant will actually deliver the payment. Once the Flemish merchant has the wool, he has the choice of transferring the money to England or not. But why should he? The shadow cast by the future will not be sufficiently strong to enforce cooperation if the two merchants are not expected to regularly trade with each other in the future. Knowing this, the English merchant will never agree to trade unless he can be paid up front and immediately. The potential gains from trade are never realized.

Greif (2000) called this the fundamental problem of exchange. Trade is limited to cases where either a spot exchange can take place or merchants trust each other enough to trade on credit. This insight is generalizable: in the absence of this trust, trade is extremely costly. A lack of information about the quality of goods could generate similar problems. Manufactured goods might have suffered from defects that were hard to detect on purchase but only became apparent later on. Purchasers alone bore the consequences of defective purchases, because people who purchased defective merchandise had few remedies (Richardson, 2008). Merchants had an incentive to pass on defective goods to traders they met anonymously and to retain quality products for personal exchange.

Greif used game theory to explain how merchant communities in the Middle Ages attempted to resolve this fundamental problem of exchange. First, he considered the Maghribi traders – Jewish traders in Muslim North Africa – who were prominent in Mediterranean trade during the 10th and 11th centuries (Greif, 1989, 1993, 2006). Conducting long-distance trade in the absence of a reliable and centralized legal system, these traders faced a version of the problem of exchange. To conduct their business in different parts of the Mediterranean, they needed to hire agents. But what guarantee did a merchant have that the agent would not cheat him?

The key to the Maghribi traders' success was their ability to utilize a multilateral punishment strategy. This is a situation in which multiple parties agree to punish anyone who cheats any individual in the group. The effectiveness of this punishment hinged upon the nature of their close-knit community. Greif provides evidence that the Maghribi traders were able to disseminate information about the behavior of commercial agents among a coalition of merchants.

In the 11th and 12th centuries, the Maghribi traders were displaced from Mediterranean trade by Italian merchants. Greif (2002, 2006) documents that community responsibility enabled these merchants to overcome the problem of exchange. Community responsibility meant that individual merchants were made responsible for the behavior of their peers. The goods of a merchant could be seized simply because another merchant from his town had refused to repay a loan or had cheated another merchant. Under this system, the cost of an individual merchant cheating was borne by the community. This meant that internal community enforcement could be used to deter domestic merchants from cheating foreigners. The court of the Flemish merchant had an incentive to uphold complaints from the court of the English merchant, which in turn only championed genuine complaints. This allowed borrowers to credibly commit to repaying lenders even though they might never trade again in future.

Greif's models help to explain how trade worked without widespread rule of law. Although these institutions differed over time and place, they had one common element: they incentivized people to follow through with their promises. They thus allowed trade to flourish long before states were capable of providing the rule of law over the entirety of their domains.

Between the State and the Market: Guilds

Not all institutions are formal ones emanating from the state. The rules of the game come from many facets of life. One important set of institutions that played a role in the Commercial Revolution were *guilds*. Various craft and merchant guilds regulated large swaths of the European economy from the late Middle Ages to the Industrial Revolution. Indeed, the story of the medieval economic efflorescence is impossible to tell without some mention of guild activity.

Craft guilds dominated urban life for much of the period between the 12th and 16th centuries. To participate in a trade, one generally had to be a member of a guild. This was true for smiths, tanners, butchers, bakers, brewers, clerks, and entertainers, among many others. Guild membership was restricted, and one had to serve a lengthy apprenticeship before becoming a master. Craft guilds performed a range of different functions, including regulating goods and labor markets. They also aided local political authorities in tax collection. They kept their privileges by allying with local political authorities (Ogilvie, 2019).

Craft guilds have been the subject of considerable controversy. Were guilds rent-seeking institutions that imposed costs on the wider economy? Or did they serve an important economic function? In theory, both are possible. Guilds did restrict entry and hence generate higher profits for members than they would have otherwise obtained. At the same time, it is possible that guilds could have helped to resolve coordination problems, protect merchants from state predation, and resolve market failures.

Richardson (2008) argued that craft guilds helped resolve problems of asymmetric information such as verifying product quality. Guilds had an incentive to keep product quality high since they had a "name brand" which allowed them to sell goods well outside of the city. This is why some goods are still associated with cities. London's guild of pewterers made a particularly high-quality pewter (which we still call London pewter). The wine-makers of Burgundy made a particularly rich and sought-after red wine. The cheese-makers of Parma made a very nice cheese.

Craft guilds served other purposes as well. Epstein (1998) argued that the craft guilds and the apprentice system played a critical role in incentivizing investment in industry-specific human capital. The work done by master guild members required extremely high skill, taking years to learn. Epstein argues that restricting labor via the apprenticeship system was the only way for masters to recoup the costs of transferring skills. Teaching these skills entailed upfront costs with little immediate payoff. Masters needed to recoup costs later to make it worth it. The rents available via the guild system provided these incentives. They could also have incentivized innovation. Monopoly rents largely went to inventors, since not just anyone could pick up a trade. As a result, there were numerous minor improvements made to techniques and capital in the late medieval period. De la Croix, Doepke, and Mokyr (2017) show that these novel techniques slowly spread throughout Europe via journeymen. These master guildsmen would go from town to town and employ the tacit knowledge of "how to do things" gained in their previous employment. In this light, guilds may have encouraged innovation and the diffusion of best-practice techniques.

In contrast, Ogilvie (2019) argues that craft guilds were rent-seeking organizations that did best by their members but often imposed costs on the rest of society. Drawing on two databases of guild activities, she provides evidence that guilds routinely restricted the economic activity of non-guild members, lobbied governments for privileges, and used a combination of fines, fees, confiscations, and occasionally violence to enforce these privileges. They opposed innovations when they threatened guild profits. In this view, the late medieval economy was held back by guild activity. It is of course possible that the truth lies somewhere in between these opposing views.

Merchant guilds, on the other hand, dominated trade throughout most of the late Middle Ages, especially in the free towns of Northern Europe (Ogilvie, 2011). The most famous of these guilds was the German Hansa. Members of the Hansa traded with other members in cities throughout modern-day Germany, Poland, Denmark, Netherlands, Belgium, England, and beyond.

Travel to foreign lands can be dangerous, especially for merchants carrying valuable cargo. Beyond the physical dangers imposed by outlaws, local rulers have an incentive to confiscate the wares of foreign merchants. What's to stop them? To whom could merchants appeal? According to Greif, Milgrom, and Weingast (1994), one purpose of the merchant guild was to serve as a collective voice against rulers who wished to transgress upon their rights. If a merchant had his rights transgressed, the guild would boycott the city. This dried up the tax revenue that rulers received from trade, providing a huge disincentive to transgress merchants' rights. The guild could do this while an individual could not because boycotts require collective action. Any merchant caught trading with a city under boycott – a "scab" in modern parlance – could be kicked out of the guild, forgoing a lifetime of healthy earnings.

Once states became larger and able to protect the rights of more of their citizens, merchant guilds became unnecessary. They imposed a cost on society through their monopoly privileges (Ogilvie, 2011). In the medieval context, where state and legal capacity was limited, this cost was worth it, since it allowed some degree of trade to occur. But how did states gain the legal capacity to make institutions such as merchant guilds obsolete? It is to this issue that we turn next.

Parliaments and Limited Government

Among the most important changes in European political institutions in the build-up to the Industrial Revolution was the rise of *limited government*. As the name implies, in a limited government, the powers of the ruling elite are constrained. There are checks on authority in each part of government. Such checks help economies grow. They limit the ability of any one group to extract too much. There are no inclusive political institutions or open-access orders without some limits on government.

But how do societies get limited government? Throughout history, most governments were not limited. Small groups of ruling elites held most power, and the rest of society had relatively little capacity to push back. This began to change in Europe during the Commercial Revolution. In the 11th and 12th centuries, self-governing or independent cities emerged in northern Italy, the Low Countries, and then later in the Rhineland and across Germany. The absence of a single strong ruler enabled merchants to rise to political prominence. They implemented reforms that favored their own interests but were also largely favorable to the overall expansion of trade. For this reason, independent city-states were pioneers of the revival of trade during the Commercial Revolution.

The late Middle Ages also saw the rise of *parliaments*. The term "parliament" refers to political assemblies that had the ability to limit the power of the sovereign. They were generally comprised of three types of elites: churchmen, landed nobles, and the urban bourgeoisie. The first medieval parliaments, or *cortes*, emerged in medieval Spain, in León and Castile, before spreading across Europe in the 12th and 13th centuries (van Zanden, Buringh, and Bosker, 2012). Parliaments were important because, at least in theory, they allowed the interests of the broader population to be *represented* in a single body. In the ancient world, democracy always meant direct democracy. In classical Athens, the entire citizen body meeting in the assembly was sovereign. The limitation to this mode of government was that it scaled poorly. Individuals who did not reside in Athens could not attend the assembly. The development of *representative* institutions like parliaments made it possible for individuals living in much more extensive polities to participate, albeit indirectly, in the governing process.

Parliaments emerged out of the councils medieval kings called among their nobility. In England, the Magna Carta, signed by King John (r. 1199–1216) and his barons in 1215, played a crucial role in the formation of medieval parliaments.

The Magna Carta arose in response to the abuses of King John following his defeat by (and the loss of his Norman territories to) the King of France (Koyama, 2016). To understand why this led to the rise of representative institutions, one has to understand the feudal system that John presided over. One way to do this is through the lens of the natural state framework introduced by North, Wallis, and Weingast (2009).

In their framework, discussed earlier in this chapter, political elites restrict entry in areas of the economy in order to generate monopoly rents. These rents are distributed to those with enough coercive power to disrupt the existing power structure. In medieval England, these were the great barons, who had purview over significant territory. In such a setting, states cannot provide rule of law to all precisely because they rely on treating individuals differently in order to maintain political order. Instead of impersonal rules, natural states rely on personal enforcement and on identity rules to govern. This reliance on identity rules meant that individuals received different treatment depending on their religion, social class, place of birth, or residency.

In England circa 1200, the authority of the king stemmed from two sources. First, he was the largest landowner. This was crucial, as most royal revenue came from land. Second, the king was at the top of the feudal system. All other lords in the country swore him fealty. He could apportion estates in the absence of a direct male heir and was endowed with a range of prerogatives, which included the right to hold court and enforce justice. But these prerogatives did not include the right to freely impose taxes on his subjects during times of peace. In theory, he was expected to "live on his own" from the proceeds of the royal demesne.

To meet the costs of war with France, John exploited all of the revenue sources available to a feudal ruler. He sold wardships – the right to take control of the land of minors until they came of age – and sold the right to marry rich heiresses. Feudal rights such as these were traditionally employed to cement alliances among the nobility. But John exploited them for immediate profit. His position as feudal overlord enabled him to exploit his control over the royal courts to sell justice. And he mercilessly taxed England's Jewish community (Koyama, 2010b).

Through these abuses, John alienated the powerful lords who made up the ruling coalition of 13th-century England. These lords had the military power to defeat the king if they could coordinate their resistance. In forcing him to agree to the Magna Carta, they got him to acknowledge certain limits to royal authority – particularly the right to levy taxes without consent. They succeeded: the Magna Carta forcefully articulated the position that the king was subject to the law.

During the reign of John's successor, Henry III (r. 1216–72), the term "parliament" emerged to describe meetings between the king and the leading barons. The initial role of Parliament was judicial. It was employed to hear a variety of legal cases, and it soon became important in fiscal matters as well. In the reign of Edward I (r. 1272–1307), Parliament became crucial in granting the king the right to collect taxes. Importantly, Edward I regularly called Parliaments in which representatives of the urban bourgeoisie attended, in addition to the nobility and members of the clergy. For the rest of the Middle Ages, English kings relied on Parliament to grant them the taxes they needed, particularly in wartime.

During the Middle Ages, representative institutions flourished across Europe. However, they did not all become national institutions like the English Parliament. For example, the *parlement* of Paris was in origin a similar body to the English Parliament and it covered the entirety of the kingdom of France. However, during and after the Hundred Years' War, the French king devolved authority to regional *parlements* such as the those of Toulouse, Rouen, Guyenne and Gascony, Burgundy, and Provence. These *parlements* came to represent local rather than national interests. They therefore precluded the development of an institution strong enough to constrain the French monarch. Similarly, the *cortes* of León and Aragon, although they remained active, were only able to provide local resistance against the Spanish monarchies after the unification of the crowns of Aragon and Castile in 1469.

Unlike today, parliaments were only in session when they were called by the monarch. And monarchs were only likely to call parliaments when they needed something – mainly taxes. In return, parliaments could expect to receive some favorable laws, policies, or rights. Hence, the frequency with which parliaments were called reflects their power to constrain the crown, and it can thus be used as an indicator of the degree of limited governance (van Zanden, Buringh, and Bosker, 2012). Figure 3.8 depicts the frequency of parliamentary activity in several Western European states. One feature is immediately clear: parliaments in Southern Europe became less active over time while parliamentary activity in northwestern Europe rose rapidly in the 16th and 17th centuries. This was just prior to the economic rise of northwestern Europe.

Is this just a coincidence? The timing suggests not. The parliaments of northwestern Europe, especially in England and the Netherlands, became strong around the time when economic growth accelerated. This is precisely what we would expect to see if limited government played a role in forging the modern economy. Although it could be a coincidence, the literature described above suggests that the connection is causal. For this reason, the rise of limited governance is among the most important issues we will return to in Chapter 7, when we discuss the preconditions for the rise of the modern economy.

War and State Finances

How does a society get institutions that provide equal rights for individuals, enforce property rights, and allow for flourishing factor markets? One important factor dictating the path of institutional development has been warfare.

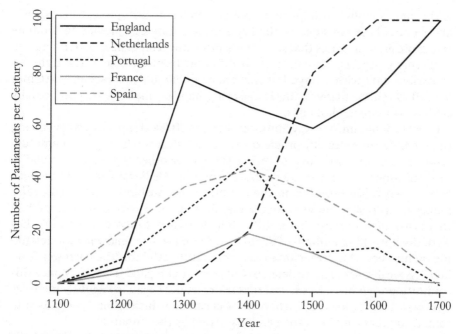

Figure 3.8 Parliamentary activity in Europe, 1100–1800

Data source: van Zanden, Buringh, and Bosker (2012). The values for Spain are the average of the number of parliaments in León and Castile, Catalonia, Aragon, Valencia, and Navarre.

In ancient Athens, the granting of the franchise to all adult male citizens was partly a response to the crucial role ordinary citizens played in maintaining the Athenian navy (Stasavage, 2020). But this was not the norm in European history. Why not? After all, prior to the 19th century, Europeans were almost constantly at war with each other. How did this shape institutional development in Europe? One set of arguments focuses on the simple fact that wars require money. And acquiring money generally requires the capacity to tax. Economists and political scientists call this a state's "fiscal capacity."

How do states acquire fiscal capacity? Raising enough revenue to support a state is a difficult problem to solve. People generally don't like paying taxes unless they feel like they are getting something in return. Even then, a major free-rider problem exists if it is difficult to enforce punishment for tax evasion. Solving this problem requires institutions that align the incentives of the relevant players: rulers, those who collect the taxes, and those who pay the taxes. Once this problem is solved, however, the state generally has to provide something besides just war in order to convince people to pay taxes. These include public goods such as transport networks, education, and infrastructure.

Perhaps more importantly, fiscal capacity does not arise in a vacuum. It is generally associated with other aspects of what scholars call state capacity. This is the state's ability to implement policy, render justice, protect its citizens, and so on. These are some of the key things a state can provide to promote economic growth. States that solve these problems tend to have better long-run economic prospects. State capacity is different from the size of the state. An expansive state with a large but inefficient public bureaucracy may attempt but fail to achieve many goals. On the other hand, a smaller state may actually achieve its more modest ends.

Over the long run, one way European states built fiscal capacity was by solving the credible commitment problem they faced. Rulers who aspire to absolute power or are unconstrained by either the law or other representative bodies like Parliament cannot make credible promises. Medieval and early modern kings often broke promises to their subjects. For instance, they might raise money for a crusade but use the revenues for their own private purposes. When they broke their promise, it was difficult to hold them to account. After all, they were the king! King Philip II of Spain (r. 1556–98) was so renowned for defaulting on his debts that Drelichman and Voth (2016) call him "the borrower from hell." As we discuss in more detail in Chapter 7, in England it was only once this commitment problem was solved that tax revenues began to seriously increase. This was done by making Parliament a permanent institution (as opposed to something that could be called and dismissed by the monarch).

Another problem for pre-industrial states is that they tended to be fiscally fragmented. As a result, they suffered from local tax free-riding. Why should one region send money to the central government when it believed the other regions would send in enough to cover expenses? Fiscal centralization helped states overcome this free-rider problem. In doing so, it enabled states to increase revenues and often complemented the expansion of markets and the division of labor. This made it easier for responsible governments to follow sound fiscal policies and thus lowered credit risk. However, there was always the chance that rulers would waste the new funds on reckless wars. Thus, it was only the conjunction of limitations on the discretionary authority of government with centralized fiscal systems that enabled states to borrow at low cost (Dincecco, 2009). This allowed a massive take-off in European government revenues between the 16th and 19th centuries (see Figure 3.9).

Why and how did some states in some places and at some times invest in fiscal capacity? In early modern Europe, parliaments played a key role in authorizing and legitimating tax collection. Because states were fiscally fragmented, rulers needed buy-in from other elites in order to collect revenue. Parliaments were the means through which they received this buy-in. Thus far, we have only focused on how parliaments limited the arbitrary power of rulers. But by constraining the arbitrary power of the monarch, parliaments also strengthened rulers by giving them the ability to make credible commitments. This enabled rulers to collect more money and fight longer and more expensive wars. For instance, after throwing off Habsburg rule in 1568, the Dutch Republic embarked upon an eighty-year war with the Spanish Empire followed by a conflict with France

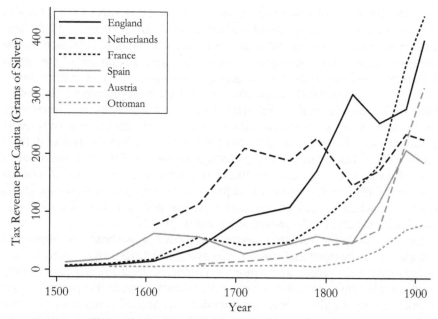

Figure 3.9 Tax revenues per capita for six European powers, 1500–1900

Data source: Karaman and Pamuk (2013).

that would last, on and off, for over forty years. For England, the Glorious Revolution of 1688 marked the start of a "Second Hundred Years' War" with France. But how and why did states form in a manner that they could conduct such long and expensive wars?

This question was asked by Tilly (1975, 1990). His statement "war made the state, and the state made war" succinctly summarizes the matter. War was the main preoccupation of medieval and early modern European states. Before 1800, states spent most of their revenue on warfare or on paying interest on debts occurred in previous wars. Nonetheless, though almost all pre-modern states were preoccupied with war, Tilly (1990) discerned three paths of state formation: a "coercive-intensive" path, a "capital-intensive" path, and a mix between the two.

The coercive-intensive path was taken by Prussia and Russia. These states were built from and for war. The Prussians and Russians did not just tax their populations. They directly mobilized labor and other resources through conscription. In the 17th century, Russia was involved in a war on its western frontier one year out of every two. On its southern and eastern frontiers, war was essentially continuous (Pipes, 1974). As war machines became stronger, they were able to exert force over a greater expanse of people and demand tax revenue from them. This, however, did not lead to positive long-run economic outcomes. There was little incentive for individuals to invest in capital in such a regime.

On the other extreme were states on the "capital-intensive" path. This was taken by many of the city-states of northern Italy, Central Europe, and the Low Countries. These states expanded as their wealth expanded. Capital-intensive states were also often involved in warfare. They generally protected the rights of their citizens, especially those engaged in commerce. They were thus able to collect tax revenue from the economic elite in return for protection. These city-states were able to borrow at relatively low rates precisely because they were run *by* merchants *for* merchants (Stasavage, 2011). Merchants had an interest in maintaining the credit-worthiness of the state, and thus the risk of default was low. This is important: access to credit is a necessary feature of the modern state. Absent natural resource windfalls, it is impossible to think of a modern state functioning well without the capacity to borrow. Yet, as Stasavage (2014) points out, when certain groups dominate the political scene for too long, vested interests eventually undermine further growth.

The late medieval Italian city-states provided a particularly important example of the institutional innovations associated with warfare. Almost continuously at war, Venice and Florence pioneered institutional innovations which enabled them to compete with much larger states and raise ever larger revenues to pay for their mercenary armies. The annual revenue of Florence in the 14th century varied between 250,000 and 350,000 florins, but historians estimate the direct cost of the three-year war between Florence and the Papacy in 1375–8 exceeded 2.5 million florins (Caferro, 2008, p. 177). To meet this shortfall, Italian city-states developed impersonal systems of public debt and permanent systems of taxation (Epstein, 2000). In these cities, the holders of capital were represented in government, ensuring that the promise to repay was credible. Thus, their political institutions allowed city-states to pay lower interest on their debts than territorial monarchies did (see Figure 3.10).

Yet, Tilly (1990) argues that the path to the modern economy did not lie in the purely capital-intensive political institutions of the city-states. Instead, it lay in those states that employed some hybrid model that combined both coercion and capital. England is a prototypical example. These states were able to encourage capital accumulation while also acquiring the capacity to tax large swaths of their population. And those with capital were willing to provide taxes in return for protection of their property rights.

Hoffman (2015) presents a modified version of this thesis. Like Tilly, he focuses on incessant European warfare as a prime mover of European economic success. But instead of emphasizing its role in state formation, he stresses the role that warfare played in encouraging innovation in military technology. These technological advances, especially when combined with gunpowder, gave Europe the upper hand in colonizing the rest of the world. But why were European patterns of warfare different? Hoffman argues that a cultural proclivity to warfare made European military competition more intense than elsewhere.

Yet another impact of warfare was its effect on the location of economic activity. Rosenthal and Wong (2011) argue that European warfare disproportionately

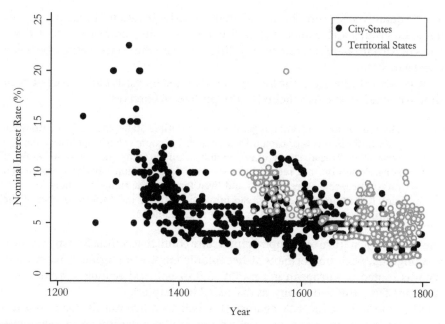

Figure 3.10 Interest rates in city-states and territorial states, 1200–1800
Data source: Stasavage (2016).

affected the countryside because cities tended to be better fortified. This contrasted with China, where less frequent warfare meant that urban and rural locations were equally affected by war. The result was that trade and manufacturing were pushed to urban areas in Europe but not in China. This in turn meant higher urban wages in Europe, which encouraged investment in labor-saving technologies. As we will see in Chapter 8, these were precisely the types of technologies that were key to Europe's industrialization.

In highlighting the role played by warfare in Europe's institutional development, we do not mean to suggest that war was "good" for the economy. Naïve historical accounts that sometimes suggest this are usually mistaken. Warfare is destructive. The direct costs include the destruction caused by war and the opportunity costs of investment in defense, walls, weapons, and armies. There are also harder to ascertain indirect costs that include the effect of warfare on institutional quality or culture.

In any case, warfare was hardly unique to Europe. For instance, conflict was endemic to the Indian sub-continent. Nath (2018, p. 245, quoted in Dincecco, Fenske, Menon, and Mukherjee, 2019) notes that "the Mughals fought their enemies ceaselessly ... war was a constant preoccupation of the Mughal Empire." The Mughal state was also almost entirely devoted to military activity. In Southeast Asia, the Toungoo Empire in Burma warred more or less continuously with Pagan, Ava, and Siam. As we discussed in Chapter 2, there was also frequent warfare on China's northern frontier between China and various nomadic groups and confederacies. The critical point, however, is that these types of warfare were fundamentally different from interstate warfare between European states.

Warfare in Europe from the late medieval period onwards took place between similarly sized states. As Scheidel (2019, pp. 338–9) observes:

> The fall of Rome ultimately gave rise to multiple states that did not dramatically differ in terms of capabilities (smaller but more cohesive polities balanced less-well-organized larger ones), mobilization intensity (Roman-style levels of conscription did not return until the French Revolution), mode of production (most Europeans were farmers and lived far from the steppe frontier), and religion (Christianity steadily spread into the northern and eastern reaches of the continent while Islam failed to make much headway).

The symmetric nature of European interstate conflict accounts for why warfare was ongoing, with no permanent hegemonic empire emerging. This symmetry was rooted in European geography and in political economy factors that stemmed from this geography, as discussed in Chapter 2.

Other authors push back against this bellicose hypothesis. One counter-argument is that frequent warfare did not promote urbanization, economic development, or the rise of more inclusive institutions in other parts of the world (Centeno, 1997). Another criticism is that when population density is low, warfare may promote slave raiding rather than state-building (Herbst, 2000). We discuss this latter point in the African context in Chapter 6.

Even in Europe, not all states invested as much in fiscal capacity as England did after 1688. To account for why some European states built much more fiscal capacity than others, Gennaioli and Voth (2015) laid out a model in which the incentive to build capacity depended on the chances a state had of defeating its rivals. In this account, interstate competition provided incentives for some states – those for whom the relative payoff to such investments wass high – to standardize their fiscal systems and invest in more capital-intensive forms of war. But other states, which faced higher initial costs of centralizing because they were more heterogeneous, might not find this worthwhile. Nations that did not have a robust military tended to be gobbled up by their rivals, as was Poland-Lithuania.

Chapter Summary

In this chapter, we assessed the role of *institutions* in economic development. Institutions form the "rules of the game" that people play in their day-to-day lives. They come in many forms: political, economic, legal, social, and religious. They form the incentives which shape how people act. Institutions differ across societies and throughout history. They can therefore help explain why different societies have had varying degrees of economic success.

Among the most important institutions a society can have to facilitate growth are those that uphold the rule of law and protect property rights. Whether a society has such institutions is a result of some nexus of their political and legal institutions. Understanding why some societies have had institutions at (or near) this nexus and others have not is an inherently historical question. This chapter has provided insight into why some societies have achieved this and others have not.

Yet, unresolved questions remain. Most importantly, why do institutions work differently in different parts of the world? Democracy is a prime example. Democratic institutions have broadly succeeded in some countries, especially in Europe, in facilitating open exchanges of ideas, empowering a broader set of citizens, and addressing broad-based economic needs. But democratic institutions have failed in other settings, such as many post-Soviet transition states or the post-Arab Spring Middle East. Why do similar institutions work in some settings but not in others? Does culture play some role in the efficacy of institutions? More generally, is a society's culture an important independent determinant of a society's economic success? We turn to these issues in the next chapter.

4

Did Culture Make Some Rich and Others Poor?

What Is Culture and Why Does It Matter?

Henrich (2015) defines culture as a set of learned rules of behavior. These rules are the short-cuts we apply to make sense of a complex world. Our brain power is limited. It is impossible to think through the implications of every action we take. How do we interact with strangers? When do we move forward at a stop sign? What type of food is healthy to eat? The answers to these questions are embedded in a society's culture, and different cultures have come to different conclusions regarding the best ways to answer them.

The mental shortcuts provided by one's culture are *learned* through both imitation (of successful people) and direct transmission. This insight goes back to the work of Hayek, among others. For Hayek (1982, p. 157), the "mind is embedded in a traditional impersonal structure of learnt rules." Human beings are dependent on learned rules because our "capacity to order experience is an acquired replica of cultural patterns which every individual mind finds given." Culture shapes the way we view the world. From this perspective, cultural learning is key to explaining the success of humans as a species. Indeed, some cultural anthropologists contend that cultural evolution allows humans to leapfrog genetic evolution (Boyd and Richerson, 1985; Henrich, 2015). Through culture, we are able to pass down to future generations what works and what does not. As Richerson and Boyd (2010, p. 109) describe it: "[T]he wheels of cultural evolution roll on the time scale of millennia, even though, when we look closely at any one society over short periods of time, change is often readily perceptible."

Different societies have different cultural norms. This statement should be obvious to anyone who has traveled even a bit outside of their home town. Not only does culture evolve differently across countries and continents, but even within countries cultural norms can diverge immensely. Within the US, Woodard (2011) identified eleven regional cultures, which range on issues regarding individual liberty, the role of the state, views on education, and religion (see Figure 4.1). Within the states of California and Texas, a number of

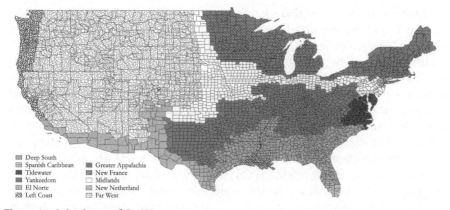

Figure 4.1 Subcultures of the US

Data source: Woodard (2011).

widely different subcultures exist, covering all degrees of the political spectrum and a wide range of ethnic backgrounds and religiosity.

Why might culture help explain how the world became rich? The answer to this question is often addressed by considering its converse: what aspects of culture have *inhibited* economic development? Because the learned norms and beliefs we acquire through cultural evolution develop slowly – often more slowly than economic and technological change – cultural beliefs can become maladapted to their economic environment. In other words, cultural beliefs that benefited economic growth under one set of circumstances may hamper it in another. And because cultural norms are slow to change, societies may not be in a position to take advantage of the new opportunities afforded to them.

Culture also matters because cultural beliefs can affect how institutions function. Recall that this was a key insight of Greif's discussion of institutions in Chapter 3. From this perspective, cultural beliefs matter because they explain why people do what they do and therefore why institutions encourage certain patterns of behavior in some contexts but not in others. This may explain, for instance, why democracy has had such a tough time taking hold in the Middle East, even in the wake of the Arab Spring. If democratic norms of accountability and abiding by the outcomes of elections are not well established, democratic institutions are unlikely to function as they are supposed to.

Before we proceed, we want to be clear that, with respect to the effect of culture on "why the world became rich," we are *not* speaking of (and certainly not endorsing) a "Eurocentric" view of history. This view, common among historians of the early 20th century, attributes some aspect of Western culture – such as being hard-working, innovative, or willing to take risks – as being superior and the cause of much that is good in the modern world. Not only are many of the views of this ilk offensive, but they are unsatisfying as social science. Even if we are to believe that such cultural traits differ between societies, *why* did such differences arise in the first place?

Most of the supposed cultural differences pointed to in the early 20th century may have reflected as much about the cultural norms of Western observers as about their subjects. For example, in the late 19th century, Westerners in Japan commented on the indolence and laziness of Japanese workers. Chang (2008) notes that "in his 1903 book, *Evolution of the Japanese*, the American missionary Sidney Gulick observed that many Japanese 'give an impression . . . of being lazy and utterly indifferent to the passage of time.'" Gulick was no casual observer. He lived in Japan for twenty-five years (1888–1913), fully mastered the Japanese language, and taught at a Japanese university. After his return to the US, he campaigned for racial equality on behalf of Asian-Americans. Nevertheless, he saw ample confirmation of the cultural stereotype of the Japanese as an "easy-going" and "emotional" people who possessed qualities like "lightness of heart, freedom from all anxiety for the future, living chiefly for the present." But by the late 20th century, similar observers claimed that the discipline, industriousness, and punctuality of the Japanese reflected a deep-rooted Confucian culture.

An aversion to such cultural stereotyping understandably led economists of the late 20th century to dismiss culture as a cause of economic differences between societies. Yet, going too far in the opposite direction may have been a mistake. Research over the past twenty-five years has demonstrated the insights that studying culture offers. In this chapter, we focus on recent scholarship that has presented a more nuanced view of how and why certain cultural traits differ across societies and what this means for economic development. Such cultural traits include those related to trust, family structure, individualism, and (perhaps most importantly) religion. In none of these cases are one set of cultural traits "superior" to others, although some do affect economic growth differently than others.

Can Culture Explain the European Take-off?

Was there something about European culture that allowed it to become wealthy before the rest of the world? This is a thorny issue. On the one hand, it invites ethnocentric or racist theorizing: that is, that Europeans have something about them that is just "better". These arguments tend to be flawed upon even casual inspection, and we will not consider them in this book. On the other hand, this should not dissuade us from asking whether there are cultural attributes that may have helped propel the European take-off in the 18th and 19th centuries. Recent research suggests that culture can play an enormous role in all sorts of economic outcomes. We should not rule out the possibility that culture played a role in Europe's rise.

The answer to the question posed in the title of this section depends on one's assessment of how and why modern economic growth took place. To the extent that one views the onset of sustained economic growth as a pan-European phenomenon, then the cultural factors that we should study will be ones common to all of Europe, or at least Western Europe. But to the extent that one views modern economic growth as beginning in northwestern Europe, specifically in the British Isles, then one should be most interested in cultural traits that permeated Britain but not the rest of Europe.

Just how important are values to a society's economic potential? Could a society take off economically in the absence of values praising hard work, risk taking, and wealth accumulation? McCloskey (2006, 2010, 2016) argues that such values were essential for northwestern Europe's take-off in the 17th and 18th centuries. According to her, one of the primary impediments to growth in history was the way people thought and talked about work and profit. For the ancient Greeks and Romans, for example, work of any type was among the lowest-valued pursuits. Wealth was valued because it brought freedom and permitted leisure (Finley, 1973). The middling classes – the bourgeois – had little prestige in ancient society. If you were at all successful, you were supposed to strive to own a landed estate and live off of its returns. Indolence was what a Roman social climber strove towards.

A society with such cultural values is unlikely to have sustained economic growth. As we will see, technological innovation is essential for growth to persist in the long run. But innovation requires detailed knowledge of production processes and what can make production more efficient. Any society that frowns upon hard work will be unlikely to have a robust class of innovators. Any society that disparages finance will be unlikely to have a thriving entrepreneurial class or significant investment in capital. Although the Roman Empire had a sophisticated market economy and, as we saw in Chapter 2, a developed road network, it did not experience sustained economic growth.

Cultural values that disparaged hard work persisted through the medieval period, especially among the European elite. To the extent that the elite were supposed to get their hands dirty, it was through warfare, not work. Those lucky few from the lower classes who were able to rise up the economic ladder were supposed to use their wealth to gain social status, perhaps by acquiring a noble title. Once acquired, nobles were supposed to live off the fruits of their land, leaving behind the professions that gave them their wealth. McCloskey claims these cultural values changed in northwestern Europe in the 17th and 18th centuries. In the Netherlands, and later in England, the bourgeois pursuit of profit became lauded, not demonized. The rhetoric concerning the bourgeois elevated financiers, innovators, and merchants to a place where people aspired to these professions. Rising up the economic ladder also placed one higher on the social ladder – it was not simply a means to social prestige. These cultural changes, in turn, encouraged the best and brightest to engage in productive pursuits. A class of well-to-do merchants, financiers, and manufacturers emerged and entered into the British elite – individuals like Sir Robert Peel (1750–1830), who made his fortune in the textile industry before entering Parliament and becoming a baronet, or Joseph Chamberlain (1836–1914), who was a shoe manufacturer before becoming a politician.

On the flip side is China. For most of the last two millennia, China was the world's leader in technology and science. But by 1850 it had unquestionably fallen behind Europe in technology, science, and engineering. This gave rise to the famous Needham puzzle, named after the great British chemist and historian Joseph Needham (1995). How did China go from being the world's scientific leader in ancient and medieval times to a technological laggard by the 19th century?

One prominent answer to this question is culture. Landes (2006, p. 7) summarized this line of thinking when he noted that China failed to "realize the economic potential of its scientific expertise involved the larger values of society." While Landes does point to institutional factors such as the absence of political competition, the power of the state, and the lack of institutions that allowed for free debate, he dwells on cultural differences between China and Europe. He argues that China lacked "this peculiarly European joy in discovery. . . . This pleasure in the new and better. . . . This cultivation of invention" (Landes, 2006, p. 9).

Does this explanation hold water? It is hard to square a Chinese cultural disinclination for invention with the facts. For one, it does not explain the Needham puzzle. China was the world's innovation leader for much of the last two millennia! In any case, the evidence in support of Landes's assertion is thin. The primary piece of evidence he brings to bear is the mission of George Macartney to the Qing Empire in 1793. Qing China restricted trade with the West and Macartney's mission was to persuade the Qianlong emperor of the benefits of more extensive trade with Britain. When Macartney presented the latest manufactured goods in order to impress the emperor, Qianlong was notoriously underwhelmed, replying: "Strange and costly objects do not interest me. . . . We possess all things. I set no value on objects strange or ingenious, and have no use for your country's manufactures." As Platt (2018, p. 97) relates, however, this statement need not represent a negative cultural attitude towards science and innovation:

> Privately, . . . Qianlong was deeply fascinated by Western inventions. [He] had a cherished collection of seventy intricate English clocks gathered over the years, and had written poetry on the loveliness of foreign glass as well as several poems about telescopes. He periodically addressed edicts to the customs commissioner in Canton asking him to send European goods or artisans to the capital. He was a patron of the Catholic missionaries he employed at court as astronomers and cartographers, and though he allowed them little freedom, he valued the skills they brought. When James Dinwiddie was assembling the scientific equipment that Qianlong would so publicly dismiss, he did so without knowing that the emperor had actually ordered the missionaries to watch closely what Dinwiddie was doing so they could replicate his work after he was gone.

The problem with Landes's argument is not that there is no evidence of a cultural disinclination towards innovation or new ideas in 18th-century China. Rather, Landes does not provide a systematic explanation for the differential incentives facing rulers and intellectuals in China versus Europe. No European ruler in the 18th century would have acted as the Qianlong emperor did. But this may be better explained by geopolitics than by culture. In the late 18th century, China still did not have to fear any serious military competition. Qianlong's focus was on maintaining order within his empire. As a Manchu outsider, it was more important for him to pose as a guarantor of traditional Confucian culture than it was to acquire technologies from a foreign power.

Does Religion Affect Economic Growth?

Another cultural feature that can impact economic growth is religion. While social scientists have largely eschewed simplistic theories stating that certain religions are the reason some (Protestant) societies are ahead or other (Muslim) societies are behind, recent research suggests there are more subtle ways that religion can affect economic growth. These include incentivizing education, affecting family formation through marriage regulations, and impacting political development. This section examines the leading theories tying religion to economic growth.

The Protestant Work Ethic and the "Spirit" of Capitalism

Perhaps the most famous argument that "culture matters" was made by Weber (1905/1930) in The Protestant Ethic and the "Spirit" of Capitalism. According to Weber's hypothesis, the Calvinist doctrine of predestination – which stated that one's eternal fate was decided regardless of one's actions on earth – encouraged people to work harder and save more. This is how they would show that they were one of the "elect" who would enter heaven. This ideal became secularized in places with Calvinist influence (the US, the Netherlands) and was the root of a "capitalist spirit" that permeated these societies. For Weber, people like Benjamin Franklin were the ideal type exhibiting the capitalist spirit. They were hard-working, organized, frugal, and always engaged in productive pursuits (never mind that Franklin often indulged in the luxuries of life).

The inspiration for Weber's hypothesis came from his home in Germany, where Protestants seemed to do much better than Catholics. This correlation extended beyond Germany, though. Since the 16th century, the world's leading economy has been Protestant: the Dutch Republic from the late 16th through early 18th centuries, Great Britain from the 18th through early 20th centuries, and the US since. More generally, Protestantism is strongly and positively correlated with modern per capita GDP, while the correlation is weaker

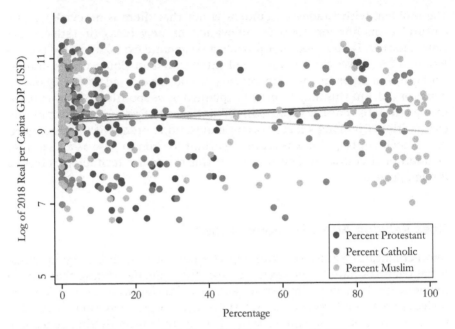

Figure 4.2 Percentage Protestant, Catholic, and Muslim vs. per capita GDP

Data sources: Rubin (2017) for religion shares, Bolt and van Zanden (2020) for GDP per capita.
Every country is listed three times, once for each of the religions.

for Catholicism and negative for Islam (see Figure 4.2). But is Weber's *causal* argument correct? Did Protestantism (and specifically Calvinism) *cause* economic growth via some capitalist work ethic, or is this just a case of "correlation does not equal causation"?

There are two issues with Weber's hypothesis. First, it needs to be established that a "work ethic" can indeed be responsible for economic growth. On this front, there is some evidence in favor. In his book *A Farewell to Alms*, Clark (2007) argued that a taste for hard work became more prominent in England during the late medieval and early modern periods. This happened in England because the hard-working bourgeois had more surviving children, to whom they passed their cultural values. Doepke and Zilibotti (2008) formalized Clark's account. They derive a model in which some people are thrifty and thus accumulate capital (which takes time to see returns). Ultimately, these people become the economically dominant group in society. However, increased thrift alone is unlikely to have been the driving factor in the economic divergence between northwestern Europe and the rest of the world. One problem is that individuals work harder *in response to incentives*. Therefore, a lax work ethic – such as the one the Westerner observed of 19th-century Japan – is likely to be a response to low wages and opportunities for work as much as a reflection of intrinsic preferences towards work.

The second, and larger, issue with Weber's hypothesis is sorting out causation from simple correlation. The first prominent critic of Weber's thesis, Tawney (1936), pointed to an obvious flaw in the argument: the "capitalist spirit" existed in certain places long before John Calvin came on the scene. In the late medieval period, the Italian city-states, the independent cites of Germany, and the cities of Flanders were hotbeds of capitalist activity. Akçomak, Webbink, and ter Weel (2016) present similar evidence from the Netherlands, which suggests that it was well on the path to modern capitalism prior to the Reformation. They cite pre-Reformation religious innovation (the Brethren of the Common Life), responsible for improved literacy, as a key factor. Likewise, Andersen, Bentzen, Dalgaard, and Sharp (2017) trace the roots of the work ethic, which Weber ascribed to Calvinism, to the pre-Reformation spread of Cistercian monasteries. Cistercians were the prototypical hard workers. Where they went, productivity improved and populations grew.

Cross-country studies connecting Protestantism to economic growth have produced more mixed results. McCleary and Barro (2006, 2019) find that religious beliefs are correlated with economic growth across countries. But cross-country analyses reveal little about the relevant mechanisms through which these cultural or religious values affect economic outcomes. Protestant countries may be richer than non-Protestant countries, but how do we know that it is Protestantism that is responsible for these differences? A more disaggregated approach is required.

If Not a Work Ethic, Why Did Protestant Countries Grow Faster?

If a unique "Protestant work ethic" seems like a stretch as an explanation of long-run economic differences across the world, are there alternative channels connecting Protestantism and economic growth? One channel proposed by Becker and Woessmann (2009) is literacy. Martin Luther stressed the importance of reading the Bible. Indeed, he produced the first widely used translation of the Bible in the German vernacular. However, literacy (and education more generally) has benefits far beyond being able to read the Bible. Might Protestant economic success have been an unintended consequence of Luther's desire to spread the Word of God?

Becker and Woessmann test this connection in the context of 19th-century Prussia – precisely the setting that inspired Weber's initial observations. They find a strongly positive relationship between Protestantism and education. This relationship is readily apparent in Figure 4.3, which shows the relationship between the proportion of Protestants and school enrollment rates for each Prussian county in the early 19th century. The question is whether this connection enabled greater economic output in Protestant regions. The evidence suggests that it did. Becker and Woessmann find there was a strong positive relationship between Protestantism and income and industrial employment. Likewise, Becker, Hornung, and Woessmann (2011) find that Protestant regions

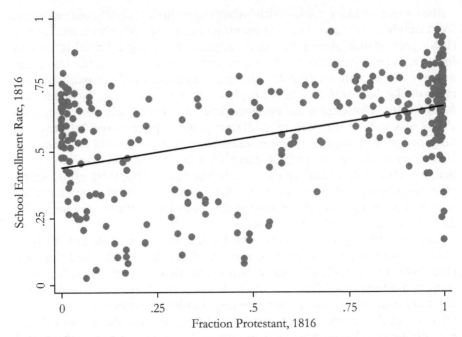

Figure 4.3 Percentage of Protestants vs. school enrollment rate in early 19th-century Prussia
Data source: Becker, Hornung, and Woessmann (2011).

had an advantage in adopting industrial technologies. The Protestant educational advantage had additional consequences. Becker and Woessmann (2008) find that the incentives for Protestants to learn to read translated into a smaller gender gap in literacy rates and school enrollment in Protestant areas. Dittmar and Meisenzahl (2020) find that Protestant cities that also implemented compulsory schooling laws tended to be hubs for people with elite levels of human capital to congregate.

These findings raise the question: was industrial growth *due to* Protestantism or was it a result of something else? The answer appears to be the latter. These studies find that the Protestant advantage is *completely explained* by higher Protestant education levels. In other words, once the Protestant edge in education is accounted for, there is no additional special edge that Protestant regions have. It is thus unlikely that the Protestant economic advantage has anything to do with a unique "work ethic," but may have been the result, in part, of a tradition that values education. Such values are not unique to Protestants. Botticini and Eckstein (2012) find that Jews historically had high levels of human capital due to religious reforms following the destruction of the Temple at Jerusalem in 70 CE.

The Reformation and Religion as a Source of Political Legitimacy

Another channel through which Protestantism may have affected economic growth is through politics. The Reformation upended the political status quo. States and cities that adopted the Reformation tended to kick out the prevailing Church establishment and confiscate its wealth. Henry VIII (r. 1509–47) initiated what was probably the most famous confiscation when he dissolved the English monasteries. The resulting wealth transfer into royal coffers was the second greatest in English history, following only that of 1066, when William conquered the whole of England. But what did the removal of the Church mean for politics? And why should we expect this to have affected economic growth?

Rubin (2017) argues that the Reformation undermined the capacity of Protestant rulers to gain legitimacy via the Church. In the medieval period, the Church played an important role in providing kings and queens with legitimacy. A ruler in bad standing with the Church was not likely to last long. The Church's ultimate punishment – excommunication – could be a death knell to an insecure ruler. Although the power of religious legitimation had weakened by the end of the 15th century, the Reformation was the proverbial straw that broke the camel's back. Protestant rulers could no longer turn to an independent, established Church to prop up their regime. Sure, religion remained important in the minds of the people. But Protestant religious elites tended to be under the thumb of the Crown. England's newly formed Anglican Church was a case in point. As such, religious authorities lost much of their power to legitimate rule, at least in the Protestant lands.

If Protestant rulers had limited capacity to legitimate their rule via religion, how could they stay in power? Rubin (2017) argues that they turned to *parliaments*. We already saw in Chapter 3 that the rise of parliaments in the 16th and 17th centuries played a key role in the economic rise of northwestern Europe. It is no coincidence that these places also happened to be Protestant. Parliaments tended to be comprised of powerful people: nobility, churchmen, lawyers, and merchants. The more that rulers needed parliaments to stay in power, the more these powerful people had a say in governance. This is why the secularization of politics affected economic growth. Parliaments tended to represent the interests of the economic elite, who desired things (for self-interested reasons) such as secure property rights and investment in infrastructure. Their interests aligned with those type of things that bring economic success more broadly. Giving them a greater say in politics meant that more of their interests would become policy.

According to Rubin, this is why England and the Dutch Republic began to take off after the Reformation, while places like Catholic Spain lagged behind despite tremendous inflows of silver and gold from the New World. Cantoni, Dittmar, and Yuchtman (2018) find a similar transition of power from religious to secular elites in the wake of the Reformation in Germany. They show that university graduates in Protestant regions took more public sector jobs, and construction shifted from religious to public and administrative buildings. This meant that Protestant rulers had a larger group of competent bureaucrats to draw from. Coinciding with the increased bureaucratization of Protestant states was a shift in legal thinking from religious to secular. Protestants relegated religious law to spiritual affairs, leaving the state to deal with worldly issues (Berman, 2003). Combined, these changes helped create the basis for the bureaucracies and legal formalism that are the hallmarks of the modern state, especially in Northern and Central Europe. Unlike Weber's theory, these explanations have little to do with the *content* of Protestant doctrine, but instead focus on the role religion played (or ceased playing) in politics.

Is Islam the Cause of Middle Eastern Economic Stagnation?

If Protestantism was good for growth (for whatever reason), might other religions have been bad for it? The answer is dependent on time and place, and it is unlikely that one religion was uniformly bad for economic growth. For instance, the negative correlation between the presence of Islam and economic development may be true of the last few centuries (see Figure 4.2), but it has not always been the case. During the "Golden Age of Islam" – roughly the 7th through 10th centuries – the Islamic Middle East was far ahead of Western Europe in terms of wealth, technology, and culture. One indication of the Muslim economic advantage is that it was much more urbanized (see Table 4.1). Urban populations can only be large if there is a surplus of food, and urban areas are generally where thriving markets and trade arise. Hence,

Table 4.1 Most populous cities in Western Eurasia, 800 CE

City	Current country	Population	Muslim?
Baghdad	Iraq	350,000	Yes
Constantinople	Turkey	250,000	No
Basra	Iraq	100,000	Yes
Fustat/Cairo	Egypt	100,000	Yes
Kufa	Iraq	100,000	Yes
Wasit	Iraq	100,000	Yes
Alexandria	Egypt	95,000	Yes
Córdoba	Spain	75,000	Yes
Damascus	Syria	50,000	Yes
Kairouan	Tunisia	50,000	Yes
Naples	Italy	50,000	No
Raqqa	Syria	50,000	Yes
Rome	Italy	50,000	No

Data source: Bosker, Buringh, and van Zanden (2013).

it is tough to swallow theories of economic growth that blame some attribute of Islam – such as its "conservative" or "mystical" nature (Weber, 1978; Landes, 1998; Lewis, 2002) – but do not also explain the Muslim advantage that existed for centuries following the spread of Islam.

This does not mean that we should automatically discard theories that attribute economic growth, or lack thereof, to Islam. Islamic law covered numerous aspects of commercial life and was the law of the land in many Middle Eastern states. If the secularization of law may have led to Protestant economic growth, might religious law have led to Middle Eastern economic stagnation? Kuran (2011) argues that it did, but for reasons more nuanced than "religious law bad, secular law good." Kuran argues that numerous aspects of Islamic law were progressive and benefited economic growth in the 7th- to 10th-century context in which they emerged. These features include a relatively egalitarian inheritance system, an extensive corpus of partnership law, and a law of trusts (*waqf*). Why might these laws, which served Middle Eastern economies well in the Islamic Golden Age, also have been a source of stagnation?

Kuran argues that Islamic law was relatively slow to respond to changes in economic conditions. But religion had little to do with it. There was simply little desire to change laws regarding commerce. A telling example comes from Islamic laws of inheritance and partnerships. The Islamic inheritance system was quite egalitarian for its day: women received a share (while only half that of men, this was better than zero, which was the norm in many parts of Europe) and numerous heirs were dictated by a pre-ordained formula. This mattered for economic growth because of its effect on partnerships. Islamic partnership law dictated that partnerships were to be broken up upon the death of any partner. Partnerships could in theory re-form, but this would take the cooperation of most of the partner's heirs. If any of the heirs were in a bind, they could seek liquidation of the partnership's assets, potentially costing all involved. In response to these incentives, Muslim merchants and entrepreneurs kept their partnerships small and of limited duration. The logic is simple: the more partners who were added or the longer the duration of the arrangement, the more likely it was that one of the partners would die, thereby creating a forced dissolution. More importantly, this also meant that there was little demand for change in the law. Even as European business arrangements were growing more complex – especially with the introduction of tradable shares and the widespread use of the corporate form – there was little incentive for Muslims to demand changes to the law. When business is small by design, things like tradable shares or the corporate form – both of which help big businesses grow – are unthinkable.

Politics was another arena through which Islam may have affected economic growth. One reason is that Islam is good at legitimating rule. There is a corpus of Islamic doctrine stating that Muslims should follow any ruler who acts in accordance with Islam but should depose those who do not (Rubin, 2011, 2017). This made religion an attractive source of legitimacy for rulers who faced threats to their power. In return, Muslim religious authorities had their voices heard in political decision-making (Rubin, 2017; Kuru, 2019). While this is not necessarily a bad thing, it can have detrimental consequences. For instance, it helps explain why there was no printing press capable of printing in the Arabic script in the Ottoman Empire for nearly *three centuries* after Gutenberg's invention. The printing press threatened the monopoly the religious establishment had on the transmission and interpretation of religious knowledge. Since the clerics were a powerful interest group, they were able to have this invention blocked, despite it arguably being the most important invention of the last millennium (Coşgel, Miceli, and Rubin, 2012).

The outsized importance of religious authorities in Muslim societies also meant that rulers supported religious education at the expense of secular and scientific learning. Chaney (2016) finds that, following the consolidation of the Muslim religious establishment and the rise of the madrasas (Islamic schools) in the 11th–12th centuries, religious book production dominated output in the Muslim world, while scientific production fell off a cliff. As with restrictions on the printing press, the decline in Muslim science was likely due to the increased political bargaining power of religious elites.

Blaydes and Chaney (2013) argue that a critical feature of Muslim politics was that rulers had access to slave soldiers. This meant they did not need to negotiate with other elites for military service or resources. Because medieval and early modern European rulers did not have access to slave armies, they had to cede rights to feudal lords (in the medieval period) and parliaments (in the early modern period). This relative lack of executive constraint was a source of political instability that is still a feature of Middle Eastern politics in the 21st century. Since power was not dispersed in the Middle East, there was always a group of people – those without political power – who benefited from a change in the status quo. Revolt was therefore common. On the contrary, in Europe, dispersed power meant that powerful people tended to have an interest in maintaining the status quo, and revolt was less common. As a result, European rulers tended to last longer, especially after the feudal revolution of the 9th–10th centuries institutionalized the dispersion of power (see Figure 4.4).

A related explanation of Middle Eastern political instability is provided by Platteau (2017), who argues that the decentralized nature of Islam (as opposed to the centralized nature of the Catholic Church) meant that there would always be clerics, likely radical ones, left out of the ruling coalition. These clerics were precisely the ones who could spark a revolt against entrenched powers, as was the case during the 1979 Iranian Revolution.

In short, recent scholarship does not implicate Islam in all of the problems of the Middle East. Nonetheless, it does suggest that the intermingling of politics and religion, characteristic of many Muslim societies, and the persistence of Islamic law severely restricted the possibilities for economic growth. Economic stagnation and political instability in the Middle East are byproducts

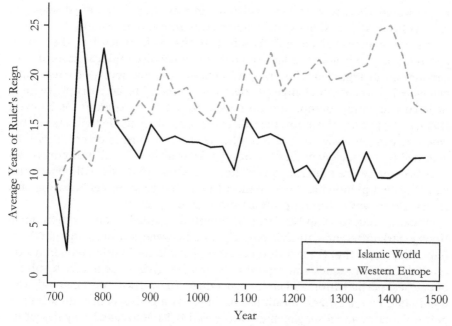

Figure 4.4 Ruler duration in Western Europe and the Islamic world

Data source: Blaydes and Chaney (2013).

of how Islam was instrumentalized by powerful elites. This is not necessarily a reflection of Islam per se, as many other religions including Christianity have also been used in this way.

The Long-Term Persistence of Culture

The primary reason culture can have such a large impact on economic growth is that it is so *persistent*. Even in the face of changing economic and technological conditions, cultural values are slow to change, regardless of whether this means a society is left behind. In what follows, we give a taste of some of the recent research that shows just how persistent cultural norms can be.

The North–South Italy Divide

In 1954–5, the anthropologist Edward Banfield and his family lived in a village in southern Italy. To describe what he found among the peasants he and his wife encountered, he coined the term "amoral familism." Amoral familism refers to a nexus of cultural beliefs. Amoral familists, according to Banfield, maximize the material short-run interests of their families and assume others will do the same. The society he described was one in which public goods were not provided, there were few or no civil organizations, people were disengaged from politics, and trust between strangers was almost non-existent.

The consequence of amoral familism at the societal level is the under-provision of public goods, a lack of checks and balance on local government, corruption, disregard of the law, and endemically low levels of trust. Such behavior is difficult to change. If everyone is *believed* to be corrupt, there is little cost to being corrupt and no benefit to not being corrupt. As Banfield (1958, p. 94) put it: "The amoral familist who is an office-holder will take bribes when he can get away with it. But whether he takes bribes or not, it will be assumed by the society of amoral familists that he does." Cultural norms can thus become self-reinforcing: given the expectation that one will behave cor-ruptly, a corrupt individual has no incentive to change his or her behavior. This is one reason why cultural norms are often highly persistent.

Putnam, Leonardi, and Nanetti (1993) built on Banfield's observation, iden-tifying stark differences in civic participation between southern and northern Italy. They argue that these differences trace back to the Middle Ages. In north-ern Italy, free city-states and republics flourished, giving rise to a rich culture of political participation and civic engagement. In contrast, southern Italy was dominated by feudal and absolutist regimes. As a consequence, a culture of political apathy and disengagement arose. Guiso, Sapienza, and Zingales (2016) provide further empirical evidence for this hypothesis. They show that civic engagement, as measured by the number of non-profits in a region, is posi-tively associated with the existence of a medieval commune. Combined, these studies show that cultural differences generated about a millennium ago *still exist* today, despite significant political and economic development in the inter-vening time.

But why did these cultural differences arise in the first place? Schulz, Bahrami-Rad, Beauchamp, and Henrich (2019), Henrich (2020), and Schulz (2020) argue that the marriage policies of the medieval Catholic Church are to blame. The Church sought to break kin ties, forbidding marriages between cousins (up to the sixth degree!). As a result, kin groups became smaller in places with deeper Church influence. These places were therefore more likely to have governance institutions that relied on cross-kin cooperation. In the context of Italy, these governance institutions were precisely the communes at the core of the the-ories proposed by Putnam, Leonardi, and Nanetti (1993) and Guiso, Sapienza, and Zingales (2016). Like those studies, Schulz (2020) shows that differences in cultural norms persist to the present. In southern Italy, where the influence of the Catholic Church was much weaker during the early Middle Ages, cousin marriage rates are higher, and trust, voter turnout (a measure of civic engage-ment), and judicial efficiency are all lower (see Figure 4.5).

Greif (1994, 2006) provides further insight into why these types of cultural differences may have affected economic growth. He compares the "individual-istic" culture of Genoa (one of the most powerful medieval Italian city-states) with the more kin-based culture of Jewish merchants in northern Africa. Greif

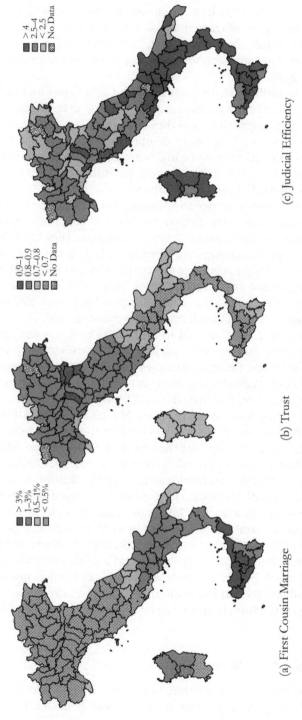

(a) First Cousin Marriage

(b) Trust

(c) Judicial Efficiency

Figure 4.5 The north–south Italy divide: cousin marriage, trust, and judicial efficiency

Data source: Schulz (2020).

shows that kin-based cultures have an advantage in establishing trade networks when the total level of trade is small, since they can trade within their kin networks and punish those who cheat. This is one major advantage that kin-based cultures have: interactions requiring *cooperation* are more likely to take place (Enke, 2019).

Societies with an individualistic culture are not able to punish cheaters this way. Instead, they must set up *institutions* to do this and to facilitate trust. Such institutions are costly to establish, and they may not be worth it when the scale of trade is small. However, as more trade opportunities arise, the benefits of establishing such institutions may be high enough to convince individualistic societies to adopt them. Once in place, these institutions permit trade with a much larger set of potential exchange partners.

On the other hand, what was once an advantage in kin-based societies becomes a disadvantage. Since their networks are kin-based, there is little incentive to adopt costly, impersonal institutions. Yet, by not doing so, they limit their trade partners to those within the kin group, forgoing trade with much of the outside world. The consequences for economic growth are clear. As inter-regional trade became more widespread and lucrative, those societies that were able to take advantage of trading with as many partners as possible grew, while those that remained confined to old (kin-based) trade networks stagnated.

A similar argument can be applied to China. The clan was the key unit in China for risk sharing and resource pooling. Clan members supported each other in time of need and brought resources together for bigger projects. This was rooted in a Confucian ideology that was centered on clan-based obligations. This meant that there was little demand for larger financial markets that could distribute capital more broadly (Chen, Ma, and Sinclair, forthcoming). Why engage with someone you cannot trust when there are a bunch of your kin for you to deal with? This was not the case in Western Europe, where there were no larger family units to provide access to capital. Eventually, financial markets emerged in Europe to fill this void (Greif and Tabellini, 2017).

The importance of individualistic culture extends beyond the type of trade and financial institutions a society has. Individualistic culture rewards personal achievement. It stands to reason that innovators therefore gain greater social status in individualistic societies than they do in collectivist societies. Gorodnichenko and Roland (2011, 2017) find that societies that are more individualistic have much higher income per worker, and much of this comes from greater productivity and innovation. This is important: as we will see in Chapters 7 and 8, innovation is one of the keys to modern, sustained economic growth.

The Persistence of Trust Norms

Economists have long recognized that *trust* is an integral part of economic exchange. Trust is important because most exchange is sequential. One party gives the other party something, with the expectation that the latter will give something back in return, possibly at a later date (Greif, 2000). We discussed this in Chapter 3 in the context of the fundamental problem of exchange. This is as true today as it was in the past. When you buy something online, you provide your credit card number, and then money is immediately taken from your account. The online merchant is then supposed to send you whatever you purchased over the course of the next few days. But what if they do not send it to you? They already have your money. Especially if they never expect to sell to you again, why should they send you the goods?

In the example of the online retailer, it is obvious why they would send the goods to you. Any company that regularly cheated customers like this would be sued and made to pay damages. They would also get a bad reputation and would likely not be in business for long. But court systems and means of reputation building have not always been available. In their absence, why would one trust that the entity they are dealing with will fulfill their end of the bargain?

This is where trust comes in. If I trust that the online merchant is not going to cheat me – regardless of my ability to sue – then I may go through with the exchange. Of course, the merchant also needs to be likely to come through on his or her promises. This is why societies that have high levels of trust tend to do better economically (Tabellini, 2010). Trust enables mutually beneficial exchanges that would not otherwise occur. In the words of Arrow (1972, p. 357): "Virtually every commercial transaction has within itself an element of trust, certainly any transaction conducted over a period of time. It can be plausibly argued that much of the economic backwardness in the world can be explained by the lack of mutual confidence." Perhaps variation in trust across countries can help explain why some countries are rich and others are poor? Social scientists have in fact frequently noted differences in trust across countries. People in richer countries are both more trusting and more trustworthy than people in poorer countries (see Figure 4.6).

The question is: why are some societies more trusting than others? Trust does not come from thin air. People are more trusting in environments that are safer and when the likelihood of being cheated is lower. So, on the one hand, levels of trust might reflect institutional quality rather than a separate and identifiable cultural trait. On the other hand, recent work by economists and political scientists has also shown that trust norms tend to persist long after the reason they emerged in the first place. Thus, historical events which affected trust in the past may help explain economic prosperity today.

Natural experiments can help parse out the role of history in the development of trust norms as opposed to modern factors like contemporary institutions. Natural experiments, like the partition of Korea discussed in Chapter 3, occur when some people in a population are "treated" with some event and others are not, much like a clinical trial in a medical experiment. History is full of natural experiments, often due to shifting national borders. One day, a group is under the dominion of one state, the next day part of the population

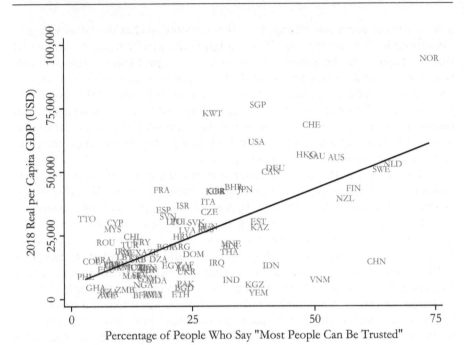

Figure 4.6 The relationship between trust and per capita GDP

Data sources: Inglehart, Haerpfer, Moreno, Welzel, Kizilova, Diez-Medrano, et al. (2018) for trust data, Bolt and van Zanden (2020) for per capita GDP data. Qatar dropped to make the rest of the data more visible.

is under the dominion of another. If there is reason to believe that this change might affect trust, we can compare people on opposite sides of the border to see whether trust was indeed affected by the border change and whether these differences persisted. For instance, Becker, Boeckh, Hainz, and Woessmann (2016) find that people who live on the Habsburg side of the old Habsburg–Ottoman–Russian border trust government officials, courts, and police more *in the present day*. In the 18th and 19th centuries, the Habsburgs provided public services more efficiently than their eastern neighbors, increasing trust in government. The fact that these trust norms exist in the present day strongly suggests that cultural norms persist after their original cause is long gone.

Lowes, Nunn, Robinson, and Weigel (2017) find evidence for the persistence of cultural norms in a study of rule following by individuals living on opposite sides of the old borders of the Kuba Kingdom, a state established in the early 17th century in what is now the Democratic Republic of the Congo. Contrary to expectations that the presence of a relatively powerful state might have encouraged and reinforced pro-social norms, they find that Kuba descendants are less likely to follow rules and more likely to steal. They reason was that those living under Kuba rule had less need to generate norms of rule following. Those who did not follow rules could be punished by the institutions of the kingdom.

Again, a key takeaway is that culture *persists* long after the institutional and political environment under which it emerged has changed.

Gender Norms

Most societies in history have had cultural norms that restrict the capacity of women to work. For this reason, it is possible that women have historically been the greatest untapped source of potential economic growth. Yet, although most societies have restricted women in one way or another, some societies placed greater restrictions than others. Why?

Cultural norms regarding female labor likely date to the Neolithic Revolution, which saw the spread of settled agriculture. Boserup (1970) argued that plow agriculture precipitated the emergence of a sharp gender division of labor. Plows required significant upper body and grip strength, both of which favored men over women. As a result, men gained significant bargaining power over women in societies practicing plow agriculture. It is therefore possible that gender norms favoring men emerged in such societies.

Alesina, Giuliano, and Nunn (2013) tested this hypothesis. They document that a social norm arose in societies with plow agriculture whereby men worked outdoors in the field and women were confined indoors. The sexual division of labor that arose in plow-dominant agricultural civilizations proved to be self-reinforcing. In societies where grain provided the majority of calories and society was organized around agriculture, the fact that women played a subordinate role in the agrarian economy reinforced their inferior social status. The evidence provided by Alesina, Giuliano, and Nunn testifies to the persistence of these norms even today, in societies where the vast majority of people work outside agriculture. In the 21st century, societies with more traditional plow use have lower female labor participation, lower female firm ownership, and less female participation in politics (see Figure 4.7). Alesina, Giuliano, and Nunn also show that the children of immigrants living in the US and Europe exhibit more unequal beliefs about gender if *their parents* came from a country with a heritage of plow use. Similarly, Fernández and Fogli (2009) find that the work and fertility behavior of second-generation American women is affected by gender cultural norms in the country of their ancestry. Combined, these results point to a detrimental consequence of social norms that persist long after the reason they emerged in the first place was relevant.

Cultural attitudes towards female labor can also shift due to economic change. For instance, Xue (2020) studies the introduction in China of the treadle-operated spindle wheel, which tripled the productivity of female cotton spinners beginning in 1300. In cotton textile producing regions, female incomes rose substantially. Their earning power increased many times over, to the point where female incomes were comparable to or even greater than those of men. Consequently, women began to be seen as more important members of society. Pomeranz (2005) uses the term "economics of respectability" to

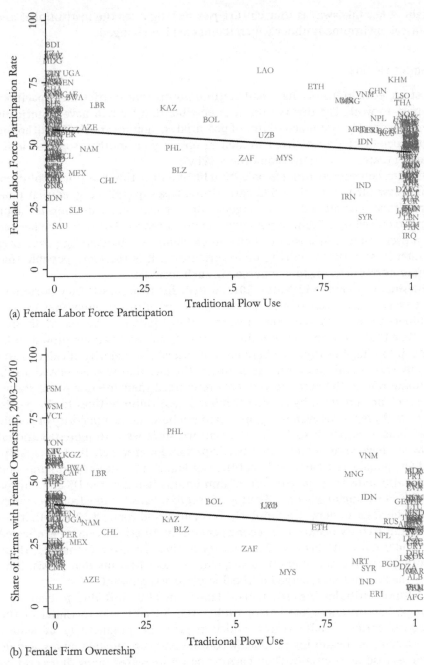

(a) Female Labor Force Participation

(b) Female Firm Ownership

Figure 4.7 Traditional plow use, female labor force participation, and female firm ownership
Data source: Alesina, Giuliano, and Nunn (2013).

describe women's rising status. For parents, as women became productive members of the economy in their own right, it became less financially costly to have a daughter. The prospect of daughters being self-sufficient lowered the cost of having them. Xue (2020) provides evidence that cultural attitudes towards women were transformed in the affected counties. Today, in counties with pre-modern cotton textile production, sex ratios are less biased against women. Additionally, individuals in counties with pre-modern cotton textile production are more likely to disagree with the statement that men are naturally more capable, or that women should focus on family, and are more likely to have preference for daughters over sons.

The status of women mattered for economic growth in the past and continues to do so. The studies cited above show how cultural norms may have been a channel through which female status affected economic growth. We will return to a discussion of gender and economic growth in Chapter 5, which studies demographic trends and investment in human capital.

Chapter Summary

This chapter summarized the growing literature on the role that culture plays in economic growth. Recent cultural explanations are much more nuanced than those of the early 20th century, which were Eurocentric at best and racist at worst. Modern theories tend to think of culture in the way that anthropologists view culture: it is those aspects of society which forms people's worldview. This shapes how people respond to incentives, how they interact with others, how and whom they marry, how many children they have, and so on. Modern economic studies of culture focus on things such as the role of trust, gender norms, and marriage norms in determining outcomes. Religion may also affect economic development, often through its effect on politics or law. One key reason that culture can affect long-run economic development is that it *persists*. Even after the reasons certain cultural traits emerged are long a thing of the past, they tend to shape the outlook of the descendants of those past societies. For this reason, culture tends to interact with some of the other determinants of long-run economic development, such as institutions and demography. As we shall see in Chapter 7, these interactions are at the heart of most societies' long-run economic trajectories, for both good and bad.

5

Fewer Babies?

It is January 24, 1700. A cold winter air blows through Westminster Abbey in the center of London. Even open fires and coal braziers struggle against the winter chill. Princess Anne, heir to the throne of England, is silently sobbing into her bedclothes, surrounded by her maids and ladies-in-waiting.

Anne had miscarried again. Though only 33, this was her seventeenth and last pregnancy. She had not produced a living heir. Of her four live births, only one outlived early childhood. But Prince William died aged 11 of pneumonia, having been bled and blistered by his doctors. We do not know the reasons for Anne's failed pregnancies. But her own health was fragile. Historians have suggested that she may have suffered from a host of ailments including Lupus, diabetes, or Rhesus autoimmunization (Emson, 1992). By her early thirties, she suffered from severe gout, which would prevent her from walking and ensured she would have to be carried to her coronation in 1702. Anne would die at 49.

Anne could afford the best medical treatment of her time. But it hardly availed her and her family. Her mother only lived to 34. Her sister Mary died at 32 of smallpox. Anne's tale was not uncommon. Even for the rich, life in the pre-industrial world was dominated by births, deaths, and disease.

This is clearly no longer the case. Even in the poorest parts of the world, life expectancy is higher than it was in the wealthiest parts of the world during Anne's time. In 1703, average life expectancy in England was 38.5 years (Roser, 2021c). In 2015, no country in the world had an average life expectancy less than 51 years (see Figure 5.1). What changed? Might these changes have affected growth?

For most of human history, families had many children, a few of whom would make it to adulthood. These conditions led Thomas Malthus (1798/2007) to famously conclude that this was the permanent condition of humanity. He reasoned that most people would not be able to eke out much more than a subsistence living. Malthus wrote in the late 18th century and was not wrong about the human condition up to that point in time. His ideas relating demography to economic development explain much about the pre-industrial economy. But they cannot account for the incredible transformations in

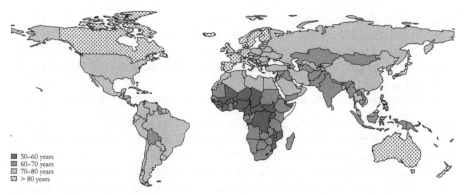

Figure 5.1 Life expectancy around the world, 2015
Data source: Roser (2021c).

the human condition that have arisen in the last two centuries. What changed?

In this chapter, we discuss the role that demography played in making some parts of the world rich. We consider the theories of Malthus and consider the extent to which the world he envisioned aptly describes the economic realities of our ancestors. Then we ask: how did some parts of the world first moderate and then escape the forces Malthus highlighted? What factors made a transition from a Malthusian world to modern growth possible? In particular, how did demographic change lead to investments in education and human capital, and how did these investments foster economic growth?

Malthusian Pressures

The most frequently cited cause of persistent poverty in the pre-industrial world is population pressure. There were simply too many mouths to feed. This theory is most commonly attributed to Malthus (1798/2007, p. 13), who put it succinctly:

> That population cannot increase without the means of subsistence is a proposition so evident that it needs no illustration.
>
> That population does invariably increase where there are the means of subsistence, the history of every people that have ever existed will abundantly prove.
>
> And that the superior power of population cannot be checked without producing misery or vice, the ample portion of these too bitter ingredients in the cup of human life and the continuance of the physical causes that seem to have produced them bear too convincing a testimony.

To explain these principles Malthus proposed a simple model:

1. As income rises, more children survive to adulthood.

2. As income rises, fewer people die each year.
3. As population increases, income per capita decreases. This is due to the diminishing marginal product of labor. This is the idea that when there are only so many jobs to do, every additional person added to the workforce will be less productive than the last.
4. Hence, in the long run, population growth will absorb any gains in income.

The Malthusian model can be depicted in a simple diagram (Figure 5.2). Income per capita is on the horizontal axis. The vertical axis in the top panel measures the birth rate and the death rate. Where these two lines cross, the population is stationary. The lower panel depicts the relationship between population and per capita income. It captures assumption (3). If resources such as land are relatively fixed, population growth reduces the marginal product of labor and results in each worker earning a lower income.

Suppose per capita income exceeds y^*. In this case, the birth rate will exceed the death rate and population will grow. Population growth, however, puts pressure on resources and causes per capita incomes to fall. As incomes fall, the death rate rises and the birth rate falls (as fewer children survive to adulthood), thereby returning the economy to equilibrium at y^*.

Occasional positive shocks such as a one-off improvement in technology or the introduction of a new crop increase productivity, enabling a period of population growth and temporary higher incomes. In the long run, however, per capita incomes will return to y^*. People will have more babies, and those babies will eat up all the surplus. Countries with more fertile land or better

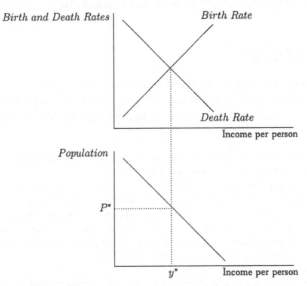

Figure 5.2 The Malthusian model

Note: This figure is adapted from Clark (2007).

technology are therefore characterized by higher population densities, not higher living standards.

What happens if there is a demographic change? Consider the effects of a fall in the birth rate (from *Birth Rate* to *Birth Rate'* in Figure 5.3). Since the death rate schedule is unchanged, the population falls. As the population falls, the marginal product of labor rises. In equilibrium, per capita income increases to y^{**}. This increase is permanent. Similarly, an increase in the death rate also raises per capita income.

But why might the birth and death rates change? Dramatic shifts in death rates have been a common theme in human history. The "great levelers" that are plague, war, revolution, and state collapse have repeatedly brought massive and rapid deaths to human populations (Scheidel, 2017).

The Malthusian logic suggests that these tragic circumstances may have a silver lining: they increase average income. Clark (2007, p. 101) draws out the stark and counter-intuitive implications: "[T]he plague was not the harsh judgment of a vengeful Old Testament God on a sinful Europe, but merely a mild reproof by a beneficent New Age-style deity ... [that] raised living standards all across Europe." On the flip side, Clark lists cleanliness, peace, charity, hard work, and parental solicitude as "Malthusian vices." These practices enabled a larger and healthier population that would eat away any gains in productivity.

There are reasons to be skeptical of the starkest Malthusian predictions. Plague was only beneficial if we ignore the costs of elevated mortality in assessing living standards. It also obviously does not account for the social and

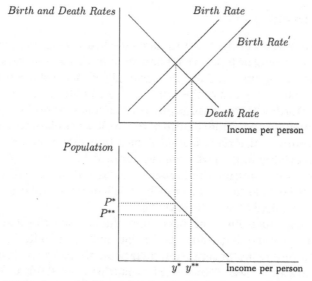

Figure 5.3 The Malthusian model: illustrating the effects of reducing the birth rate

Note: This figure is adapted from Clark (2007).

political disruption caused by frequent and unexpected deaths. But enough truth is captured by the simple Malthusian framework to make it a compelling lens through which to view the past.

Ashraf and Galor (2011) show that a Malthusian framework explains many features of the world up to 1500. Specifically, they find that countries that underwent the agricultural transition earlier had more productive land and higher population densities in 1500. But they did not necessarily have higher per capita incomes.

Yet, Malthusian forces operated gradually and in conjunction with other factors. Even in a Malthusian environment there is variation in living standards and economic growth is possible. As we saw in earlier chapters, there were periods of relative prosperity in pre-modern Europe. There were also episodes when per capita income rose well above subsistence in Classical Greece, the Roman Empire, and Song China.

The fact that the long-run dynamics of the world economy are broadly consistent with the Malthusian model does not mean that Malthusian dynamics provide a complete explanation of short- or medium-run growth fluctuations. The Malthusian feedback mechanism operated gradually and a given economy could be "out of equilibrium" for many decades or longer. Other factors such as epidemics of contagious diseases and warfare impacted pre-industrial populations much more rapidly and with greater effect than did gradual Malthusian feedback loops. The result was that pre-industrial societies fluctuated around their Malthusian equilibrium, but sometimes with significant variation.

The Black Death

How can we test whether the Malthusian model had any bite in the pre-modern world? One way would be to see what happens following a massive demographic shock. The most famous – and deadly – example of such a shock was the Black Death, which ravaged much of the world in the mid-14th century.

The Black Death was the most deadly pathogen to ever hit Europe and Asia. Contemporaries estimated that a third of the world's population died. For much of the 20th century, historians scoffed at such high figures and suggested that the overall mortality must have been significantly lower, say 5 or 10%. Recent research, however, confirms the higher previous estimates, with some historians going as far to argue that as much as 60% of the population in Western Europe may have died (Benedictow, 2005).

Scientists have identified the bacterium that caused the Black Death as *Yersinia pestis*, or bubonic plague. As Europe and the Middle East had been spared plague outbreaks for centuries, their populations had little or no immunity to the disease. It was transmitted to Europe from Kaffa in the modern Crimea, and from there to Italy and Western Europe. The mortality rate of the disease was not related to pre-existing characteristics. At least as many died in the countryside as in the cities. Southern Europe and the Mediterranean were hit especially hard, and so were the British Isles (see Figure 5.4).

The medieval population of Europe peaked in the early 14th century, several decades before the Black Death. Between 1315 and 1322, excessive summer rains led to successive harvest failures. As a result, a terrible famine swept through much of Northern Europe. Bruce Campbell (2010, p. 287) describes it as possibly "the single worst subsistence crisis, in terms of relative mortality, in recorded European history." It was accompanied by a bovine plague that

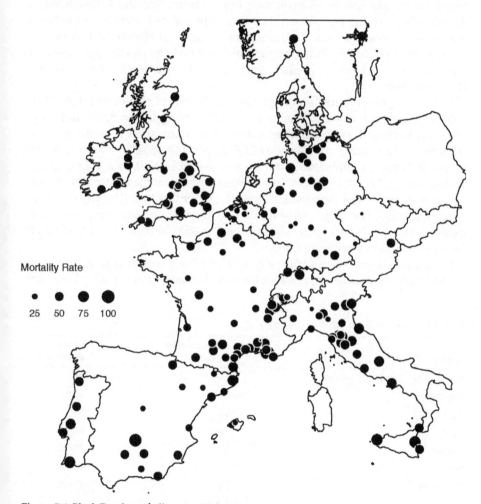

Figure 5.4 Black Death mortality rates (%) in 1347–52

Notes: This map plots the location of all existing cities (i.e. localities ≥ 1,000 inhabitants) in 1300 for which we know their Black Death mortality rate (%) in 1347–52 as well as the modern boundaries of eighteen Western European countries.

Source: Jedwab, Johnson, and Koyama (2019).

wiped out livestock. The population barely had time to recover before the Black Death struck. As a consequence, the population of England fell from between 4.5 and 6 million in 1300 to around 2 million by the middle of the 15th century (Smith, 1991; Campbell, 2010). A similar population collapse occurred throughout Europe (see Table 5.1) and the Middle East.

A tragedy of such scale is difficult to comprehend. There were clearly many consequences that fall well outside the scope of conventional economics, such as social dislocation and psychological trauma. But this does not mean we should ignore its economic implications. The Black Death was a massive shock to the population. Nor was it an isolated occurrence: bubonic plague reoccurred sporadically across Europe and the Middle East in the following three centuries. This permanently elevated the death rate. And as a Malthusian model would predict, an increase in the death rate raised per capita incomes.

The initial period following the pandemic was one of economic crisis. Trade collapsed and real wages fell as food was left rotting in the fields and crops were not harvested. Political elites across Europe also tried to prevent wages from rising. In England, the Statute of Laborers (1349) sought to limit nominal wages. In France, a comparable statute was passed in 1351 to regulate wages, prices, and guilds admittances. In Florence, wages were permitted to rise for urban workers but not for rural laborers. The latter faced particularly stringent regulations and saw their real wages fall as they had to purchase basic commodities at hyper-inflated prices (Cohn, 2007, p. 468). Individuals who left their farms to seek new work were fined.

But economic pressures ultimately trumped the political will of the elites. In the following decades, real wages increased. Pamuk (2007, p. 292) finds that

Table 5.1 Black Death mortality by country

Country	1300 population (millions)	Mortaliy estimate (%)
Austria, Czech Republic, & Hungary	10.0	20
Belgium	1.4	22.5
England	6.0	55
France	16.0	50–60
Germany	13.0	20–25
Italy	12.5	50–60
Netherlands	0.8	30–35
Poland	2.0	25
Scandinavia	1.9	50–60
Spain	5.5	50

Source: Jedwab, Johnson, and Koyama (2019). Original data from Ziegler (1969), Gottfried (1983), and Benedictow (2005).

the Black Death caused urban real wages to rise by as much as 100% in the decades after 1350. They remained above their earlier levels until late in the 16th century. This was true not only in Western Europe and the western half of the Mediterranean but also around the eastern Mediterranean.

Land use also changed. Marginal lands were abandoned and landowners shifted away from arable farming (which was relatively labor-intensive) towards pastoral farming (which was more land-intensive). To paraphrase Sir Thomas More (1516/1997), sheep devoured men. Jedwab, Johnson, and Koyama (2019) find evidence for substantial geographic mobility in the wake of the plague as people moved in search of better economic opportunities.

The most important institutional consequence of the Black Death was the demise of serfdom in Western Europe. In England in 1300, half of the rural population were serfs. They owed labor and other feudal dues to their lords. This changed in the aftermath of the Black Death. Bailey (2014) finds that, in England, serfdom was in sharp decline from the 1350s onwards. This suggests that labor scarcity and falling land values were critical to the decline in serfdom. On the manors studied by Bailey, there was no attempt to reimpose serfdom after the Black Death. The sharp demographic shock of the plague simply made it impossible for landlords to maintain or reinstate servile institutions and impose feudal dues on recalcitrant peasants. A serf fleeing oppressive fines and labor requirements on one manor would easily find work on the land of another lord. Landlords throughout Western Europe were unable to coordinate their response. As a consequence, serfdom disappeared in most of England by 1500, even though it was never formally abolished.

Brenner (1976) argued that when serfdom ended in England, it permitted the rise of agrarian capitalism. Former serfs became tenants and paid rents to their landlords. They were thus easily dispossessed, allowing landholdings to be consolidated. It was this agrarian capitalism that in Brenner's telling made possible the increases in agricultural productivity that he sees as critically enabling the Industrial Revolution. In contrast, French peasants gained control of their land. This impeded the development and consolidation of large estates. The specifics of the argument Brenner developed do not need to detain us here. Subsequent research has qualified or undermined the factual basis for many elements of his broader argument. What is indisputable, however, is that the impact of the Black Death and the ensuing demographic retrenchment differed in Western Europe relative to Central or Eastern Europe. While serfdom disappeared in England and France in the 14th and 15th centuries, it did not disappear and in many cases became more firmly entrenched in Germany, Poland, and Russia.

Why did the Black Death have this effect in Western Europe but not in Central or Eastern Europe? Acemoglu and Wolitzky (2011) provide a model in which landlords can use carrots (wages) or sticks (coercion) to incentivize peasants. The incentive to use one or the other depends on how scarce labor is, the outside options peasants have, and the costs of using coercion. From this perspective, a massive demographic shock like the Black Death could have countervailing effects. On the one hand, the resulting scarcity of labor increased the incentive landlords had to use coercion and to defend or reassert serfdom. On the other hand, labor scarcity also greatly improved the outside options peasants had, and this reduced the incentive to use coercion. Which effect dominated depended on their relative magnitude. Acemoglu and Wolitzky interpret their model as indicating that in Western Europe the costs of reliance on coercion ultimately outweighed the benefits. This was largely due to the fact that peasants had good outside options. They could go to the city or work on another manor. Thus, keeping peasants enserfed was too expensive to justify the costs. Meanwhile, in Central and Eastern Europe, coercion proved a more viable strategy. This is because there were fewer cities, and those cities that did exist tended to be smaller. This meant fewer outside options for peasants. This, in turn, made coercion a viable strategy for landlords.

Voigtländer and Voth (2013b) argue that the shock of the Black Death pushed Europe into a Malthusian steady-state characterized by higher per capita incomes. Higher incomes increased the demand for manufactured goods, including luxuries. As workers' incomes rose, they spent a higher proportion of their income on manufactured goods produced in cities. Greater demand led to higher levels of trade and urbanization in many parts of Europe. The intensification of warfare in Europe after 1350 also pushed people into urban areas. Greater levels of urbanization then pushed up the death rate further as cities were unhealthy population sinks. Thus, the origins of Western Europe's relatively high incomes in the centuries prior to the Industrial Revolution can be found in the "Three Horsemen of Riches": war, plague, and urbanization (Voigtländer and Voth, 2013b, p. 776).

The late Middle Ages was a relative golden age for workers. Ordinary people could afford richer and more varied diets. Meat consumption increased, housing improved, and more money was available to be spent on clothing and fashion (Dyer, 2005). Labor scarcity gave workers increased bargaining power, which they used to demand both higher wages and greater freedom.

After 1500, population growth resumed. In line with a Malthusian model, the result was a gradual fall in real wages from the heights achieved in the late Middle Ages. The period between 1550 and 1650 was "an iron century" in which ordinary people's standards of living fell (Kamen, 1971). This is exemplified in England, where there was a clear inverse relationship between wages and population prior to industrialization (see Figure 5.5).

Household Formation and the European Marriage Pattern

In a simple Malthusian model, living standards are determined by the intersection of fertility and mortality. As we saw in Figure 5.3, higher income per capita

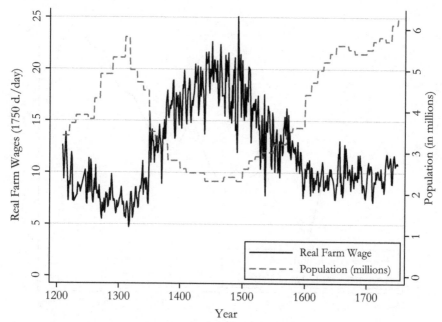

Figure 5.5 Population and wages in England, 1209–1750
Data sources: Galor (2005) and Clark (2010).

can be obtained if fertility can be restrained. Malthus himself considered this possibility, distinguishing it as a preventive check (as opposed to a positive check, which refers to disease and starvation).

One example of the preventive check was the practice of late marriages. For women, teenage marriage was common in many parts of the world since the dawn of the institution of marriage. However, in parts of late medieval Europe, women tended to marry in their mid-twenties. Hajnal (1965) labeled this practice the *European Marriage Pattern* (EMP). This marriage pattern, which was characteristic of most of Europe in 1900, had its origins in northwestern Europe several hundred years earlier. Common in Scandinavia, the British Isles, the Low Countries, Germany, and northern France, it was less evident in Southern Europe and entirely absent in Eastern Europe. Why might this marriage pattern matter for economic growth?

Before the modern period, female age at marriage was important in determining aggregate fertility (see Figure 5.6). Childbirth outside of marriage was rare. But birth control within marriage was not widely practiced. Since fertility within marriage remained high, aggregate fertility was significantly reduced by delayed marriages. Every two years a woman was not married reduced the number of children she had, on average, by one child. Malthusian theory therefore suggests that the EMP helped keep per capita incomes higher than they would have otherwise been. Some scholars have gone further and argued that

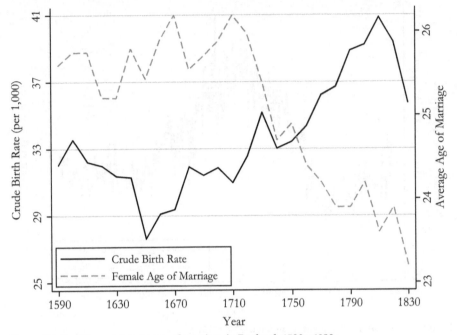

Figure 5.6 Fertility and female age of marriage in England, 1590s–1830s

Data sources: Wrigley, Davies, Oeppen, and Schofield (1997, p. 130) and Galor (2005).

the EMP could have played a decisive role in the transition to modern economic growth. We consider both claims here.

The EMP was associated with small, nuclear households, based on a single married couple. After marriage, the husband left his parents' home and became the head of a new household. Prior to marriage, young people worked in other households as servants or wage laborers. While working, "women were not under the control of any male relative. They made independent decisions about where to live and work and for which employer" (Hajnal, 1982, p. 475). This contrasts sharply with pre-industrial societies outside of northwestern Europe. There, joint households, comprising two or more married couples, were common. These households were characterized by universal and early marriage and high fertility.

These two systems reacted differently to population pressure. In joint households, an increase in the population might increase the underemployment of married adults. In contrast, in northwestern Europe, population pressure would have simply caused delayed marriages. The characteristics of the EMP can therefore be summarized as follows:

- High age of first marriage: ≈ 25 for women.
- Very low levels of illegitimacy.
- ≈ 10% never marry.

- Nuclear families rather than stem families (adult married children live with one set of parents in the latter).

One consequence of the EMP was that a considerable proportion of women were able to earn money independently prior to entering into marriage. Late marriage enabled young men and women to choose their own spouses independent of the decisions of their parents (de Moor and van Zanden, 2010). Labor markets played a critical role in this development.

The EMP also had implications for how inheritances and marriages were arranged. In Southern Europe, women received their inheritances through dowries. The dowry system created an incentive for early marriage for both the bride and her parents since a woman who waited too long to marry became less desirable in the marriage market and thus required a large dowry in order to compensate the groom. However, in Northern Europe, women were not disinherited at marriage and dowries mattered less. Conjugal inheritance, common in Northern Europe, meant that women could expect to inherit a fair share of the household's resources in the event of separation or widowhood. This ensured that woman had an incentive to earn money and accumulate resources within marriage.

The origins of the EMP are difficult to discern. It became prominent in the centuries following the Black Death. The demographic collapse of the second half of the 14th century increased the demand for labor and increased both the opportunities women had for wage labor and the remuneration they received. Without a functioning market for workers, it would have been difficult for young people to set out on their own, save money, and form households independent of their parents.

Did the EMP Spur Economic Growth?

Two distinct claims are made on behalf of the EMP. The weak claim is that it played an important role in restraining fertility and hence *maintaining* per capita incomes in a Malthusian economy. The stronger claim is that it played a crucial role in the transition to modern economic growth. To address this claim, we have to move beyond a simple static model like that in Figure 5.3. Let us consider the evidence in favor of the stronger claim.

Theoretically, we have seen that the EMP could raise the equilibrium level of income by a moderate amount in a Malthusian world. How might this translate into a sustained increase in economic growth? Voigtländer and Voth (2013a) argue that the demographic shock of the Black Death had a differential effect in Northern Europe – where the land could be turned over to pastoral agriculture – than in Southern Europe, where the land was more suited for arable farming. As pastoral farming increased the demand for female labor, this contributed to labor and marriage market outcomes in which individuals married late and restricted fertility (the EMP).

In a related argument, Voigtländer and Voth (2006) simulate a model of the English economy between 1700 and 1850. They find that industrialization was dependent on England's low-pressure demographic regime. Their model suggests that in a high-fertility regime, faster population growth during the early stages of economic expansion pushes down per capita incomes and reduces the effective demand for manufactured goods. This prevents sustained economic growth from getting started in the first place. England was saved from this fate because of its low birth rates.

Another channel linking the EMP to growth is human capital investment. Foreman-Peck (2011) argues that by lowering birth rates, the EMP also lowered death rates and encouraged investment in human capital. This argument builds on the claim of Becker and Lewis (1973) that families trade off the quantity and quality of their offspring in response to relative prices. Foreman-Peck (2011) provides suggestive empirical evidence that in 19th-century England, low birth rates were associated with lower infant mortality and greater human capital investments.

Reasons for Skepticism

Dennison and Ogilvie (2014) dispute the argument that the EMP had any relationship with sustained economic growth. They argue that the EMP was actually most developed in parts of Central Europe that saw economic stagnation rather than growth in the early modern period. They dispute the claim that England had a unique demographic regime and that fertility was especially responsive to economic conditions. In support of this claim, they show that when measured at the age at first marriage, the EMP was less extreme in England than elsewhere. This was particularly true of the parts of Central Europe that grew more slowly. They argue that "[w]hat is needed is a theoretically coherent and empirically satisfactory account of how particular aspects of the EMP were connected to the wider institutional context, and which demographic and institutional features were responsible for which economic outcomes" (Dennison and Ogilvie, 2014, p. 687).

Taking into account the wider institutional context is not necessarily antithetical to EMP arguments. In fact, proponents like Carmichael, de Pleijt, van Zanden, and de Moor (2016) argue that the EMP was a reflection of a wider institutional package based on joint households and the idea of marriage based on consent. Accordingly, it cannot simply be measured narrowly as age at first marriage. The institutions of the EMP which emphasized consent and participating in the workforce raised the age at first marriage. But more prosperous economic circumstances lowered this. According to Carmichael et al. (2016, p. 202), economically successful regions with EMP institutions had lower marriage ages than those with stagnating EMP regions.

However, it is clear that the EMP did not always simply reflect a voluntary decision between bride and groom. Dennison and Ogilvie (2014) are on stronger ground when they contest whether the EMP was good for women's economic opportunities or status. They contend that women's rights and status varied greatly within societies characterized by a high age of first marriage: in "many regions of Switzerland, Germany, and France, as local studies indicate, the EMP prevailed but women's work, wages, property rights, and in some cases even their consumption choices, were restricted by local communities" (Dennison and Ogilvie, 2014, p. 674). Local institutions such as guilds excluded women, and economically independent women were often harassed by landlords.

Many instances of enforcement of the EMP involved coercion. Marriages were policed by local communities, pre-marital sex was harshly punished, and labor markets were not always welcoming places for women. Ogilvie (2003) documents the extent to which guilds and local elites controlled women's ability to work in early modern Germany. Far from freeing women, the highly regulated and guild-dominated labor markets of 17th-century Germany were places where women's labor was frequently exploited.

Another criticism of the EMP argues that many East Asian societies also restricted fertility. If fertility restrictions were not unique to northwestern Europe, then it can hardly have been crucial to its economic rise. Lee, Campbell, and Feng (2002) provide evidence that the Chinese regulated fertility through a range of different practices. Infanticide, for example, was widely practiced. Female babies were often exposed and the resulting unbalanced sex ratio meant that as much as 20% of the male population did not marry and reproduce. Moreover, it was common in China for young married couples to spend time apart, a practice that further reduced fertility. Chinese families also practiced spacing and targeted a certain number of children (Campbell, Feng, and Lee, 2002). As a result, marital fertility was lower in China than in much of Europe. Similarly, in Tokugawa Japan, fertility restraint was widely practiced through abortion, infanticide, and male migration (Hanley and Yamamura, 1977, p. 25).

These practices were certainly important in shaping Chinese and Japanese demography. They fall somewhat flat, however, as criticisms of the significance of the EMP. What advocates for the importance of the EMP like Carmichael, de Pleijt, van Zanden, and de Moor (2016) emphasize is that the EMP was not simply a means of restricting fertility. It was also a set of institutional arrangements that orientated households, and particularly women, towards the market and human capital accumulation. Practices such as infanticide may have constrained fertility, but they did so in a costly way. These practices do not appear to have been part of a package of institutional innovations that were favorable to economic development.

Demographic Change and the Transition to Modern Economic Growth

It is possible for the beginnings of modern economic growth to arise in a Malthusian economy. Our examination of the EMP suggests how different demographic regimes can affect levels of per capita income. But, as we will discuss further in Chapters 7, 8, and 9, *sustained innovation* is the key to unlocking the modern economy. Not all societies have been innovative. Innovation can take a stroke of brilliance. Innovation is also more likely to occur when a society has the capacity to transmit knowledge of the past to future generations. Larger populations likewise breed innovation (Kremer, 1993; Henrich, 2004). How does sustained innovation emerge in a Malthusian economy?

The transition from Malthusian stagnation to modern economic growth has been studied by Galor and co-authors (Galor and Weil, 2000; Galor, 2005, 2011). Galor proposed a unified theory of the transition from Malthusian stagnation to sustained economic growth based on the interaction of demography and the incentive to invest in human capital. He called this theory *unified growth theory*.

Unified growth theory accounts for two important developments: (1) the gradual increase in growth rates that occurred during the Industrial Revolution; and (2) the demographic transition of the late 19th and early 20th centuries. The demographic transition saw fertility rates plummet and ensured that as incomes rose, the rate of natural population increase declined. Today, population growth in many rich countries is below the rate of natural replacement.

Galor's theory begins with the fact that for most of history, the rate of technological progress was low. Consequently, the returns to investment in human capital were also low. Parents thus had little incentive to invest in education. They invested in the quantity rather than the "quality" of children. The economy remained Malthusian. Improved technology led to more people but not to higher per capita income.

Investment in human capital therefore occurs only when the stock of human knowledge is large enough that technological improvement is common. But how and why does the stock of human knowledge increase in the first place? All else being equal, the larger the population is, the higher the chances of a major invention or a new idea.

Over time, as the stock of knowledge increases, it eventually raises the returns to human capital. As a result, it becomes worthwhile for parents to invest in their children's human capital. Consequently, the rate of economic growth increases further. The returns to human capital increase to the point that parents start to have fewer children. This induces a demographic transition to a modern growth regime. In this regime, parents focus on the "quality" of their children rather than the quantity. Hence, according to this argument, the second phase of the Industrial Revolution after 1850 led to a widespread increase in the demand for more educated workers. We will return to these ideas in Chapter 9, when we discuss the role that population growth played in the rise of the modern economy.

Chapter Summary

The basic facts of births and deaths dominate much of economic history. A casual look at the travails of the English royal family demonstrates that the rich and powerful were not exempt from these basic facts. At the macro-level, historians have seen the ups and downs of pre-industrial history as dictated, at least in part, by demography.

Perhaps the most dramatic example of this is the Black Death. It culled Europe's population and led to higher wages for ordinary workers. But demographic factors did not operate in isolation. The birth rate was largely determined by patterns of marriage and household formation (that is, by institutional and cultural practices). In ancient Rome, women married as soon as they reached sexual maturity. The consequent high birth rate was partly responsible for the low average incomes earned by unskilled workers in the Roman Empire (Harper, 2017). In late medieval Europe, and especially after the Black Death, age at first marriage rose. This European Marriage Pattern helped moderate demographic pressure and keep wages relatively higher than they would otherwise have been, though its importance for long-run growth is debatable.

The Industrial Revolution was followed by a demographic transition. Per capita incomes grew modestly during the Industrial Revolution as population growth accompanied the overall increase in GDP. With the demographic transition, as population growth slowed, per capita income began to rise in a sustained fashion. We will return to the demographic transition in Chapter 9. It is one of the key reasons that economic growth has become *sustained*. Above all, the demographic transition encouraged investment in human capital. According to unified growth theory, as technological progress accelerates, the returns to human capital increase, and this induces parents to switch from large families and low levels of education to smaller families with highly educated children. This is one of the reasons that demographic factors enabled parts of the world to become rich. But was it decisive? Did demography interact with other factors such as institutions and culture? We will return to these issues in Chapter 7.

6

Was It Just a Matter of
Colonization and Exploitation?

In the 15th century, sailors from Portugal – a small, peripheral kingdom on the edge of Europe that had only recently overcome the threat of Muslim invasion from the south – began to explore the coast of Africa. Each year they sailed further. Their motivations were mixed. Initially, some came in search of Christian allies to join the wars against Islam and hoped to find the legendary Prester John, ruler of Ethiopia. Others traveled in search of exotic products from the east, particularly spices. Others still were in search of precious metals like the gold that was produced along the West Coast of Africa. Yet others sought slaves.

It was these Portuguese successes under Prince Henry the Navigator (1394–1460) and the subsequent rounding of the Cape of Good Hope by Bartolomeu Dias in 1488 that inspired Christopher Columbus. Columbus hoped to reach India and China by sailing westwards across the Atlantic. Instead, of course, he reached the Americas. In 1498, Vasco da Gama became the first to reach India directly from Europe by sailing east. These early voyages laid the foundations for Spain's Atlantic empire and Portugal's empire in Southeast Asia and for the later colonial ventures of the Dutch, French, and English. From the very beginning, many of the violent and exploitative practices characteristic of European colonialism were evident. Da Gama harassed local shipping, bombarded cities, and demanded that Muslims be expelled from Indian cities. On one occasion, he burned to death all the passengers of a captured ship.

The opening of trade routes to Asia and the Americas was a landmark event in world history. It led to the formation of global empires and gave rise to new patterns of trade and settlement. But was it crucial to the origins of modern economic growth? A final set of explanations for how Western Europe became rich hinge on the importance of colonization.

The process of European colonization was episodic. Following the Portuguese ventures in Asia and the Spanish conquest of the Aztec and Inca Empires in the Americas, other European powers outfitted and armed fleets. They also encouraged settlers to search for new territories to exploit. Initially, European colonies were located either in the Americas, where epidemic disease rapidly depopulated the continent following contact with Europeans, or in the periphery of Asia and Africa. Europeans were unable to venture far into sub-Saharan Africa. Nor were European states powerful enough to overcome the Mughal emperors of India or the Ming emperors of China. It was only in the late 19th century that large parts of Africa, Southeast Asia, and the Middle East also came under European purview.

The most common explanation for why colonization made Western Europe rich is *exploitation*. The colonial powers exploited the natural resources of their colonies. These included precious metals (South America), rubber (Congo), spices and sugar (Indonesia), oil (Middle East), and slaves. This had two consequences. First, cheap inputs and labor from the colonies allowed for dramatic economic expansion in Western Europe. In one telling, European industrialization is impossible to imagine without its vast colonial empires. Second, the colonized countries were impoverished due to the exploitation of their natural resources. Had they never been colonized, many parts of the world (Africa, South Asia) would have been much better off than they currently are. Hence, theories that rely on colonization attempt to explain both why Europe became rich first *and* why much of the rest of the world has been relatively slow to catch up. Do these explanations survive upon further scrutiny? Colonization was brutal and extractive. Its legacy is still with us in many respects. But was it responsible for modern economic growth?

We focus in this chapter on the *economic* consequences of colonization. This is certainly not a full accounting. The costs and benefits of colonization cannot solely be calculated in monetary terms. Colonization entailed a wide spectrum of actions and outcomes. At their worst, Europeans committed genocide, enslaved Africans and natives, and tore up the pre-existing social fabric of the colonies. These costs are unquantifiable. Yet, if we want to consider colonization as a key cause of why the world became rich, we must consider it relative to the counter-factual world where European colonization never took place. Would Britain still have had an Industrial Revolution? Would India and sub-Saharan Africa still be relatively poor? Recent research in the social sciences has asked these and related questions. Here, we examine their findings.

How Did the Colonizers Benefit?

Empire is as old as history. When the Assyrians captured Israel in the 8th century BCE, and the Babylonians conquered Judah a century later, loot and slaves enriched the cities of Nineveh and Babylon. The city of Rome grew large and Roman elites grew wealthy on the back of an empire established across the Mediterranean and Western Europe. The Mongol conquests of the 13th century saw the populations of China and the Middle East collapse. The Ottomans enslaved Europeans and Africans on a large scale in the 15th and 16th centuries. But none of these empires saw sustained economic growth. Looted wealth was simply a transfer from one place to another.

Nonetheless, one popular explanation attributes the rise of Europe to the resources plundered from the Americas (and later Africa and Asia). There was undoubtedly much plunder. Individuals like Thomas "Diamond" Pitt and Robert Clive became extremely wealthy from looting India, as did the Conquistadors who looted Mexico and Peru. Yet, the amount of wealth taken from the Americas and British India is small compared to the increase in overall national income that took place after 1800.

Previous episodes of empire building did not result in modern economic growth. Nor did all of the colonial powers experience sustained economic growth – Spain and Portugal stagnated in the 17th and 18th centuries. Nevertheless, it is possible that colonization contributed significantly to the onset of sustained economic growth in Britain and its spread to northwestern Europe and North America.

The ultimate source of many of these arguments is Karl Marx. He outlined his theory of primitive accumulation in his landmark work of political economy *Das Kapital* (1868/1990, p. 915):

> The discovery of gold and silver in America, the extirpation, enslavement and entombment in mines of the aboriginal population, the beginning of the conquest and looting of the East Indies, the turning of Africa into a warren for the commercial hunting of black-skins, signaled the rosy dawn of the era of capitalist production. These idyllic proceedings are the chief moments of primitive accumulation. On their heels treads the commercial war of the European nations, with the globe for a theatre. It begins with the revolt of the Netherlands from Spain, assumes giant dimensions in England's Anti-Jacobin War, and is still going on in the opium wars against China, &c.

According to this argument, colonization provided the initial capital required for the construction of the modern economic system. It was also a trying ground for capitalist practices. Thus, says Marx (1868/1990, p. 918), "The colonial system ripened trade and navigation as in a hothouse." The trading monopolies that dominated colonial trade

> were powerful levers for the concentration of capital. The colonies provided a market for the budding manufactures, and a vast increase in accumulation which was guaranteed by the mother country's monopoly of the market. The treasures captured outside Europe by undisguised looting, enslavement and murder flowed back to the mother-country and were turned into capital there.

We will review some of the arguments specifically linking colonization with the British Industrial Revolution in Chapter 8.

More recently, the book that made famous the term "the Great Divergence" claims that one of the keys to Europe's rise relative to China was all of the new land ("ghost acreage") in the New World. New land relieved population pressures in Europe and brought in new natural resources (for more on Pomeranz's [2000] argument, see Chapter 2).

Certainly, there is much to the argument that Europe benefited from the resources of the New World. For instance, Nunn and Qian (2010) show that the potato was one of colonization's great finds. The potato was a New World crop that was much more nutritious and more efficiently grown than Old World crops (see Table 6.1). Nunn and Qian estimate that the introduction of the potato was responsible for about one-quarter of Old World population growth and increase in urbanization between 1700 and 1900. Such numbers make it clear that the flow of goods from newly "discovered" lands played an important role in the economies of early modern Europe. But were such factors decisive in generating modern economic growth?

How important colonization was for economic growth depends on which parts of the world we are talking about. From Figure 6.1, we can see that a large fraction of the world's landmass was at some point under European control. For some countries, the period of colonial rule was short and transitory. For others, it was long-lived. Europeans had a negligible impact on East Asian societies like China and Japan until after 1800 and so it is hard to see how colonization had a negative effect on them prior to the Great Divergence. Arguments pertaining to this divergence therefore focus on the *benefits* of empire to Europeans.

Table 6.1 English crop yields, 18th century

	Average yield per acre (kg)	Acres of land needed to feed a family for one year
Wheat	650	1.7
Barley	820	1.4
Oats	690	1.6
Potatoes	10,900	0.5

Energy needed to feed one family for one year provides 42 megajoules of energy per day, or approximately 10,000 calories.

Data source: Nunn and Qian (2010).

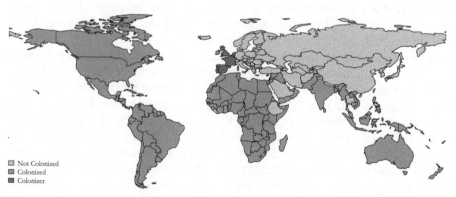

Figure 6.1 Countries colonized by Great Britain, France, Spain, Portugal, the Netherlands, or Belgium, 1500–1950

With respect to the Middle East, although some arguments center on the negative aspects of colonization (focusing on, for instance, the Sykes–Picot agreement of 1916, which split the region into various spheres of influence with little respect for pre-existing ethnic divisions), Kuran (2011) notes that the timing of such arguments is off. The divergence between Western Europe and the Middle East happened well before the colonization of the latter. It is therefore an unlikely culprit in the divergence.

Strong claims are made that conquest by the East India Company and the establishment of the British Raj had catastrophic effects on the Indian economy. These claims, however, are not supported by the facts. While British rule brought Indians little improvement in per capita income, the evidence suggests that the Indian economy was in deep decline decades prior to the British takeover (Broadberry and Gupta, 2006; Clingingsmith and Williamson, 2008; Broadberry, Custodis, and Gupta, 2015; Gupta, 2019). We further examine Indian economic growth in Chapter 10.

With respect to Africa and Latin America, the colonizers certainly benefited from the resources and slave/coerced labor provided by the regions. Meanwhile, these regions also fell further behind because of colonization. Some arguments focus on the role of the colonies and slavery in Britain's industrialization. Britain was far from the first to engage in the transatlantic slave trade: Portugal sent millions of slaves to its Brazilian colony from the 16th century onwards. But Britain came to dominate the slave trade as it proved increasingly successful in acquiring Caribbean islands and their access to sugar, tobacco, and cotton (see Figure 6.2). For this reason, many scholars – most notably Williams (1944), Solow (1987), and Inikori (2002) – have seen something singular in the connections between slavery, the Caribbean sugar economies, and subsequent industrialization.

The role that slave and coerced labor played in Britain's industrialization has been the source of heated discussion for decades, if not longer. This is an important debate. After all, Britain's industrialization played a key role in how the world became rich. But in order to discuss this issue, we need a better understanding of Britain's Industrial Revolution. This is the focus of Chapter 8. We will therefore hold off on discussing this until then.

In the remainder of this chapter, we focus on the varying detrimental consequences of colonization for those that were colonized. If colonization benefited the colonial powers, its negative effects on those parts of the world that were colonized may have been greater still. A large literature has emerged in recent years that attempts to explain the lingering effects of colonization on the colonized. Some places subject to colonial rule clearly ended up quite well-off (the US, Canada, Australia, New Zealand, Hong Kong, and Singapore), while others remain poor today (much of sub-Saharan Africa and Southeast Asia). What accounts for these differences? What role did colonization play, if any? Why has poverty *persisted* in many of the colonies?

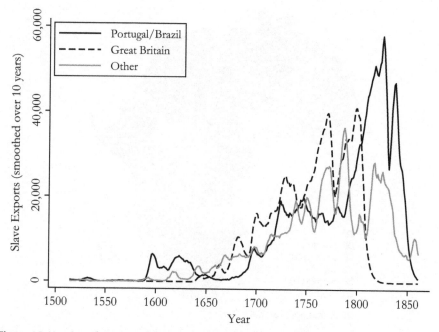

Figure 6.2 Number of slaves in the transatlantic slave trade by carrier

Data sources: The Transatlantic Slave Trade Database at www.slavevoyages.org, downloaded March 23, 2021. Also see Whatley (2018).

The Slave Trades

Of the many odious aspects of colonization, the most odious was the slave trade. The slave trade is as ancient as history. During the expansion of the Roman Empire, millions of slaves were transported to Italy. In just one episode, Caesar sold 53,000 individuals into slavery following the defeat of the Atuatuci. According to his own estimates, over 1,000,000 individuals were killed or enslaved during his conquest of Gaul. The Arab Conquests of the 7th–8th centuries also saw a revival in slavery in Europe and the Middle East.

Between 1400 and 1900, Africa experienced four slave trades: the transatlantic trade (to the New World), the trans-Saharan trade, the Red Sea trade, and the Indian Ocean trade. The colonial powers were the primary participants in the transatlantic trade, which brought over 12 million slaves to the New World (Nunn, 2008). This number does not include those killed in slave raids or those who died on the journey to the port. It is thus an underestimate of the total number of Africans lost to the slave trade. Most of these slaves came from the west coast of Africa (see Figure 6.3). It is hard to overstate the impact of the slave trades on economic and demographic growth. According to Manning (1990), by 1850, Africa's population was only half of what it would have been had the slave trades never taken place.

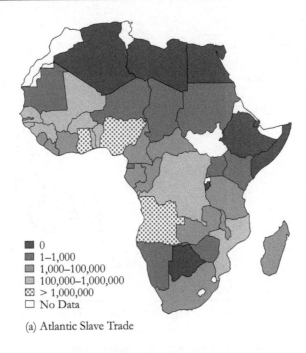

(a) Atlantic Slave Trade

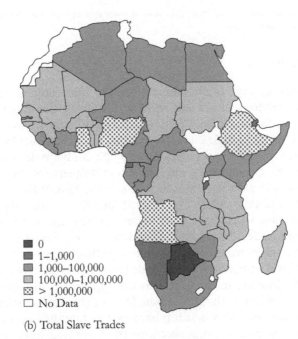

(b) Total Slave Trades

Figure 6.3 Number of slaves taken in the slave trades

Data source: Nunn (2008).

Many of the costs of the slave trades were not directly economic. The psychological costs of being enslaved are incalculable. The sociological costs of what the slave trades did to African communities, as well as the damage done to slave families torn apart in the New World, may well be greater than the economic costs of forgone development. Yet, this does not mean that we should be uninterested in the economic costs of the slave trades. They play a significant role in Africa's continued poverty. Nunn (2008) finds that countries that had high levels of slave "exports" (an unfortunate term when speaking of human beings) have lower GDP, greater ethnic fractionalization (which itself is associated with lower income in numerous economic studies), and worse political institutions (see Figure 6.4). The gap grew following the collapse of European colonial rule. Between 1950 and 2000, the per capita GDP of high slave export countries was nearly constant (at a low level of less than $3 a day), while the per capita GDP of low slave export countries nearly doubled from around $4 to $8 a day. This suggests that the slave trades might be responsible for *both* the relative poverty of sub-Saharan Africa *and* differences of income within Africa. But the slave trades have ceased to exist for well over a century. Why would their residue still be with us?

One reason the slave trades still affects outcomes is that they shaped the culture of societies damaged by them. As we noted in Chapter 4, culture can persist long after the original impetus for the cultural trait has disappeared. One of the most lasting cultural impacts of slavery arose from the way in which slaves were captured. Some were captured through state-organized raids and warfare, while many others were kidnapped or tricked into slavery by people such as close friends or family members. This produced a culture of mistrust and uncertainty in those regions affected by the slave trades. Nunn and Wantchekon (2011) found that people whose ancestors belonged to ethnic groups that were heavily exposed to the slave trades *still* have lower trust today of relatives, neighbors, co-ethnics, and local government. This negatively impacted Africa's economic development and may explain some of Nunn's results cited above linking the slave trades to long-run economic outcomes. As we noted in Chapter 4, trust is a crucial component of exchange, especially with previously unknown persons. The dearth of trust in sub-Saharan Africa, engendered by the slave trades, is therefore an impediment to the region's development.

Other consequences of the slave trades abound. Whatley and Gillezeau (2011) find that places more heavily affected by them have higher ethnic fractionalization today. That is, there are more ethnic groups living in close proximity to each other in these regions. Africa does in fact have *many* ethnic groups (see Figure 6.5). But what does this have to do with the slave trades? The logic is straight-forward: where slave raiding was profitable, local groups would raid each other rather than form larger, cohesive states. Ties across villages and ethnic groups were weakened. Inter-ethnic alliances and marriages were less common. This led to more ethnic groups over time.

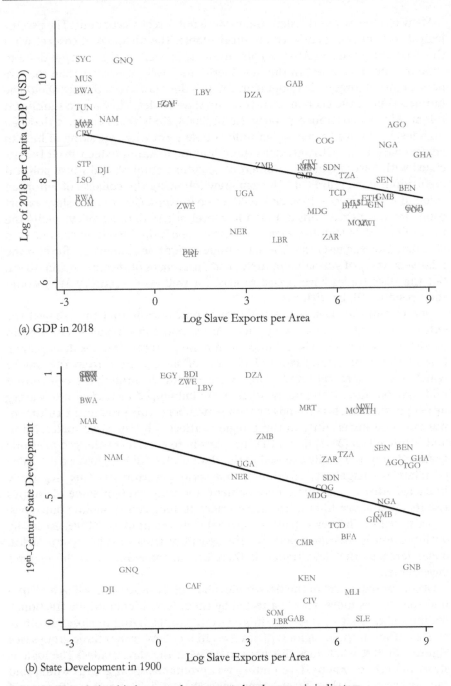

Figure 6.4 The relationship between slaves exported and economic indicators

Data sources: Nunn (2008) for slave exports and state development, Bolt and van Zanden (2020) for GDP.

Figure 6.5 Africa's ethnic boundaries prior to colonization
Data source: Nunn (2008).

There are many reasons that ethnic fractionalization might be negatively associated with economic growth. In fractionalized states, some groups rule over others. This can be disastrous, especially if these groups have a history of animosity towards each other. In these settings, fractionalization can cause civil conflict, less public good provision, and lower trust. In fact, Easterly and Levine (1997) find that ethnic fractionalization is responsible for around 25% of the differences in African and Asian economic growth. As the results of Whatley and Gillezeau (2011) suggest, this may be a residue of the slave trades.

The Resource Grab

From the point of view of long-run economic growth, perhaps the most damaging aspect of colonialism was the institutions the colonizers established. As we saw in Chapter 3, institutions can be hard to change. They also tend to stick around well beyond the time their original purpose is relevant. This can be really bad for economic development if the original institutions were exploitative in the first place.

European colonizers mostly set up institutions in their colonies to maximize the amount of resources extracted. Some of these institutions built off of institutions that were there prior to colonization. Others were completely new to the environment. Extraction often required forced labor and brutal means of suppression. In the Belgian Congo, for instance, local chiefs were given rubber quotas. If coerced laborers failed to meet these quotas, they could be imprisoned, burned, or murdered (Lowes and Montero, forthcoming). The Spanish set up similar forced labor institutions in their South American colonies, where natives were forced to work in silver mines – most notably in Potosi. These institutions were *extractive*. Their primary purpose was to extract resources, most of which went back to the colonizing country.

Where extractive institutions were established, rights for the native population were limited (if they existed at all), and investments in public goods tended to be restricted to those that facilitated extraction (such as roads leading from mines to ports). Unfortunately, many post-colonial governments found these extractive institutions useful as well. As a result, these institutions often persisted after independence. This is one of the reasons why "bad" governance – in terms of checks and balances and freedoms secured – is more common in the formerly colonized world than in Western Europe. However, not all of the former colonies got bad institutions. For instance, Australia, New Zealand, Canada, and the US all have institutions that place limits on the extractive ability of the state. Why did some colonies end up with "good" institutions and others end up with "bad" ones?

Acemoglu, Johnson, and Robinson (2001) were among the first to offer a comprehensive answer for the large variation in contemporary institutional quality and economic outcomes in the former colonies. They argue that colonizers set up different types of institutions depending on how frequently settlers died in the colonies. In places with climates poorly suited for European settlement – such as Africa's "malaria belt," where European mortality rates were extremely high – the incentive for Europeans was to extract as much as they could. There was little reason to set up European-style institutions, since this would limit their capacity to exploit the native populations. On the other hand, in more temperate climates similar to those found in Europe – such as the US or the east coast of Australia – there was more incentive for Europeans to settle. As more Europeans came over, they brought with them the type of legal, political, and religious institutions that were so vital to their continent's economic growth. The analysis conducted by Acemoglu, Johnson, and Robinson supports these relationships. They find that places with higher settler mortality *still* have worse institutions today, and those places with worse institutions are also poorer (see Figure 6.6). This might also be responsible for the "reversal of fortunes" that they found in a follow-up study (Acemoglu, Johnson, and Robinson, 2002: discussed in Chapter 1, see Figure 1.8). Those places that were the wealthiest in the world in 1500 were among the poorest by the end of the 20th century. It was precisely those places with easily exploitable natural resources that got the bad colonial institutions associated with poor long-run economic development.

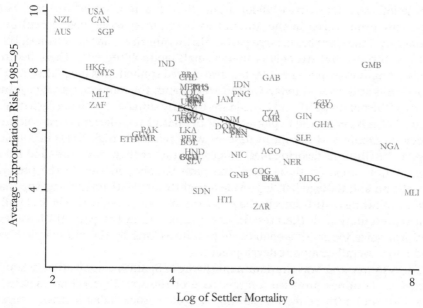

(a) Settler Mortality vs. Expropriation Risk

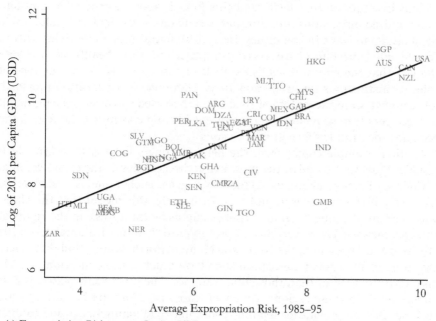

(a) Expropriation Risk vs. per Capita GDP

Figure 6.6 Settler mortality, institutions, and long-run development

Data source: Acemoglu, Johnson, and Robinson (2001) for settler mortality and expropriation risk, Bolt and van Zanden (2020) for GDP.

Sokoloff and Engerman (2000) argue that the reversal of fortunes was especially pronounced in the Americas, where places with good agricultural suitability – the Caribbean, large parts of Latin America, and the southern US – got institutions that strongly favored a small landholding elite. These institutions brought wealth to the elite, but also caused tremendous inequality, much of which is still present today. On the other hand, the more marginal farming lands of the northern US and Canada were poorly suited for growing cash crops. Instead of relying on the exploitation of the native population, these colonies relied on laborers of European descent with relatively high levels of human capital. Institutions favoring local enterprise, rather than cash crops and labor exploitation, arose in these areas and have largely persisted to the present day. Bruhn and Gallego (2012) provide a slightly alternative view, arguing that labor-exploiting institutions in the Americas are associated with a lack of political representation in the present. Areas exploited in the past still have less political voice today. This enables more rent-seeking by the plutocratic class and lower overall economic development.

The resource grab was the dominant theme of Spanish colonization in South America. Its mines provided a large share of the world's precious metals in the 16th and 17th centuries. Mining is a dangerous, labor-intensive enterprise, hence, the Spanish forced natives to do this work. One of the most pernicious institutions that facilitated this forced labor was the *mita*, a system that required indigenous communities to send one-seventh of their adult male populations to work in the mines. Dell (2010) found that those living within the old *mita* boundaries have less consumption and worse health *today*, despite the fact that the *mita* was abolished in 1812. This is likely due to the type of colonial institutions set up in *mita* areas. There was less education provided, less connection to the system of roads, and increased subsistence farming. All of these persist in some form to the present day and continue to hold back the economic potential of former *mita* regions.

Another example comes from the Belgian Congo. Belgian King Leopold II (r. 1865–1909) set up one of the most extractive colonies of the entire colonial period. As discussed above, local chiefs were given rubber quotas, and violence was likely if the quotas were not met. Ultimately, this meant that the chiefs who were most prone to enforce rubber quotas by transgressing the rights of their people stayed in power. This is a prototypical "bad" institutional design. Its effects are still present today. Lowes and Montero (forthcoming) find that places that were in the rubber concession zone have much worse education, wealth, and health outcomes than those that were not. The most likely reason is that village chiefs in these regions – many of whose positions are hereditary – are still less likely to provide local public goods like road maintenance and conflict arbitration.

Colonial institutions were established not only to extract natural resources, but also to tax the local populations. How these taxation systems worked was important. Some gave significant power to local authorities in return for tax collection. This tended to be bad for long-run economic development. Local power brokers wanted to keep their rents flowing after independence, and thus extractive institutions tended to persist. Banerjee and Iyer (2005) studied these taxation institutions in colonial India. They found that, even decades after independence, places in which rights were given to local landlords continued to have greater inequality, lower agricultural productivity, and less investment in health and education. These differences were mostly due to differences in government spending. Places where landlords dominated in the past tend to irrigate and fertilize less in the present, leading to lower crop yields (see Figure 6.7).

India provides a fertile testing ground for examining the effects of colonial rule. Not only was it by far the most populous of the European colonies (colonial India also included modern-day Pakistan and Bangladesh), but only parts of it were ruled by the British. The rest of the subcontinent, known as the "Princely States" because they were ruled by local princes, maintained some degree of political autonomy. Iyer (2010) found that areas that were formerly under British rule have much less access to schools, health centers, and roads. They are also no better off in terms of agricultural productivity or investment. One explanation for these results is that local princes funneled less tax revenue into their own pockets than did the British, instead spending more on public goods. Another reason is that the British removed the worst princes in the colonial period. This gave an incentive for princes to be relatively good rulers. It is not clear if this result extends beyond India, however. Lange (2004), on the other hand, finds that former British colonies that were under direct rule (that is, they were ruled by the British administrative apparatus) tend to have more political stability, bureaucratic effectiveness, rule of law, and freedom from government corruption than do those that were under indirect rule (like the Princely States).

Another set of negative consequences from colonization stemmed from poor political design. Colonial powers sought to rule groups of people they knew relatively little about. This led to some disastrous decisions. In the US, Native Americans were placed on reservations at the tribal level. However, most Native American political decisions were historically determined at the sub-tribal level. Dippel (2014) studied the impact of this forced coexistence on Native American tribes and found that reservations that combined multiple sub-tribal bands are around 30% poorer today than those that did not. The primary explanation is poor local governance. These reservations have more political corruption and internal conflict, while having less certainty about the contracting environment and less investment by local government.

Michalopoulos and Papaioannou (2016) find further evidence of poor colonial political design in the "scramble for Africa." In the late 19th century, much of sub-Saharan Africa remained among the last places on earth that had not come under some type of colonial rule. The European powers sought to change this. Meeting in a board-room in Berlin (the Berlin Conference of 1884–5), they partitioned Africa among Great Britain, France, Germany, Italy, Belgium,

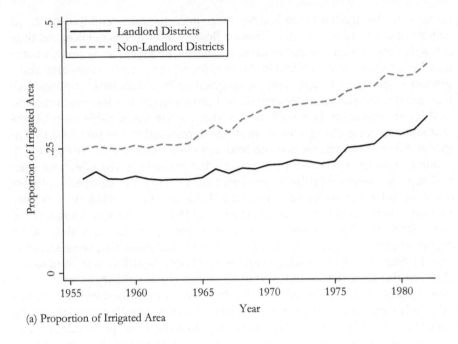

(a) Proportion of Irrigated Area

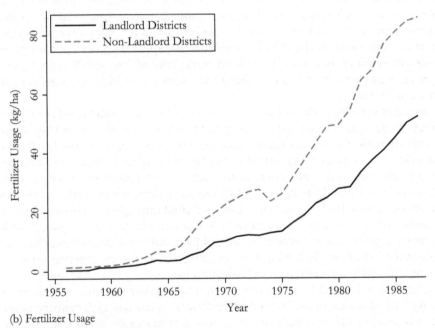

(b) Fertilizer Usage

Figure 6.7 Agricultural investment in India

Data source: Banerjee and Iyer (2005).

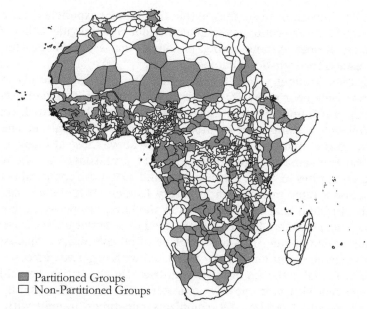

Figure 6.8 Ethnic partitioning and the "scramble for Africa"
Data source: Michalopoulos and Papaioannou (2016).

Portugal, and Spain. The people in charge of dividing Africa into spheres of influence had little knowledge of the continent. The consequences were disastrous. The colonial powers gave little thought to pre-existing ethnic divisions. They just wanted to maximize their own share of the pie. This meant that rival ethnic groups were placed in the same states – a situation that continued after independence as these colonial borders largely remained. Michalopoulos and Papaioannou find that these partitions (which affected many ethnic groups throughout Africa: see Figure 6.8) triggered political violence, political instability, discrimination, and ethnic wars. This was bound to happen in an environment where some ethnic groups rule over others, especially when there is a long history of animosity between them. Michalopoulos and Papaioannou also find that ethnically partitioned groups are worse off on a host of economic outcomes, including education and wealth.

Some Silver Linings of Colonialism?

On balance, the effects of colonization on the colonized world were almost certainly negative. This is true of Africa, where the economic costs of the slave trades are only one part of the overall costs faced by those enslaved and their descendants. It is also likely true of Latin America, South Asia, and Southeast

Asia. Yet, it is important to emphasize that the colonial experience was highly heterogeneous. Some economies stagnated under colonial rule. Others developed rapidly. It goes without saying, of course, that economic development does not excuse the injustices that took place.

Colonization brought some economic benefits, even in those places that remain relatively poor today. During the colonial period, Frankema and van Waijenburg (2012) find that real wages grew considerably in British colonial Africa. This was accompanied by urbanization and structural change. As a result, incomes in many African countries were above those of many parts of Asia in 1950. Frankema and Van Waijenburg (2012, p. 912) note that "the average annual growth rates in Accra between 1900 and 1960 were comparable to the average growth rates in nineteenth-century London (1840–1900)." Likewise, in a study of islands that were colonized by the European powers, Feyrer and Sacerdote (2009) find that former colonies tend to be better off the *longer* they were under colonial rule. This was not true of all colonizers – Spanish and Portuguese colonization tends to be associated with negative outcomes. Why might the colonial activities of other countries (Dutch, British, French) have been associated with more positive outcomes? These countries hardly colonized for benevolent reasons. Yet, colonizers sometimes brought with them modern transport technologies (such as railroads), access to education, and modern medicine. A literature has recently emerged that tries to understand how these aspects of colonization have affected modern economic outcomes.

Public Goods and Education

Even if one takes that view that colonialism was mostly about extraction, it is still true that some of the colonial powers invested in their colonies – even if the point of investment was to enhance extraction. Some of these investments lasted after independence, either because they were fixed, like railroads, or because they took minimal upkeep, like schools and health clinics. Although we often do not know what types of public goods would have been provided *in the absence of colonization*, the fact that some of these goods were in fact provided is a silver lining of colonization.

Among the most important goods provided by some of the colonial powers were railroads, which they built largely for military and (self-serving) economic reasons. Despite this, they are one of the lasting legacies of colonialism. Donaldson (2018) studied the effect of British investment in Indian railroads, which began in 1853 (soon before the mutiny of 1857, which highlighted the usefulness of railroads for military purposes). By 1930, there were 67,247 kilometers of track laid in India, making it the fourth largest network in the world (see Figure 6.9). This was by far the dominant form of public investment in British India. While the primary reason the British laid so much track was military, there were economic benefits to railroad expansion. Previously isolated parts of India became connected with both local and international markets.

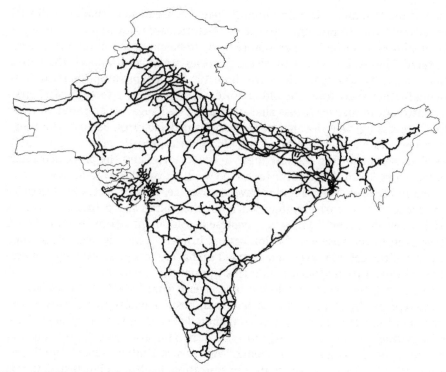

Figure 6.9 The Indian railroad network, 1930
Source: Map provided by Dave Donaldson from Donaldson (2018).

Donaldson finds that investment in railroads increased income, trade, and market integration throughout British India. Chaudhary and Fenske (2020) provide additional evidence that the spread of the railroad improved literacy. In a study on Ghana, Jedwab and Moradi (2016) find that places that received colonial railroads are more developed today *despite* the fact that many of the railroads went into disuse after independence. This is because the network encouraged urbanization around the railroad lines. Investment and economic activity followed where urban populations were relatively dense.

Sometimes, extractive institutions can have unintended positive benefits in the long run. Dell and Olken (2020) study one such institution: the Dutch Cultivation System imposed in Java (Indonesia). Under this system, peasants were forced to cultivate sugar, which was then processed in nearby factories before being shipped to Europe. This was an extremely lucrative trade, accounting for up to one-third of Dutch government revenue. The cultivation system reorganized economic life in Java. Millions of Javanese worked (often by coercion) in the sugar factories, a major shift away from the predominantly agricultural society that had previously dominated. Villages surrounding the factories were reorganized to grow sugar cane. Although the Dutch did this to maximize extraction, Dell and Olken find unanticipated consequences that are still with us. People living in proximity to the old factories are *today* much less likely to be employed in agriculture and more likely to be employed in manufacturing or retail. That is, areas near those old factories are more developed than areas that are not. These households have about 10% higher consumption than those living further away from the old factories. Why do these effects persist? First, downstream industries (those that used processed sugar as an input, such as food processing) were located near the old sugar factories. Second, the transport network was better around the old factories, mostly because the Dutch needed ways of getting the raw sugar to the factories and the processed sugar to the docks. Third, some of the increased wealth around the factories was reinvested in the area. These regions have, on average, greater access to electricity and schools than nearby regions. Much like the studies above, this study comes with a caveat. It is *not* comparing Javanese development against what it would have been in the absence of colonization. Instead, it merely notes that some aspects of the colonial experience ended up having less negative long-run economic impacts than others, even if this was not the intention.

In general, the types of colonial investments that have lasted consisted of some type of physical facilities or had local positive externalities. This is why transport infrastructure may have contributed to economic development. Once railway track is laid, it is costly to take away. This also goes for schools and health facilities. In a study of French West Africa, Huillery (2009) found that around 30% of current performance in education, health, and infrastructure is explained by colonial investment. She provides evidence suggesting that physical investment in these facilities and increased demand for local public goods are the reasons these investments persisted over time. Within colonial Africa, Grier (1999) finds that former British colonies outperform former French colonies. Much like the studies noted above, investments in public goods – in this case, education – can explain the differences in performance.

Frankema (2012) warns, however, that we should not view this as some benevolent policy of the British. It was hardly a top priority of their colonial policy to educate their colonial subjects. Most of the education advantage of the British colonies was instead due to missionaries, who set up schools in order to gain converts to Christianity. The British tended to provide better environments for missionaries to work in, which explains the British education advantage. More generally, missionaries provided a host of (non-religious) goods that benefited the colonies. Because of this, they can be viewed as one of the "silver linings" of colonialism. We turn to them next.

Missionaries

As we have mentioned before, some former colonies have done much better than others. It is not just the wealthier, former British colonies that are better off than others (the US, Canada, Australia, New Zealand). Argentina, Brazil,

Costa Rica, and Botswana are middle-income countries whose economies are likely to continue to grow in the coming decades. Meanwhile, other former colonies, such as Haiti, Mali, Sudan, and Niger, remain desperately poor. What can account for these differences in outcomes among the colonized? Why have the riches of economic development spread to some but not others?

One feature of the colonial experience can account for much of this variation: the presence of missionaries. As part of the colonization process, Christian churches sent missionaries to far-off lands with the goal of converting the local populations. To be clear, this literature does *not* claim that it was something about Christian values or theology that enabled some of the colonies to eventually escape the poverty trap. Instead, it emphasizes the various other things that missionaries did in order to achieve their conversion goals, many of which had unintended long-run economic effects.

Woodberry (2012) finds evidence of one important channel through which missionaries may have prevented some of the worst outcomes of colonialism: democracy. He claims that the placement of Protestant missions helps explain about half of the variation in democracy in Africa, Asia, Latin America, and Oceania. The reason democracy was more likely to flourish in regions with missionaries was not due to any religious doctrine or because missionaries promoted democratic thinking. Much more important was that Protestant missionaries helped promote mass education, mass printing, newspapers, and civil society. Probably the most important of these is education, which Lankina and Getachew (2012) find was positively associated with missionary activity in India.

Why is education related to democracy? Highly literate societies with strong civil societies tend to be where democracies prosper. In these societies, a larger part of the population wants a say in government and has the means to fight for it. This links back to missionaries not because they valued education for its own sake or what it could contribute to economic well-being. The primary goal of missionaries was conversion, and they promoted education largely because they wanted people to read and interpret the Bible. This is yet another example of unintended consequences playing an enormous role in shaping long-run political and economic development.

More broadly, one of the common themes in this literature is that *contemporary* educational attainment is greater in places where missionaries set up shop. For instance, in Africa, Cagé and Rueda (2016) find that places near Protestant missions with printing presses have numerous contemporary socioeconomic outcomes that are much better. These include more education, greater trust, greater political participation, and higher newspaper readership. In South America, Valencia Caicedo (2018) finds that proximity to (Catholic) Jesuit missions is associated with higher education attainment today – and thus higher income – despite the fact that Jesuit missionaries were kicked out in 1767 (see Figure 6.10). This is likely due to the fact that, as in other missions around the world, Jesuit missions placed emphasis on reading and writing. In Mexico, Waldinger (2017) finds that places with Mendicant missions – which

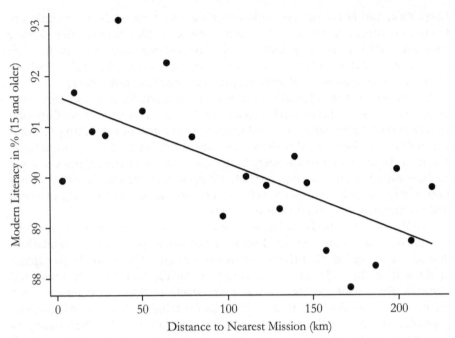

Figure 6.10 Modern literacy and proximity to Jesuit missions in Argentina, Brazil, and Paraguay Binned scatter plot.

Data source: Valencia Caicedo (2018).

were committed to alleviating poverty by educating the native population – have higher contemporary literacy rates and educational attainment. Bai and Kung (2015) report a similar finding for Protestant missions in 19th-century China.

We want to be clear that the claim in this literature is by no means that colonization was a good thing for local populations just because missionaries promoted education and other public goods associated with higher incomes. The point is simply that places with missionaries tended to do better than *other places that were also colonized*. This is because they were *more developed*. History is rich and complex. The economic consequences of colonialism were highly heterogeneous. It was very bad in some places, less bad in others, and probably good in a few others. Appreciating these nuances is important to gaining a better understanding of how colonization contributed to modern wealth and the distribution of wealth. In the best case, missionaries may have played a positive role on development and education. In the worst case, they may have merely mitigated some of the damaging effects of the broader colonial enterprise.

Chapter Summary

Colonization played a large role in the making of the modern world. It brought vast riches to some in Europe, and it still has an effect in the present on parts of the world that were colonized. But is it responsible for how the world became rich? Here, the evidence is mixed.

Yet, there is little controversy regarding the damaging role that colonization played on the colonized. A large literature has emerged showing various mechanisms through which the colonial legacy is still with us in many parts of the world. This includes institutional development, trust norms, human capital accumulation, and public good provision. All of these are key factors in either promoting or inhibiting economic catch-up with the leading economies. By this metric, the colonial legacy is dark indeed.

Part II

Why Some Parts of the World Became Rich First, Why Other Parts Followed, and Why Some Are Not There Yet

7

Why Did Northwestern Europe Become Rich First?

In attempting to answer the question "How did the world become rich?" we have considered the roles played by geography, institutions, demography, culture, and colonialism. Among the factors we have studied, which best explain the timing and location of the onset of modern economic growth?

To begin to grasp these issues, it helps to restate the problem. During the 19th century, Western Europe and some of its offshoots (the US, Canada, Australia) began to experience sustained economic growth. They were followed by countries like Japan and Russia and later other countries in East Asia. McCloskey (2006) calls this the Great Enrichment. How did this happen? In 1700, no economy in the world showed signs that it was capable of sustained economic growth. This typically involved structural change in the economy: a movement away from agriculture and towards industry and services. It came with much greater levels of urbanization. In the long run, it was aided by a demographic shift to lower birth and death rates. Most of all, it required a massive increase in the rate of innovation. These factors coalesced in northwestern Europe in the 18th and 19th centuries and ultimately led in the mid-19th century, to modern, sustained economic growth. Why did this happen when and where it did?

You may suspect that the answer is "the Industrial Revolution." You would not be completely wrong. It is certainly true that Britain's Industrial Revolution was a key stepping stone on the path to the modern economy. Britain industrialized first, beginning in the second half of the 18th century, and was followed in the 19th century by the US and a few European countries. Once this industrial transformation occurred, it created a new global division of labor, in which countries like Australia and Denmark could become rich by specializing in non-industrial sectors of the economy like commercial agriculture.

But industrialization is just a proximate cause. Why did industrialization and sustained innovation – and the modern economy that followed in their wake – first take place in northwestern Europe? Why not Southern Europe (which dominated Europe's economy in the medieval period)? Why not the Middle East (which was ahead of Europe for centuries following the spread of Islam)?

Why not China (which was technologically dominant until around 1500)? Why didn't the pace of innovation slow down, as occurred in prior growth spurts around the world?

So far, this book has presented a survey of some of the most well-known and meticulously researched answers to these questions. Some do a better job than others. In our view, a good answer needs to address at least three questions. First, why was Europe behind most of the rest of Eurasia for centuries following the fall of the Western Roman Empire? Most answers that assume European economic dominance was inevitable have a hard time addressing this question. Second, what happened in Europe in the two to three centuries prior to the 19th century that set the stage? The modern economy did not arise out of nowhere. By the 18th century, Britain was clearly in a comparatively favorable position to achieve sustained economic growth. Why? Third, why did modern economic growth first happen in *northwestern* Europe? Modern economic growth was not a pan-European phenomenon. Simple comparisons of "Europe vs. elsewhere" are misleading. In the 19th century, Southern and Eastern Europe were closer to the Middle East or East Asia on most economic dimensions than they were to northwestern Europe. By 1700, the center of Europe's economic geography had moved northwards away from Italy and the Mediterranean and towards economies that faced the Atlantic – especially to the Dutch Republic and the British Isles. A convincing explanation must account for this.

Hopefully we have given the reader a dispassionate view of the dominant theories of long-run growth. In this chapter, we pull together arguments from Chapters 2–6 to provide our own view of the origins of modern economic growth. Something as complex as the origins of the modern economy is not monocausal. In our view, the most convincing explanations bring together multiple arguments, considering how they interact and fill in each other's blanks.

A comprehensive explanation for the onset of sustained growth has to explain both the divergence between Europe and the rest of Eurasia and the divergence within Europe. It also has to be consistent with the timing of growth. Chronologically, many of the institutional developments that distinguished early modern Europe from elsewhere can be traced to the Middle Ages. These include the rise of representative institutions, city-states, the rediscovery of Roman law, and the development of the corporate form. They preceded the onset of modern economic growth by many centuries. But modern economic growth was dependent on these developments.

Our favored arguments draw on multiple chapters in this book. First, we view institutions as being of central importance. But institutional developments did not occur in a vacuum. For example, the possibilities for both economic growth and institutional change were constrained by geography. Europe's fractured geography and distance to the steppe frontier led to persistent political fragmentation. Political fragmentation explains several important institutional developments that were unique to medieval Europe. These include the rise of representative institutions such as self-governing city-states and parliaments, public debt, and the notion of separation between religion and the state.

Another key interaction was between institutional development and culture. Culture should not be seen as isolated from institutional, political, and economic factors. For example, one of the lasting legacies of the Catholic Church in the High Middle Ages was in breaking down kinship groups. Catholic scholars also played a critical role in the revival of Roman law. In contrast, Islamic law constrained institutional developments, particularly the corporate form, in the Middle East (Kuran, 2011). In both cases, Catholic and Islamic legal institutions are difficult to fully disentangle from Catholic and Islamic cultural values and norms.

In this chapter, we outline why, for a host of reasons, Western Europe was on a distinctive institutional path from the late Middle Ages onwards. To be clear, we distinguish here between *institutional* and *economic* trajectories. Even the richest parts of Europe at the end of the medieval period were poor by modern standards. The continent as a whole was probably less developed than China, even if it had overtaken the Middle East by this point. The major economic divergence did not occur until later.

Several factors were important in explaining the divergence between northwestern Europe and the rest of the world. Many of these factors were also responsible for the mini-divergence between northwestern and Southern Europe. These include the rise of Atlantic trading networks as well as cultural and religious developments. Perhaps the most important religious development was the Protestant Reformation. But this was not because of a superior work ethic, as Weber famously suggested (see Chapter 4). Rather, it was the institutional consequences of the Reformation that helped ensure the rise of representative institutions in northwestern Europe.

In the final part of this chapter, we sketch the most important preconditions for the onset of sustained economic growth *as it emerged in Britain*. By this we mean those institutional features that ultimately played an important role in the structural shifts characteristic of Britain's economy in the 18th and 19th centuries. None of the preconditions were enough by themselves. In fact, the Dutch Republic shared many of these preconditions with Britain. But it did not achieve sustained economic growth until much later. We save our explanation for Great Britain's economic rise, especially its Industrial Revolution, for Chapter 8. Here, we are interested in understanding the conditions that enabled the modern economy to arise in the first place.

How Geography Shaped Institutional Development

Chapter 2 examined the importance of geography in the origins of economic growth. The arguments we reviewed suggested that geographic factors were even more important historically than today due to the limitations of pre-industrial transportation and communication technologies. Yet, geography on its own can at best explain only the *location* of economic activity. It has little to say about the *timing* of economic growth. The most important effects of geography work through economic and political institutions.

It is not always obvious that "good" geographic endowments lead to economic success. In fact, good geographic endowments can sometimes be a *detriment* to economic development. There is a large literature on what is known as the "resource curse" (Sachs and Warner, 2001; Mehlum, Moene, and Torvik, 2006; Robinson, Torvik, and Verdier, 2006; Ross, 2015; Desierto, 2018). The resource curse explains the observation that many countries that are plush with resources are still very poor. This is a particular problem in sub-Saharan Africa. Why are some countries unable to use their natural endowments as a gateway to wealth? The answer lies primarily in a society's *political institutions*. Where political institutions are extractive, to use a phrase from Chapter 3, natural resources strengthen the ruling elites' grip on power. They can use those resources to pay off friends and enrich themselves. This can lead to even more extractive institutions down the road. In short, natural resources can sometimes be a blessing, but they can also very much be a curse.

The resource curse is just one example of how geography and institutions interact with each other. Geography can also lead to institutional developments that, in the long run, promote economic growth. One such example is the "fractured land" hypothesis. Developed by Diamond (1997) and Jones (2003), this hypothesis suggests that Europe's geography explains its persistent political fragmentation. This fragmentation, in turn, had important consequences for future institutional development. The topographical structure of Europe, with "its mountain chains, coasts and major marches, formed boundaries at which states expanding from the core-areas could meet and pause. . . . [T]hese natural barriers helped to hold the ring between the varied ethnic and linguistic groups making up the European peoples" (Jones, 2003, p. 226).

In particular, the location of Europe's mountain ranges ensured that there were several distinct geographic cores of roughly equal size that could provide the nuclei for future European states (Fernández-Villaverde, Koyama, Lin, and Sng, 2020). The Alps separate the Italian Peninsula from the rest of Europe, and the Pyrenees do the same for the Iberian Peninsula. Meanwhile, China is dominated by a single large northern plain between the Yangtze and the Yellow Rivers. Fernández-Villaverde et al. find that the presence of a core region of high land productivity in China – the North China plain – and the lack thereof in Europe was crucial for the emergence of political unification in China and fragmentation in Europe.

A related geographic factor that can explain Europe's persistent fragmentation in comparison to China is the location of the Eurasian steppe. This vast highway of grassland that links Eastern Europe and East Asia (see Figure 7.1) played a key role in state development. After steppe nomads domesticated horses in the first millennium BCE, they provided a perennial and unresolvable

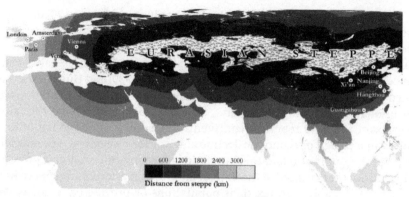

Figure 7.1 The steppe and state formation in China and Europe
Each shade represents 600 kilometers from the steppe. *Source*: Ko, Koyama, and Sng (2018).

threat to sedentary populations until the 18th century. While Genghis Khan and the Mongols may have been the most famous of these groups, they were only one in a long chain of predatory steppe nomads. The fragile ecology of the steppe meant that during periods of drought or cold weather, steppe nomads were more likely to invade neighboring populations (Bai and Kung, 2011). China's proximity to the steppe meant that a strong, northern-based, Chinese state had to arise if it were to protect its frontier. If such a state were capable of fending off the threat from the steppe, it would also be powerful enough to unify the rest of China (Ko, Koyama, and Sng, 2018).

On the other end of Eurasia, the Western European city most exposed to the steppe (Vienna) is as far from the steppe as the least exposed major city in China (Guangzhou). The "steppe threat" was therefore not nearly as potent in Western Europe. But this did not relieve Europe from invasion. On the contrary, settled people in post-Roman Europe could be invaded from multiple directions. And indeed they were: Huns, Avars, Magyars, Arabs, Moors, and Vikings invaded Europe for centuries from nearly every direction. Any prospective empire builder in Europe would thus face a multidimensional threat that would strain his resources. This is one reason why attempts to build a large centralized state in Europe failed after the fall of the Roman Empire.

Why did Europe's persistent political fragmentation matter? From the point of view of Smithian economic growth, introduced in Chapter 2, empires could be good news. The Roman Empire was able to create a fairly unified market economy that spanned the Mediterranean. It suppressed piracy, limited internal trade duties, and introduced a standardized monetary system (Temin, 2006). Similarly, the "Pax Islamica" and the "Pax Mongolica" allowed trade to thrive in the Middle East and Central Asia for centuries. Chinese dynasties also invested in transport infrastructure, as we saw in Chapter 2. From estimates for the mid-18th century, we know that levels of price integration in China were relatively high (Shiue and Keller, 2007; though it declined quite sharply in the late 18th century – see Bernhofen, Li, Eberhardt, and Morgan, 2020). In contrast, Europe's endemic fragmentation was accompanied by frequent warfare which often disrupted inter-regional trade.

But European fragmentation also had positive and unforeseeable consequences. Scholars dating back to Montesquieu (1748/1989) and Hume (1762) have argued that the most important consequences of Europe's fragmentation were institutional. As we saw in Chapter 3, Scheidel (2019) argued that the failure of European rulers to rebuild a continent-wide empire after the fall of Rome resulted in a period of economic decline and military weakness – the so-called "Dark Ages" – but it also laid the foundations for long-run economic growth.

The polities that succeeded the Roman Empire in Western Europe were weak. They lacked the ability to tax their populations or provide basic goods. As a consequence, political power became unbundled from economic and military power. Ideological power became the near-monopoly of the Catholic Church. The separation of sovereignty between rulers, the Church, and the nobility was an important precondition for the emergence of parliaments, independent cities, and other representative institutions that we discussed in Chapter 3. These dispersed pockets of power were unique to Europe in the medieval period. Ironically enough, it was the very weakness of European rulers that allowed these alternative sources of power to arise. Within states, it meant that rulers had to cede more to elites to stay in power (Blaydes and Chaney, 2013; Salter and Young, 2019). It also meant that there was more interstate competition, which gave impetus to economic, political, scientific, and technological breakthroughs (Hoffman, 2015; Mokyr, 2016; Scheidel, 2019; Kitamura and Lagerlöf, 2020). As we shall discuss below, these were important preconditions for future economic growth.

Why Was There No Medieval European Take-off?

During the 11th and 12th centuries, self-governing or independent cities emerged on the edges of what had been the Carolingian Empire – in northern Italy, the Low Countries and then later in the Rhineland and northern Germany. As we saw in Chapter 3, the absence of a single strong ruler enabled merchants to rise to political prominence. They implemented reforms that favored their own interests but also, by and large, were favorable to the overall expansion of trade. This made possible the European Commercial Revolution. The new cities were manufacturing centers and trade entrepôts. Trading networks based on the market economy emerged in the absence of a central authority. These cities were characterized by what McCloskey (2006) calls "bourgeois values."

Unlike in either the Byzantine Empire, the Islamic world, or China, Europe's political polycentricity allowed for multiple sources of power. In addition to merchants, the Catholic Church took on an unprecedented political role. This had important intellectual and cultural consequences. For instance, Fukuyama

(2011) notes the role the Church played in undermining the claims of clans and extended families. Focusing on the emergence of the individual, Siedentop (2014) sees Christianity as critical to the emergence of liberal societies. The research we touched on in Chapter 4 by Schulz, Bahramni-Rad, Beauchamp, and Henrich (2019), Henrich (2020), and Schulz (2020) provides empirical support for the specific claim that the Church undermined traditional kinship networks. They link the Church's prohibition on cousin marriage to the formation of medieval communes. It was precisely in these communes that the great medieval city-states were born. These were the political units that relieved Europe of its post-Roman economic doldrums. It is difficult to see how such independent, free cities could have emerged under the thumb of the type of strong ruler who ruled over much of the rest of Eurasia.

If the preconditions for sustained economic growth emerged in the medieval period, why didn't Europe take off then? Medieval Europe did experience several centuries of growth during the Commercial Revolution. Could these developments have led to sustained economic growth in the Middle Ages? What was holding the medieval European economy back?

Answering these questions with certainty is impossible. In history, we lack controlled experiments. For example, we do not know how the European economy would have developed had Europe not been hit by the Black Death (as discussed in Chapter 5). The Black Death may have had positive institutional implications in the long run, but its immediate impact on trade and the medieval economy as a whole was devastating. In any case, it is possible that the medieval economy was already on the verge of crisis prior to the Black Death. Many medieval historians have long thought that an economic crisis was all but inevitable even before the Black Death struck (Postan, 1973).

Economic growth did occur in the Middle Ages. But it was not sustained, and it was prone to reversals. To see why, we need to consider *how* medieval economic growth occurred. Trade and the expansion of markets were an important source of economic growth during the Commercial Revolution. Van Zanden and Prak (2006) argue that medieval city-states were able to successfully create political communities based on trust and cooperation. City-states were able to overcome free-rider and other agency problems and to elicit high contributions in money and time from their populations through a concept of active citizenship. They enforced property rights and supplied market-supporting public goods.

But was this enough? Medieval city-states such as Florence, Genoa, and Venice saw rapid economic growth in the 12th and 13th centuries. But even before the Black Death, there is evidence that the economic dynamism of these cities was on the wane. These city-states may have grown, but they did not develop. Their growth was subject to reversals. Stasavage (2014) finds that autonomous city-states grew more rapidly than non-autonomous cities in the initial years of independence but more slowly thereafter. Growth was not sustained. The primary reason was that merchant oligarchs tended to put in place barriers to entry in order to consolidate their own positions and the positions and fortunes of their heirs. In other words, they did not transition to a fully open-access social order.

In this respect, medieval city-states contained the seeds of their own ruin. Florence illustrates this. Although it remained a center for international trade and banking in the 15th century, its prowess as a manufacturing center peaked a century earlier. Florence manipulated and restricted market access to maintain its regional primacy within Tuscany at the cost of impeding regional economic integration (Epstein, 1991, 2000). It also imposed large and distortionary taxes on its peasantry. The financial services offered by Florentine bankers became increasingly monopolized in the hands of a few banking families, of whom the Medici were the most powerful. In the 15th century, Florence's competitive political institutions were subverted by the Medici (Belloc, Drago, Fochesato, and Galbiati, 2021). All of these were consequences of a rent-seeking ruling elite.

Another example comes from the city-state of Venice. Venice eventually built an empire on the basis of its commercial success. From the 10th and 11th centuries onwards, the prosperity associated with trade gave rise to a new Venetian merchant class. These merchants became powerful enough to influence and shape the political system. Trade promoted social mobility. Puga and Trefler (2014) show that there was increasing movement of families into and out of the Great Council (a ruling body) before 1297, suggesting a fluid and competitive political elite. However, more open access to politics also threatened the profits the elites earned as a result of their control over Venice's foreign trade. The reaction of existing elites led to a period known as the Serrata ("closure") in the early 14th century. During the Serrata, established merchants used their power in the Council to pass laws to restrict access to trade. First was a law in 1297 restricting new entrance into the Council. Then another law in 1323 restricted entrance into long-distance trade. As a result, Council seats became fully hereditary among the nobility. The nobility then used state power to monopolize international trade by collectivizing control of the galleys, which were previously privately owned. The rights to use these ships were auctioned off among the nobles.

These accounts suggest that prosperous Italian city-states became increasingly restrictive and exclusive after around 1300. Rent-seeking among commercial elites increased. Economic growth began to decline. Incidentally, the cultural flowering of Renaissance Italy occurred perhaps a century and a half after its economic peak.

The technological base of the medieval economy was also limited. There was some innovation in the late Middle Ages, notably in clock-making, spectacles, and later printing. Navigational techniques also improved, paving the way for the voyages of discovery that would begin in Portugal and Spain in the 15th century. But the rate of innovation remained too slow to overwhelm demographic and other retarding factors (Mokyr, 1990, chs. 3, 8). An important reason for this was that the costs of reproducing knowledge remained high prior to the invention of movable-type printing (Buringh and van Zanden, 2009).

In short, many of the preconditions for Europe's eventual economic rise emerged in the medieval period. The multiple centers of power that character-ized medieval European life set the stage for the continent's eventual economic rise. But this rise was by no means pre-ordained, and it took centuries to come to fruition. Nor was it certain by the end of the medieval period that Europe would eventually take this path. History is not deterministic. Had a few things gone differently, modern economic growth might not have begun in Europe. Indeed, many of the wealthiest parts of Europe at the end of the medieval period, such as northern Italy and Spain, did not experience modern economic growth until the 20th century.

But this does not mean that the history is impossible to understand or that some events are just as likely to happen in one place as another. As we will argue below, the political conditions characterizing Europe at the end of the medieval period did indeed matter for subsequent events. Even if these events were not pre-ordained, they are difficult to imagine without the medieval her-itage. But how and why did this heritage matter? What happened in the early modern period (roughly 1500–1750)? Understanding what happened in this period is probably even more important for understanding why northwestern Europe was the first part of the world to become rich. It is this period we turn to next.

Divergence within Europe Just before the Take-off

By the end of the medieval period, Europe was no longer obviously behind the rest of the world. The medieval European resurgence was led by the trading and manufacturing centers of northern Italy: Venice, Genoa, Florence, Milan, and many others. Yet, over the course of the 16th and 17th centuries, the economic center of Europe moved away from the Mediterranean. By 1800, the Italian city-states had long lost their independence and prosperity, and Italy was among the most economically backward areas in Western Europe. The reversal of for-tunes became clear during the 17th century, when the Italians were driven out of textile production by the English and Dutch. Historians have debated over whether or not this decline resulted in an absolute decline in living standards or merely a relative decline (Braudel, 1949/1973; Cipolla, 1952). The real wage and per capita GDP estimates compiled by Malanima (2003, 2005, 2007) suggest that this decline was absolute.

One dramatic event was the discovery of the Americas and the Cape Route around Africa. This shaped the economies of both Europe and the Middle East. The old trade routes between Asia and Europe lost much of their value, leading to a decline in the economic fortunes of cities in Central Asia and the Middle East as well as in Italy (Blaydes and Paik, 2021). In the 16th and 17th centuries, the Atlantic economy rose to prominence. This was true relative both to Europe and to the rest of the world. It was this shift that ultimately set the stage for the modern economy. What can explain this transformation in economic fortunes?

One factor often cited in explaining this mini-divergence within Europe was demography. Chapter 5 considered the role of late and voluntary marriage – the European Marriage Pattern (EMP) – in European development. While this demographic pattern may have deep roots in European history, it appears to have become prominent after the Black Death.

The labor scarcity that resulted from that catastrophe encouraged women to enter the workforce and helped produce active markets for agricultural labor. The high wages that followed should have resulted in a rapid population recovery. But the practice of late and voluntary marriage and small, nuclear families moderated this recovery. It dampened Malthusian pressures and enabled wages to remain higher than would otherwise have been the case. Europe's particular demography is clearly part of the reason why its real wages were higher than those recorded for Asian countries like China, India, and Japan as far back as the Middle Ages.

Demographic factors help explain why real wages tended to be higher in Northern Europe, where the EMP was strongest, than in Southern Europe. But it is also evident that demographic factors were not sufficient by themselves for sustained economic growth. Otherwise, the Industrial Revolution would have happened in northern Germany, which was economically stagnant. It is also difficult to reconcile the timing of the emergence of modern economic growth with purely demography-based explanations. The EMP preceded industrialization and sustained economic growth by at least four centuries.

But this does not mean that demography was unimportant for the eventual emergence of sustained economic growth. Indeed, it may be a key reason why industrialization did not immediately lead to a rise in incomes. We will return to this issue in Chapter 8.

Many explanations for Europe's economic rise focus on the opening of the Atlantic. And with good reason. This was one of the key economic and political events of the three centuries preceding the onset of sustained economic growth. It makes sense to start with the simple fact that an entirely new world opened up to Europe, and those with access to the Atlantic had a natural advantage in accessing it. But not everyone benefited equally. Nor was the opening of the Atlantic a uniformly good thing for European economies. One of the most easily visible effects of the discovery of the Americas was on the monetary base. Inflows of gold and silver from American mines enriched the Habsburg rulers of Spain and funded wars across Europe. This is not why the Atlantic economies pulled ahead, however. These inflows of precious metals ultimately led to higher prices and not higher levels of output. Inflation reached levels not known to Europeans for at least a millennium. This so-called "price revolution" led by Spain was, if anything, detrimental to the economic fortunes of the region.

The decline of Spain is an interesting case. It tells us much about what was important for the long-run economic development of Europe. Along with Portugal, Spain was the first European nation to benefit from the opening of the Atlantic. By the dawn of the 16th century, Spain had a worldwide empire, and Ferdinand and Isabella were bestowed the prestigious titles of the "Catholic King and Queen" by Pope Alexander VI. Through inheritance and marriage, the Spanish Habsburgs would add the wealthy Low Countries to their empire. Throughout most of the 16th century, Spain was probably the most power-ful nation in Europe, and among the wealthiest. Meanwhile, England was emerging from a bloody civil war (the Wars of the Roses) and was far from the European economic frontier.

Yet, it was in the 16th century that the seeds for reversal were sown. By the end of the century, England and Spain were no longer so far apart economically (even if it did take an English stroke of luck to keep the Spanish Armada out of its harbors). Within another century (by 1700 or so), Spain was clearly behind the economic leaders of Europe. England and the Dutch Republic, the latter recently liberated from Spanish rule, pulled far ahead. By the 18th century, Spain was at best a second-rate power in Europe. What happened?

Ironically enough, the decline of Spain was closely tied to the discovery of the Americas. The new trade routes opened up a new world to European manufacturing and trade. But not everyone was able to take advantage of these opportunities. How countries responded depended on their *institutions*. Acemoglu, Johnson, and Robinson (2005b) argue that where the profits from Atlantic trade were controlled by the crown, access to the Atlantic led to a strengthening of autocratic power. Rulers like the Spanish Habsburgs, espe-cially Charles I (r. 1516–56) and Philip II (r. 1556–98), used Atlantic profits to fund wars and consolidate power. The "royal fifth" – 20% of all precious metals and other commodities coming in from the Americas – went straight into royal coffers. These riches strengthened the Spanish crown relative to its parliaments.

The inflows of precious metals (largely silver) were massive. Between 1500 and 1600, precious metals imported from the Americans dwarfed Europe's stock of precious metals in 1492 almost ten-fold (Palma, forthcoming). The immediate effect of the gold and silver extracted from mines in the Americas was both to enrich the Spanish crown and to give a boost to the European economy, where specie was in short supply. In the medium and long run, however, the effect was inflation.

North (1981, 1990) attributed the decline of Spain to political institutions that encouraged the Habsburg monarchs to pursue economically inefficient policies such as granting monopoly rights to guilds, failing to tax the nobility, defaulting on debts, and confiscating property. These extractive political insti-tutions undermined the foundations of commerce: the "structure of property rights that evolved in response to the fiscal policies of the government simply discouraged individuals from undertaking many productive activities and instead encouraged socially less productive activities that were sheltered from the reach of the state" (North, 1981, pp. 151–2).

In Spain, the crown held a monopoly on colonial trade. The monopoly rents associated with colonial trading routes were enormous. For example, the cargo of the Manila galleons that took Asian goods from the Philippines to Mexico amounted to around 2% of the GDP of the entire Spanish Empire (Arteaga, Desierto, & Koyama, 2020). The costs associated with these monopolies was vast. Spanish trade was tightly restricted for the benefit of a relatively small number of elites. As Adam Smith (1776/1976) – a fierce critic of colonial empires and monopoly trading regimes – understood, this led to a severe misallocation of resources.

Recent research demonstrates that the Habsburg monarchs of Spain were hardly all-powerful. In particular, they were limited in their ability to raise taxes. But institutional explanations for the decline of Spain remain persuasive. Drelichman and Voth (2008) argue that the resource curse associated with large inflows of American silver afflicted the Spanish economy by increasing the returns to rent-seeking and undermining the institutions that limited the power of the monarch, nobility, and clerical establishment. Resources also undermined efforts to standardize or centralize a fragmented and inefficient fiscal system. This fiscal fragmentation was accompanied by institutional, legal, and economic fragmentation (Grafe, 2012).

Yet, institutional weaknesses in Spain are only part of the story of divergence. A compelling explanation must also account for why England and the Dutch Republic *pulled ahead* in the early modern period. The Dutch Republic became the world's dominant economy beginning in the late 16th century. The English economy was primed for industrialization by the 18th century. What changed in these economies? Why was the modern economy born there and not elsewhere?

Parliaments and the Rise of Limited, Representative Government

In Chapter 3, we discussed the role of institutions. One important set of institutions we discussed were *parliaments*. These assemblages of important people – nobility, clerics, and urban elite – constrained rulers and their worst whims. But parliaments were more powerful in some places than in others. As noted above, the Spanish *cortes* were relatively hapless when it came to preventing abuses by the Habsburg crown. This ended up not being the case in England and the Dutch Republic. There, parliaments grew in strength over time and ultimately were able to place significant constraints on central authorities. The period after 1600 saw the rise of representative political institutions first in the Dutch Republic and then in England. Meanwhile, in Southern Europe, monarchical power was consolidated. But why did this matter? Any why did limited governance arise in northwestern Europe but not in Southern Europe?

It is worth revisiting some of the relevant history. The most successful economy of the 17th century was the Dutch Republic. The cities of the Low Countries (modern-day Belgium and the Netherlands) became prosperous in the late Middle Ages. In the 15th century, the cities of the northern Netherlands prospered due to the wool trade and their control over Baltic trade routes. The wealth of their urban bourgeoisie is evident in the oil paintings of the era. As a result of a series of dynastic marriages and accidents, these rich cities came into the possession of the Habsburg Emperor Charles V (r. 1516–56) and they were passed down to his son Philip II, ruler of Spain (r. 1556–98). Tax revenues from these towns and cities helped to fund Habsburg expansion and warfare against the Ottomans.

The rich burghers of the Dutch cities resented paying taxes to a distant Habsburg monarch. At first, there was little they could do. The Habsburgs were powerful and had a legitimate claim on Dutch rule. But in the 1540s and 1550s, Protestant ideas began to spread throughout the Low Countries. This gave those looking to throw off the Spanish yoke an opportunity to do so. The heavy-handed Habsburg response – as many as 2,000 Protestants were burned alive as heretics – helped galvanize resistance from among the Dutch nobility and city leaders. The Reformation therefore helped kick-start a wider political rebellion. It resulted in the establishment of an independent Dutch Republic in the northern Netherlands and an eighty-year war with Spain.

This is precisely what we mean when we say that culture and institutions are often inseparable. It is difficult to imagine how the Dutch Revolt could have succeeded without the spread of Protestant (Calvinist) ideas. These motivated and legitimated the rebellion against Habsburg rule – binding the rebels together in a way that mere shared economic interests were unlikely to. Meanwhile, it is difficult to imagine how a religious movement like the Reformation could have succeeded without the political and institutional changes that secured Dutch independence from the fiercely Catholic Habsburgs.

The polity that arose as a result of the Dutch Revolt was a federal republic. William, Prince of Orange, was the most influential noble to lead the rebellion. He might have become the sovereign of an independent Netherlands, but he was assassinated. The position of sovereign was also offered to Queen Elizabeth of England. Only after these options were exhausted did the Dutch parliament (States General) assume full sovereignty. The result of the Dutch Revolt was therefore a religiously divided Republic in which merchants and commercial interests held political power (de Vries and van der Woude, 1997).

The Dutch Republic created institutions that benefited members of the economic elite. As a result, despite an ongoing war with Spain, it experienced rapid economic growth in the century following 1580. This growth was the result of structural changes to the Dutch economy. In other words, this was a period of Dutch *economic development*. Benefiting in part from the destruction of Antwerp by Spanish forces in 1576, Amsterdam became Europe's financial capital. Real wages grew faster than in the rest of Europe, despite a doubling of the Dutch population. Urbanization increased rapidly. Large-scale investments in canals and other inland transport helped ignite a trade boom. Dutch shipping dominated the Baltic. The United East India Company was founded in 1603 and soon helped win the Dutch an empire in Southeast Asia. Throughout the 17th and 18th centuries, Dutch real wages and per capita income were the highest in the world (see Figure 7.2).

Dutch economic success was a direct result of institutional change. The rise of limited, representative governance was one of the key driving forces behind the Dutch economic expansion. There was no centralized authority to extract resources, trample over property rights, or infringe on personal liberties. This is not to say the Dutch States General was perfect. It could – and did – favor some interests over others, and it wasn't exactly in favor of religious freedom once its preferred religion won the day. It was also not a modern democracy. Each of the seven provinces retained considerable power.

While the rise of limited government was an important precondition for long-run economic growth, it was not enough on its own. The Dutch ended up being relatively late to the industrialization game, although they remained among the world's leading economies. Why, then, do we place so much emphasis on limited, representative government? For one, it allowed the Dutch to

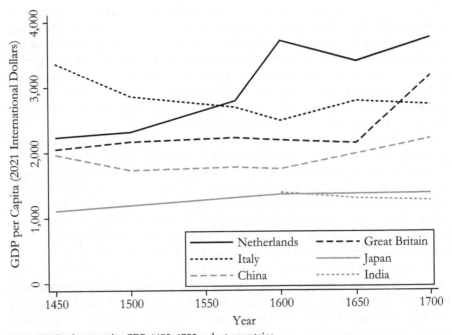

Figure 7.2 Real per capita GDP, 1450–1700, select countries

Data source: Broadberry, Guan, and Li (2018): 2021 international dollars converted from 1990 international dollars at rate of $2.03:1.

become the world's leading economy for over a century. But it was also a pre-condition for Britain's rise.

In the 18th century, the locus of economic growth moved from the Dutch Republic to England, or, as it became known after 1707, Great Britain. Even prior to the Industrial Revolution, Great Britain had emerged as one of the world's leading economies. Institutional change was critical in this development.

Changes in labor market institutions played a role in unleashing the domestic economy. While the medieval economy was dominated by craft and merchant guilds that regulated entry, by 1700 the power of English guilds had greatly diminished. Britain was, along with the Netherlands, quite different from much of continental Europe, where guild power remained entrenched. This hampered economic development by allowing insiders to block competition and innovation (Ogilvie, 2019).

The centuries leading up to modern economic growth saw the emergence of Parliament as the dominant legal and political force in England. Chapter 3 examined how Parliament emerged in 13th-century England following the Magna Carta. A particularly important development – one solidified in the reign of Edward I (r. 1272–1307) – was that Parliament came to represent urban interests and not just the nobility. As shown in Figure 3.8, the English Parliament met frequently during the Middle Ages. This was largely a reflection of how often the crown was at war. When the crown did not need additional revenues, it did not have to call Parliament. Strong medieval kings typically had the ability to dominate Parliament. When there were major challenges to royal authority, they usually came from the nobility, who still maintained their own private armies, rather than from Parliament.

This institutional arrangement began to change in the late 15th century. Following the Wars of the Roses (1455–85), the first Tudor, Henry VII (r. 1485–1509), came to the throne. Henry won the crown on the battlefield and had a very weak claim to the throne. Greif and Rubin (2021) argue that to bolster his legitimacy, he turned to Parliament, ruling by acts of Parliament much more than his predecessors. Henry also weakened the power of the noble families, particularly those whose blood might make them potential challengers (Penn, 2011). His son, Henry VIII (r. 1509–47), relied on Parliament even more frequently, especially after the Reformation further weakened one of the crown's key sources of legitimacy, the Catholic Church. Although the crown continued to employ religion as a source of legitimacy, the new Anglican Church was under its thumb. It therefore could not legitimate rule like the Catholic Church could. These factors were also present under Henry VIII's three Tudor successors, Edward VI (r. 1547–53), Mary I (r. 1553–8), and Elizabeth I (r. 1558–1603). They all came to the throne with low legitimacy. Mary and Elizabeth were the first two female monarchs in English history and had both been declared bastards. They therefore relied heavily on Parliament. As Parliament's power increased, so did its willingness and ability to limit the crown. This set the stage for the tumultuous events of the 17th century, in which

Parliament twice deposed a Stuart king whom they believed transgressed their rights.

As recent research confirms, it was in the 17th century that England's political institutions diverged from those of continental Europe (Henriques and Palma, 2020). The first key event of the 17th century was the English Civil Wars (1642–51). The Civil Wars pitted Parliamentarians against supporters of King Charles I (r. 1625–49). A vast body of scholarship considers the causes of these civil wars from a variety of perspectives. For our purposes, one can view the conflict as primarily over the proper institutional structure of English governance (Greif and Rubin, 2021). Did a king have the legitimate right to rule without Parliament (as Charles I had tried to do in the decade preceding the Civil Wars)? Or was following the law, as created by Acts of Parliament, essential to being a legitimate king? Under the Tudors, England had increasingly moved to the latter arrangement. This was not by design – both Henry VII and Henry VIII had autocratic aspirations. It occurred partly because of Henry VIII's need for Parliamentary support for his break with Rome and particularly because historical accident landed England with a minor and two women as his successors. Conflict between crown and Parliament came to a head after James I (r. 1603–25) and his successor Charles I sought to subordinate Parliament to the crown. This conflict was in large part over how powerful the monarchy should be. In the end, the Parliamentarians won and Charles I was executed.

The English Civil Wars were an important turning point. They brought about a change in the ruling coalition. Jha (2015) explores how emerging overseas economic opportunities helped the formation of a coalition in favor of constraining the crown. Many of the landed elite purchased shares in overseas trading companies, aligning their interests with the merchant class. Ownership of shares in overseas trade shifted the views of non-merchants, helping to consolidate support for reformers in Parliament. They therefore had an interest in fighting with Parliament against the king. This aligned the interests of the economic elite with a broad set of powerful people, which, in turn, gave them a central seat at the political bargaining table.

The Civil Wars sharply accelerated the ultimate pre-eminence of limited governance. Such institutional changes were important for the rise of the modern economy. However, even though the Parliamentarians won the day, this did not mean that limited governance immediately followed. The conflict between Parliament and the Stuart kings was not permanently resolved by the Civil Wars. It resulted in another conflict a generation later, between Charles I's son James II (r. 1685–8), a Catholic who aspired to create a more autocratic monarchy along French lines, and his opponents in Parliament. In 1688, a Parliamentary faction invited William of Orange and his wife, Mary (the daughter of the king), to overthrow James. James fled and William and Mary (r. 1689–1702) came to the throne with little bloodshed (at least in England; it was quite different in Scotland and Ireland). This capped off the so-called Glorious Revolution. In the process, William and Mary accepted a Bill of Rights whereby they relinquished numerous rights and agreed to limit the power of the crown. This was a major turning point in the history of limited governance.

The change in English government was part of a broader global and expensive war against France. The settlement following the Glorious Revolution helped fund this war. Because Parliament now had power over the English purse-strings, creditors were more willing to believe they would be paid back (North and Weingast, 1989). William of Orange brought with him Dutch advisors and knowledge of Dutch fiscal and financial practices (Hart, 1991). A critical event was the establishment of the Bank of England in 1694, which helped fund the war effort. Over time, it led to a substantial drop in borrowing costs (see Table 7.1). This enabled an enormous growth in state power that would become a theme of the 18th century and beyond.

By making England (after 1707, Britain) a constitutional monarchy, the Glorious Revolution laid the foundations of the party system and cabinet government (Stasavage, 2002, 2003; Pincus and Robinson, 2014; Cox, 2016). These developments did not all take place immediately after 1688. It took several decades for the implications of the Glorious Revolution to fully take shape. But they provided the political and institutional stability that was important for Britain's subsequent economic growth.

North and Weingast (1989) argued that the credibility of the English monarchy to repay its debts after 1688 translated into more secure property rights in general. While this claim has not survived subsequent scrutiny, in other respects there was an improvement in institutional quality after 1688. Rather than securing property rights, these changes made it easier to reorder property rights in order to exploit new investment opportunities.

In other words, what mattered was less the "security" of property rights in the abstract than the ability to rearrange residual claimancy as new economic opportunities emerged. Feudal property rights were secure but they were

Table 7.1 British borrowing and interest rates, 1693–1739

Date	Amount (£)	Interest (%)
Jan. 1693	723,394	14.0
Mar. 1694	1,000,000	14.0
Mar. 1694	1,200,000	8.0
Apr. 1697	1,400,000	6.3
July 1698	2,000,000	8.0
Mar. 1707	1,155,000	6.25
July 1721	500,000	5.0
Mar. 1728	1,750,000	4.0
May 1731	800,000	3.0
June 1739	300,000	3.0

Data source: North and Weingast (1989, Table 4).

designed to support feudal society and not to maximize productivity. Land rights in 17th-century England were complex and constrained. The ownership of land came with feudal entails which meant that potential heirs could veto anything that could be claimed to detract from the future capital value of the land (such as cutting down a forest or draining a lake).

Prior to the Glorious Revolution, estate bills often failed due to political conflict. However, as a result of changes brought on by the Glorious Revolution, Parliament became a forum where land could be reallocated towards more productive uses (Bogart and Richardson, 2009, 2011). As a consequence, investment in road and river transport dramatically improved, with important consequences for subsequent economic growth (Bogart and Richardson, 2011). Parliamentary regulation helped keep internal trade relatively unimpeded, especially in comparison to the Holy Roman Empire or France (Bogart, 2012). Parliament played a crucial role in regulating the tolls that maintained England's road and canal network. Tolls were kept low, in part by Parliamentary regulation and in part by market competition. Toll roads were funded by users and in competition with river and canal routes.

This was not a move towards greater democracy. Only a small proportion of adult males could vote. And after 1715, elections became less frequent (held only every seven years). In many ways, the power of the rich was entrenched and historians have often viewed the 18th-century British state as designed to favor the propertied classes. Certainly it ruthlessly enforced Enclosure Acts and penal laws against the poor (Hay, Linebaugh, Rule, Thompson, and Winslow, 1975). For the most part, early 18th-century Parliaments were characterized by unabashed rent-seeking. Parliament passed many acts that benefited specific interests – most notably the Calico Act of 1721, which banned the importation of most cotton textiles – at the expense of the larger public. None of this shocked contemporaries. Members of Parliament were expected to look out for their own material interests and to pursue what to modern eyes looks like venality (Root, 1991). This changed over the course of the 18th century. Mokyr and Nye (2007, p. 58) note that "[p]urely redistributional actions ... began losing their appeal. Many special interest groups' legislated privileges, monopolies, exclusions, limitations on labor mobility, occupational choice, and technological innovation found themselves on the defensive as the 18th century wore on."

In other words, if we are to discern the distinctive features of the British political system on the eve of the Industrial Revolution, it is less useful to focus on features such as its corruption or lack of democratic representation. These were features that it shared with almost all pre-modern states. More insight is gained from considering which factors were critical in allowing it to attain a high degree of political stability and prosperity.

In this respect, the British system was successful in constraining the independent power of the monarchy, while balancing the interests of landowning elites with those of mercantile and financial elites. It was able to mobilize tremendous resources for warfare without crushing the domestic economy. It was not a democracy, as it limited political representation to those with property. But it did provide scope for "voice" through regular elections. It also provided greater freedom for religious minorities than did its competitors in Europe (with the exception of the Dutch Republic) while also prohibiting Catholics and religious dissenters from positions of political power (Johnson and Koyama, 2019, pp. 179–83).

Chapter Summary

By around 1700, northwestern Europe had many of the necessary preconditions for sustained economic growth. Per capita incomes and real wages were high by pre-industrial standards. Markets were relatively well developed and extensive. The institutional framework was conducive to the expansion of internal trade. State institutions were strong enough to provide a measure of law and internal peace. But these factors alone were unlikely to have been enough for modern economic growth.

This is demonstrated by the example of the Dutch Republic. Though the Dutch Republic has been hailed as "the first modern economy" (de Vries and van der Woude, 1997), the Dutch pattern of commercial, Smithian, trade-driven growth more closely resembled earlier episodes of temporary growth than it did the sustained economic growth that characterized Western Europe and North America after 1800. As Goldstone (2002, p. 340) writes: "[W]hile Golden Age Holland did indeed experience an 'efflorescence' of innovation, intensification and productivity growth in agriculture, and stable per capita incomes despite substantial population growth, such a pattern is neither uniquely Dutch nor 'modern' by global standards."

In the 18th century, the Dutch Republic remained rich but its economy did not experience further rapid growth (de Vries and van der Woude, 1997). There were many factors responsible for this stagnation. Inequality rose and merchant elites based in Amsterdam were able to entrench their political power (van Bavel, 2016). Institutions like the Dutch East India Company (VOC) benefited a relative small number of shareholders. The Dutch Republic thus followed a similar pattern to Italian city-states like Florence and Venice that grew rich on the back of trade before eventually stagnating. Another factor was the high taxes and high levels of government debt incurred fighting numerous wars for survival against the French. Moreover, the mercantilist policies of the British and the comparative failure of the Dutch to invest further in fiscal capacity also contributed to their relative decline (O'Brien, 2000). Overall, the Dutch were not able to achieve a dramatic and *sustained* increase in living standards. This would not happen until the Great Enrichment that began after 1800, and it was driven by developments in Britain.

The Dutch Republic was at the forefront of the Scientific Revolution. Christiaan Huygens made important contributions to astronomy and mathematics.

Antonie van Leeuwenhoek pioneered the field of microbiology. There were also important Dutch developments in engineering, especially hydraulic engineering. Yet, the Dutch did not experience the combination of growth of industry and structural change that characterized Britain's Industrial Revolution.

Britain did experience this combination in the 18th and 19th centuries. The result was the first modern economy – one in which economic growth was *sustained* without reversal. Why did this happen first in Britain? We began this explanation in this chapter, noting that Britain had some of the important institutional preconditions. Most importantly, it had a (relatively) limited and representative government. But this was clearly not enough. If it were, the Dutch would have had the first modern economy. What else was needed for Britain to prosper? We turn to this question in the next chapter.

8

Britain's Industrial Revolution

We are now in a position to address the question "How did the world become rich?" The answer to this question begins with Britain's Industrial Revolution. Britain's industrialization set in motion a series of events that ultimately resulted in modern, sustained economic growth. Since the first few decades of the 19th century, the world has become richer and billions have been lifted out of poverty. This was due to sustained economic growth. This is why we care so deeply about it.

Figure 8.1 reports the growth of total GDP, population, and GDP per capita in England from 1270 to 1700 and then for Britain from 1700 to 1870. Between 1700 and 1870, the size of the total economy increased by a factor of 10. Population also grew roughly four-fold. Per capita GDP more than doubled. Such an economic transformation defied the logic of the Malthusian economy. By the middle of the 19th century, the British economy began to exhibit modern, sustained economic growth. Per capita GDP grew in a continuous fashion even as the population also continued to expand. Perhaps most importantly, despite the ups and downs of wars and business cycles, there were no serious growth reversals.

The first seven chapters have laid out various theories that give insight into why modern, sustained economic growth was likely to happen in some places but not others. In this chapter we go further. Answering the question "How did the world become rich?" means establishing the reasons for both the *location* of modern economic growth and its *timing*.

We begin this pursuit by exploring the causes of the Industrial Revolution. It began in Britain some time in the second half of the 18th century. This part is uncontroversial. What is more controversial is *why* it began when and where it did. Having outlined some of the institutional prerequisites for growth in Chapter 7, in this chapter we consider the development of the British economy more generally in the 18th and 19th centuries. We also consider what made the Industrial Revolution a "revolution." It was not the rate of economic growth, which remained modest. It was that growth was sustained thereafter.

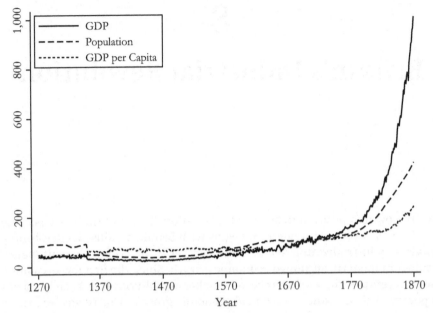

Figure 8.1 GDP, GDP per capita, and population in England/Britain, 1270–1870 (1700 = 100)

Data source: Broadberry, Campbell, Klein, Overton, and van Leeuwen (2015).

Above all else, the major revolutionary change during the Industrial Revolution was an increase in the *rate of innovation*. The acceleration in innovation ensured that economic growth continued and did not peter out. New and important technologies emerged at a rapid pace in late 18th- and early 19th-century Britain. Why? Any answer must account for how British society became particularly innovative.

We first consider the British economy on the eve of the Industrial Revolution, paying particular attention to several important preconditions. These include the rise of a market-oriented society and its implications for labor supply and consumption patterns, the size of the domestic economy, commercial agriculture, culture and social norms, and the increasing significance of the Atlantic economy. Many of these features were also shared by the Dutch Republic.

But the Industrial Revolution did not begin in the Dutch Republic. We therefore turn our attention to factors that may have distinguished Britain from its rivals. These include its high level of state capacity and its dominant role in the transatlantic slave trade. While these factors played a role in Britain's economic success, however, neither provides a full accounting of why this success led to industrialization. To answer the question "Why Britain?" we therefore focus on two important arguments. First, we consider Allen's (2009*a*) argument that innovation was a response to high wages and cheap capital and energy. Second, we consider Mokyr's (2009, 2016) argument that cultural and intellectual developments within British and European society, along with increased human capital and skills, were responsible for Britain's industrialization. But first we provide some background on Britain's economy on the eve of industrialization.

A Consumer Revolution

To identify the relevant preconditions for industrialization, we must know something about British society and its economy in the century or so prior to industrialization. There was peace (in England, though not yet Scotland) following the Civil Wars (1642–51). The domestic economy can be described as a *market economy*. That is, although problems with silver coinage meant that monetarization was far from universal, economic activities were oriented around market exchange. All large-scale societies rely on markets to some extent. Even in Soviet Russia there was market exchange, both legal and on the black market. Nevertheless, many societies that allow markets to play an important role in the allocation of final goods rely on non-market systems for allocating factors of production (land, capital, and labor).

By 1700, Britain had a fully developed market economy. The expansion and improved integration of domestic markets can account for much of the relative prosperity the country enjoyed in the 18th century. As we reviewed in Chapter 2, the integration of what was a comparatively large domestic market rested on a domestic road and canal network that was greatly improved in the 18th century (Bogart, 2014). Allen (2009a, p. 106) observes that "cities grew, London's wages were high, agriculture improved, and manufacturing spread across the countryside." Another characteristic of a market society emerged in this period: the rise of the consumer. Historians have called this period the Consumer Revolution. Put simply, households became more oriented towards the market (McKendrick, Brewer, and Plumb, 1982; Brewer and Porter, 1993).

The Consumer Revolution was a move away from within-household production and consumption to market-oriented production and consumption. It was a sea change in how people consumed goods and services. Late medieval households, while not completely self-sufficient, produced many products within the household. They might, for instance, make their own clothes from yarn or cloth purchased from a whole-seller, or they might brew their own beer. This changed in the 17th and 18th centuries. Retail shops emerged, which enabled customers to purchase goods immediately. It became possible to purchase ready-made textiles as opposed to buying them wholesale and taking them to a dressmaker or making one's clothes at home (Mui and Mui, 1989).

British consumption habits changed as a result. Weatherill (1988) found that the number of households owning durable goods in the inventories of the London's Orphans' Court increased significantly between 1675 and 1725. The frequency of goods such as saucepans, cutlery, clocks, china, pewter, and earthenware increased dramatically. Utensils for hot drinks were almost completely absent from 17th-century inventories but they were found in 80% of inventories by 1725. Lemire notes that even servants could save up the "six or seven shillings needed to purchase sufficient cotton cloth to make a gown, or the eight shillings for a ready-made gown." This created "a potentially vast market among working-women, for whom these prices meant perhaps one week's wages or less" (Lemire, 1991, p. 97).

Scholars have linked this Consumer Revolution to the growing prosperity of this period. De Vries (1993, 2008) in particular argues that new consumption opportunities created by the expansion and development of markets gave rise to an "industrious revolution." By this, he means that as households became more active participants in the market economy, they had to work harder to earn the wages to buy all of these new and affordable goods. New consumption opportunities meant that fewer goods were produced within the household economy. Households began to purchase goods that had no domestic substitute. Instead of consuming their surplus income as leisure, they spent it on an increasingly wide range of consumption goods (Koyama, 2012). The "industrious revolution" can thus be viewed as the other side of the Consumer Revolution.

According to de Vries, this "industrious revolution" originated in the Netherlands in the 17th century and spread to England and other parts of the Atlantic economy over the course of the late 17th and early 18th centuries. But why was it an important predecessor to the Industrial Revolution? Improvements in GDP per capita can either come from increased labor inputs, greater capital investment, or improvements in efficiency (often equated with innovation). Part of the growth in GDP per capita that took place during the 17th and early 18th centuries was due to an increase in labor inputs, both working hours and the number of days worked. The reason, according to de Vries, was a new "industriousness." Workers worked harder because they wanted additional income to engage in new consumption opportunities.

Increased industriousness helps resolve another puzzle involving wages and industrialization. The 19th century did not witness a dramatic rise in English real wages. Contrast this with the period following the Black Death, which saw real wages rise precipitously (see Chapter 5). Yet, following the Black Death, GDP per capita did not rise as much as real wages. And the post-Black Death rise in wages was not sustained in the long run. There were two key differences between the two periods. First, labor markets were thin in the late Middle Ages. Even though measured wages were high, this did not mean that workers could find reliable work at those wages. Second, even when wage laborers did find work, they often "consumed" their higher incomes in the form of increased leisure. So, even though daily wages were higher for some time following the Black Death, yearly incomes rose much less rapidly (Humphries and Weisdorf, 2019).

This changed between 1500 and 1700. In the Netherlands, de Vries and van der Woude (1997) find that the average number of working days increased for day laborers by 25% between 1550 and 1650. In England, Voth (2001) finds evidence of a particularly dramatic increase in the working day after 1750. While these estimates are sensitive to assumptions and to the particular data employed, there is little doubt that there was an increase in the total labor inputs in this period (Allen and Weisdorf, 2011). This increased willingness to work longer hours for the wages required to purchase new consumer goods can be seen as a precondition for the rise of the factory system (Clark, 1994). As we will discuss below, factories required large investments in fixed capital. These were only worthwhile if there was a willing workforce that could man the factories, and if necessary work long and exhausting hours.

Capitalist Agriculture

In the century preceding the Industrial Revolution, English agriculture was highly commercialized relative to the rest of Europe. Production was geared towards the market. The majority of workers were wage laborers. And farms were large compared to continental Europe, allowing them to exploit economies of scale. By the mid-18th century, England was a major exporter of food. Many historians have viewed this distinctive "capitalist" agriculture as an important precondition for the Industrial Revolution.

It is evident that labor productivity in English agriculture was comparatively high prior to the Industrial Revolution. Output per worker in England was similar to that in Italy and France in 1500. By 1750, it was higher in England and in the Low Countries than elsewhere in Europe. What was responsible for this increase in productivity?

In medieval England, the dominant form of farming was small-scale agriculture, organized around open fields and commons. Peasants farmed small, scattered plots located across the manor. These open fields enabled farmers to share risk. An individual farmer who owned several small plots of land scattered around the village was insured against idiosyncratic risk – say a hailstorm, a flood, or crop blight (McCloskey, 1976). This open-field system limited the harm that could arise from local shocks. There were downsides to this system, however. It was costly and time-consuming to move between different plots of land. Small, disjoint, and irregular plots often made it unprofitable to introduce new crop types or equipment.

We saw in Chapter 5 that the Black Death shock depopulated the countryside across Western Europe. Changing factor prices and changing patterns of demand led to a shift in land use. Land, particularly in the north and west of the country, was given over to pastoral agriculture. As a result, landowners sought to consolidate many patches of land. They did this through the process of enclosure. Many medieval enclosures occurred through private negotiation: farmers who wished to enclose the land had to buy out those who did not. It was also possible to petition Parliament for an Enclosure Act. These acts would pass if somewhere between three-quarters to four-fifths of landowners (by value) supported it. The holdouts would receive compensation. By 1500, 45% of farmland in England was enclosed (Allen, 1994, p. 99).

The trend towards larger farms, what historians like Brenner (1976) term "capitalist agriculture," accelerated after 1500. While economic historians used to think in terms of a distinct Agricultural Revolution directly preceding the Industrial Revolution, more recent evidence from labor productivity data suggests a general increase taking place over several centuries. Farms became larger and more capital-intensive. The pace of enclosures increased in the 18th century, driven by Parliamentary legislation. These enclosures had long been the subject of intense controversy. Their supporters among contemporaries and later historians saw them as contributing greatly to increased yields. They also made possible the eventual mechanization of agriculture in the 19th century with machines such as threshers. Their critics, including Karl Marx, saw them as acts of class warfare. Poor smallholders were forced off their land by rapacious, richer farmers, with scant compensation. Looking at the South Midlands, moreover, Allen (1992) finds little evidence that the late 18th-century enclosures actually improved yields.

There is evidence, however, that they led to more land being reclaimed and in the growth of larger farms and more capital-intensive agriculture. The gains from these changes, Allen contends, were largely captured by rich landlords. More recently, Heldring, Robinson, and Vollmer (2021) have studied the impact of enclosures across the whole of England. Their estimates suggest that enclosures led to an improvement in productivity. They also find that infrastructure improvements were associated with enclosures.

This rise in agricultural productivity between 1500 and 1700 in northwestern Europe was important. It helped to banish the specter of famine. It also helped sustain a dramatic rise in the proportion of the population living in cities. After all, urban development is only possible when there is a large enough agricultural surplus to feed all those city-dwellers. Improved yields and commercial agriculture may have laid the foundations of Britain's relative prosperity from 1600 onwards. But they were certainly not sufficient for sustained economic growth after 1800. When Britain did industrialize, the increase in agricultural production was not sufficient to keep up with population growth, and the agrarian economy did not offer a large market for manufactured goods. Indeed, Britain became a net food importer during the Industrial Revolution.

Do Political Institutions Explain Britain's Industrialization?

Now that we have a better understanding of some of the key features of the British economy on the eve of industrialization, we can circle back to the discussion in Chapter 7 regarding the preconditions for growth. We ended that chapter noting that the political environment in Britain and the Dutch

Republic was more conducive to economic growth than the rest of Europe (and the rest of the world). Both countries had some degree of limited, representative governance. In the British Isles, political institutions provided a measure of stability after 1688. This had both political and economic consequences. In the political realm, it allowed government borrowing to increase dramatically. It also resulted in greater fiscal and military power. Political stability enabled Smithian growth. But this is not what made Britain unique.

Political institutions alone cannot explain why Britain industrialized first. Traditionally, historians have argued that what made the Industrial Revolution a "revolution" was the wave of innovations that consumed Britain beginning in the latter half of the 18th century. Although British political stability and protection of property rights were important, they cannot fully account for this development. Britain did have intellectual property rights. A patent system existed and could be used to protect innovation. Yet, while it was ruthlessly employed by some of the Industrial Revolution's most famous innovators (like James Watt), patents were neither necessary nor sufficient to account for the wave of innovations that Britain experienced in this period. The innovator responsible for coke pig iron, Abraham Darby, for example, did not take out a patent (Mokyr, 2009). Many inventions required too much knowledge of how they worked to be copied. Other innovators kept their inventions secret or selectively revealed them to the public. None of these strategies required intellectual property rights.

Where does this leave us? There are many possibilities to consider. First, just because institutions do not fully explain why Britain industrialized, they *can* explain why other parts of the world did not. By the mid-18th century, British citizens could feel relatively secure that their property, innovations, and industrial output would not be seized by the prying hands of the government or anyone else with coercive power. Even though British political institutions were far from perfect and certainly corrupt to modern eyes, there was enough constraint on executive power that the majority of the population was reasonably well protected from infringements on property rights. This was not the case in other parts of the world, especially those with autocratic governance. The Ottoman and Qing Empires, for example, regularly infringed on the rights of their people, especially the economic elite (Balla and Johnson, 2009; Kuran, 2011; Ma and Rubin, 2019). Even within Europe, the Spanish crown was more than willing to transgress property rights, especially those of its merchants. For instance, the 16th-century kings Charles V and Philip II regularly reneged on their debts and confiscated treasure coming in from the Atlantic trade (Drelichman, 2005; Drelichman and Voth, 2011). They gave foreign merchants privileges (for a price) over domestic merchants. They trampled over the rights of religious minorities. None of this encouraged domestic production on the type of scale that would come to typify Britain.

Mercantilism and Empire

Economic policy throughout the century or so leading up to industrialization was unabashedly mercantilist. Mercantilism is the label used to describe economic policies that favored exports rather than imports. Mercantilist policies often favored domestic market integration. When it came to international trade, they supported the use of tariffs, subsidies, and monopolies for special interests to obtain a favorable balance of trade. Mercantilist economic policies were therefore embroiled with the dynastic and violent conflicts that characterized European international relations for much of the 17th and 18th centuries.

The Atlantic economy that emerged in the 18th century was the product of British success in a series of wars with France and Spain. Its origins lay in the mid-17th century, including the capture of Jamaica in 1655. After this, the Atlantic economy began to boom. It centered on the rich agricultural economy of the Caribbean. In the 18th century, the British state defeated its main rivals at sea and secured the lion's share of trade routes between the Americas, Europe, and West Africa.

The rise of the Atlantic economy changed Britain's economic landscape. The new westward orientation of international trade that came with it altered the structure and geography of the British economy. Ports like London, Bristol, and Liverpool expanded operations as Britain's growing Atlantic empire offered new opportunities. With the exception of London (which exploded, becoming the largest city in the world by 1800), the economic geography of Britain shifted to the Northwest (see Figure 8.2). Table 8.1 shows the largest English cities (excluding London) between 1520 and 1801. In 1520, Norwich was the largest city outside London. This was due to its prominence in the wool trade and proximity to the Low Countries. The only other cities with populations larger than 10,000 were York, the historical capital of the north, and Bristol, a major port. By 1801, this urban hierarchy had been transformed. The industrial center Manchester, which ranked as only the 82nd largest town in England in the 17th century with a population of around 2,000, numbered 94,876 inhabitants by 1801. By 1841, it had a population of 311,269. The only city that grew faster was Liverpool, which rose from being the 233rd most populated British city to the third most populous by 1801.

The shift of the British economy and population towards the Northwest reflects two processes. First, the rise of Atlantic trade favored ports, particularly those on the west coast. This is why cities like Liverpool grew so rapidly. Second, as manufacturing began to expand in the 18th century, it was centered in Yorkshire, Lancashire, or areas abundant with coal such as Newcastle.

Areas like the West Midlands came to specialize in metallurgy. Liverpool became the center of the watch trade (Kelly and Ó Gráda, 2016). Other centers of manufacturing arose such as Sheffield (associated with the steel industry) and Birmingham (associated with the gun trade, clocks, locks, and toys) (Kelly, Mokyr, and Ó Gráda, 2020). These manufacturing centers required many *highly*

Figure 8.2 England and its largest cities, 1520–1801

Table 8.1 Most populous English cities excluding London (with populations of at least 10,000)

1520	1600	1700	1801
Norwich	Norwich	Norwich	Manchester
Bristol	York	Bristol	Liverpool
York	Bristol	Newcastle	Birmingham
	Newcastle	Exeter	Bristol
		York	Leeds
		Yarmouth	Sheffield
			Norwich
			Portsmouth
			Bath

Data source: Clark (2001).

skilled workers to produce their goods. As we will see shortly, the agglomeration of these highly skilled workers in urban centers may have been one of the factors that set Britain apart.

The shift to the Atlantic also helped fuel the Consumer Revolution. New, exotic, addictive products were introduced to Europe by the Atlantic trade, particularly tea, tobacco, and sugar. These goods were initially luxuries, but they soon became accessible to the population at large. As Berg (2004, p. 365) describes the process: "The history of these colonial groceries is one of the transformation of exotic luxuries into necessities." In the 17th century, tea was a luxury consumed by the rich. By 1800, it had become a staple of working-class diets. Tea was consumed with sugar, which the Atlantic economy made cheaply and widely available. In fact, by the end of the 18th century, sugar was the single most important import into the British economy (de Vries, 2003, pp. 151–8).

Many of these goods were produced by slave labor. Harvesting tropical goods, especially sugar, is a dangerous and laborious task. Indentured servants tended to avoid the Caribbean, even though it offered a shorter term of servitude. The high profits made from slave labor reflected both the exploitation of the labor force and the high demand for the goods slaves produced. The Atlantic-facing British cities associated with the slave trade became important in their own right. But how crucial was slavery for Britain's industrialization? This is a heated debate. In the next section, we will discuss this debate and the extent to which the sugar–slavery nexus was a crucial ingredient for British industrialization.

Does the Transatlantic Slave Trade Explain Britain's Industrialization?

Numerous scholars have linked European colonization with the British Industrial Revolution. Two of the most powerful arguments come from Williams (1944) and Inikori (2002).

Williams (1944) first popularized the link between the slave trade and commercial and financial development in 18th-century Britain in his classic *Capitalism and Slavery*. He argued that the profits of the slave trade helped fuel the Industrial Revolution. He drew attention to the trade nexus that linked British manufactured exports with the slave trade in West Africa and the sugar, tobacco, and cotton plantations in the Americas. As Solow (1987, p. 732) describes the period before the Industrial Revolution:

> Total trade increased greatly, and the Atlantic was crisscrossed by British ships carrying manufactured goods to Africa, the West Indies, Brazil, Portugal, and British North America.
>
> The Atlantic islands were exporting wine, Africa slaves, Brazil gold, and the West Indies sugar and molasses. Some of the British North American colonies were sending rice and tobacco to Britain; others were sending fish, lumber,

horses, and flour to the West Indies and were buying British manufactures with the proceeds. Every one of these flows depended on the product of slave labor.

Slavery was at the center of this trade. Conditions on sugar plantations were exceptionally harsh. As a consequence, it proved difficult to attract free workers to settle. Initially settled by white laborers, often as indentured servants, by the 18th century the West Indies had become slave economies. Of course, slaves have no say in working conditions. Slavery enabled plantation owners to extract the entire surplus generated by forced labor in a hot and harsh climate (Wright, 2020). Given the centrality of sugar (and to a lesser extent tobacco), the 18th-century Atlantic economy was inseparable from the enslavement and exploitation of Africans.

These facts were often neglected in traditional accounts of the British economy in the 18th century. Williams's argument about the profits from the slave trade fueling industrialization established an important correlation. But was it causal?

Scholars following Williams have not established a link from the investors and landowners who benefited from exploiting slave labor in the Caribbean to the innovative developments taking place in the north of England. There are two reasons for this. First, the entrepreneurs, factory owners, and inventors who were key to the Industrial Revolution funded their firms from profits and their own savings and were not well integrated with London-based capital markets. While slavery was crucial to certain industries and made many British families rich, it was not directly linked with the more innovative manufacturing sector. Indeed, sugar was less connected to the overall economy than were coal, iron, and textiles (Eltis and Engerman, 2000, p. 140). Second, economic historians have pointed out that super-normal profits were not made in the long run due to competition, and the sugar industry was small relative to the British economy as a whole (Eltis and Engerman, 2000). The direct contribution of slavery to the British economy was small as a matter of simple accounting.

Nevertheless, perhaps the slave trade played an outsized role because of its strategic importance in the British economy? Scholars including Solow (1987) have suggested numerous other connections between slavery and the wider British economy. The slave trade ensured an elastic supply of sugar and tea, goods that helped fuel an "industrious revolution." Derenoncourt (2019) finds that cities linked with the transatlantic slave trade grew faster than other cities between 1600 and 1850. More generally, slavery raised the return on investment across the empire. This may have enabled faster structural change and industrial growth. Inikori (2002) focuses on the role played by sugar and slavery in the rise of overseas trade in the late 17th and early 18th centuries. It was this expansion in overseas trade, he claims, that drove initial increases in productivity. Technological progress built on this initial increase in productivity. To assess these arguments, however, one has to go beyond simply establishing plausible empirical linkages. What is required is a method of assessing the quantitative economic significance of these linkages.

The theoretical frameworks that Inikori (2002) and Darity (1992) propose stress the existence of linkages between overseas trade and domestic manufacturing. Slavery, by being so vital to British overseas trade, was at the heart of these linkages. However, the evidence for such important connections has not yet been provided. Hence, modern assessments do not greatly depart from Solow's (1987, p. 733) view that "[t]o argue that slavery was important for British economic growth is not to claim that slavery caused the Industrial Revolution." Eltis and Engerman (2000, p. 138) make the simple point that no industry was indispensable to the Industrial Revolution. Atlantic slavery was nonetheless a background condition tied to Britain's rise to both economic and military prominence in the 18th century.

Was It Cotton?

Williams and Inikori focused on the role played by slavery in the Caribbean economy of the 18th century. More recently, Beckert (2014) focused on cotton's role in creating the modern economic system in the 19th century. This argument has risen to prominence as part of the new "History of Capitalism."

Hobsbawm (1968) declared that, for all intents and purposes, cotton *was* the Industrial Revolution. Beckert's argument builds on this claim. Certainly cotton textile production was one of the most dynamic sectors of the industrializing economy. The outward supply shift in cotton textiles induced an 85% decrease in the price of cotton cloth between 1780 and 1850 (Mokyr, 1990). Once a luxury only for the rich, cheaper cotton goods were a tremendous boon for consumers of all classes. Almost every Brit could now afford lightweight, easily washable garments for the first time.

But how did Britain build a world-leading cotton textiles industry? Beckert's answer lies in the policies of aggressive colonialism overseas and state intervention, regulation, and coercion against the labor force at home. Thus, for him: "Slavery, colonialism, and forced labor, among other forms of violence, were not aberrations in the history of capitalism, but were at its very core" (Beckert 2014, p. 441).

One problem with this argument is that it reduces the Industrial Revolution to cotton textiles. Though cotton textiles were among the most dynamic industries in Britain during the Industrial Revolution, economic historians like Mokyr (2009, p. 296) argue that one cannot reduce the Industrial Revolution to one industry: "If there had been no cotton, there still would have been an Industrial Revolution, even if its exact shape would have differed."

So what was the link between exports and economic growth? McCloskey (2010, p. 222) observes that "[p]eople innocent of economics ... believe that trade just *is* growth." But there is no reason to privilege trade with a foreigner above trade with one's fellow citizen. Historians like Beckert focus on export industries, as these are commonly seen as key drivers of economic growth. But exports are the price we pay for imports. Harley (2004, p. 192) notes that "a person or nation fully employed ... yearns to acquire goods, not to get rid of them. Exports are an unfortunate sacrifice that people or nations must make to acquire imports for consumption."

Harley further notes that the share and prominence of international trade in national income accounts is a poor indication of its *economic* significance. To assess the economic significance of international trade, he presents counterfactual estimates of the importance of trade to the British economy. He finds that:

> Self-sufficiency in 1860 ... would have cost Britain only (50 per cent) * (0.125) or about 6 per cent of national income. Six per cent of national income – or even, if, improbably, the terms of trade effect were twice as great, 12 per cent – looks small beside bold metaphors of Britain's "dependence" on foreign trade. (Harley, 2004, p. 194)

These calculations suggest that the importance of trade to the British Industrial Revolution was sizable but not so significant to warrant being described as critical or essential.

Was It Market Size?

While certain types of institutions may have prevented other parts of the world from experiencing sustained growth, they do not fully explain why Britain *did* experience such growth. The same applies to other preconditions such as access to international markets and a large domestic market relatively free from internal taxation. Britain had both. This was in no small part due to the evolution of British political institutions, which (as we discussed in the previous chapter) increasingly favored the interests of the economic elite. We noted previously how the rise in the Atlantic trade contributed to Britain's rise as an economic power. Equally significant were the large domestic markets in which British producers could offload their goods. Important improvements in transport networks in the 18th century (see Chapter 2) lowered the cost of domestic shipping. Meanwhile, the British state was committed to free internal trade. This was no doubt due, in part, to the pre-eminence of economic elites in Parliament. This contrasted with fractured states like the Holy Roman Empire and France. In those states, internal tariffs stifled domestic trade. Along the River Rhine, merchants faced a new tariff in each of the many territories they would pass on a routine trip between cities (Johnson and Koyama, 2017, pp. 9–10). It was not until the formation of the Zollverein trade customs union in the mid-19th century that domestic trade was freed of tariffs and domestic markets became relatively integrated (Shiue, 2005).

Some economists have theorized that Britain's market size played a crucial role in providing incentives for innovation and bringing about sustained growth. This idea goes back to Adam Smith (1776/1976), who argued that the size of the market determined the extent of the market. This in turn determined both the productivity of labor and capital and the incentives for investment and innovation. Building on this insight, Desmet and Parente (2012) link increasing market size with increasing firm size and argue that these two interlinked developments were critical in accounting for the Industrial Revolution. The size of markets, particularly urban markets, expanded considerably in 17th- and 18th-century England. This played an important role in enabling regional specialization and promoting Smithian growth. Areas with poor-quality land like the Northwest and Midlands developed their comparative advantage as centers of manufacturing (Kelly, Mokyr, and Ó Gráda 2020). But this was not enough by itself.

One reason why institutions and markets were not enough is that they were not unique to Britain. Numerous studies have found comparatively high levels of market integration in parts of pre-industrial Europe (Bateman, 2011, 2012). Even in England, markets were already highly integrated by the late Middle Ages (Federico, Schulze, and Volckart, 2021). Bouts of market integration also occurred previously and in other parts of the world without inducing a sustained increase in innovative activity. For instance, under the Qing dynasty, China achieved comparatively high levels of integration (Bernhofen, Li, Eberhardt, and Morgan, 2020). Moreover, the Dutch had reasonably secure property rights and access to large international markets. Why didn't the Dutch have an Industrial Revolution? Why didn't they end up turning their trade networks, physical capital, and human capital into sustained growth and innovation?

How About State Capacity?

All of the preconditions we have discussed so far either have not been unique to Britain or were not directly related to innovation. This does not make them unimportant. They were all part of the bigger story of why Britain industrialized in the 18th century. But they leave some pieces missing. One of these missing pieces is that Britain's state capacity was second to none in Europe.

In particular, simply because it governed a much larger territory, Britain's state capacity was much greater than that of the Netherlands. The Dutch Republic was the leading economy of the 17th century. But it had to expend tremendous resources to fend off French invasions in 1672–8, 1688–97, and 1701–14. It is a testament to the resilience of the Dutch economy that it did not collapse from the fiscal challenges it faced in fighting the French. The costs were huge. De Vries and van der Woude (1997, p. 681) estimate that, in the mid-18th century, 7% of total Dutch GDP was spent on debt financing. Interest payments constituted 70% of tax receipts. The Dutch Republic remained rich – its per capita GDP exceeded that of Britain's until after 1820 – but it lacked the capacity for rapid, sustained growth.

Throughout the 18th century, the Dutch controlled a large share of world trade. Amsterdam remained a financial capital. But the large debts incurred during the French Wars had to be financed and this meant high taxes. When a renewed crisis came in the 1780s, the Dutch Republic was unable to respond. The Republic was eventually brought to an end by the French invasion of 1795.

In contrast, Britain was able to finance numerous wars with France during what historians have come to call the "Second Hundred Years' War" between 1688 and 1815. Like the Dutch Republic, the British state took on a tremendous amount of public debt (Vries, 2015). Debt as a portion of GDP soared to 250% by 1815. But unlike the Dutch Republic, the British state was able to support this debt without resorting to draconian levels of taxation. British taxes were higher than in France (about 12% of national income compared to 6–7% in France), but they were not so high so as to impede growth. As Brewer (1988) demonstrated, the bulk of taxes were raised through indirect taxation, particularly on goods like beer.

This suggests the possibility that despite having many of the prerequisites for modern economic growth, in a world characterized by interstate violence, the Dutch Republic was simply too small to support the type of economic growth that characterized industrializing Britain. The British could engage in dynastic and commercial wars with their well-funded rivals without destroying their economy. The Dutch could not. Of course, the Dutch could have tried to avoid warfare, but this was difficult in this period. Any nation that did not have a robust military, such as Poland-Lithuania, tended to be gobbled up by its rivals. Yet, state capacity merely gives us one reason why industrialization did not begin in the Dutch Republic. It does little to tell us why the British were so innovative beginning in the latter half of the 18th century. This requires knowing something more about the British people themselves.

Maybe It Was Skilled Mechanical Workers?

Another important factor unique to Britain was its large supply of highly skilled workers. These included craftsmen, printers, watch-makers, carpenters, and engineers (Kelly, Mokyr, and Ó Gráda, 2014, 2020). Britain also had a large supply of wrights, who were highly skilled mechanical craftsmen (Mokyr, Sarid, and van der Beek, 2020). These craftsmen specialized in water-powered machinery, which gave Britain an edge until well into the 19th century, when steam power finally replaced water power.

One thing tying all of these workers together was *fine mechanical skills*. These were the types of workers who would eventually create many of the innovations of the Industrial Revolution. They would also be the ones who would produce and repair these innovations at scale. Metal machines requiring precise measurement and engineering acumen were the hallmarks of the Industrial Revolution. It was these workers who made it possible (Kelly, Mokyr, and Ó Gráda, 2020). The Dutch Republic, with its strong focus on merchant activity and international trade, did not have an equivalent workforce. As we will see later in this chapter, such skilled workers were crucial to Britain's industrialization. The Dutch Republic's relative paucity in this respect likely inhibited any possibility of an industrial revolution there.

One critical factor that supported the existence of a highly skilled workforce was the system of apprenticeships. In Britain, the contract between the apprentice and a master was a private one, and hence voluntarily enforced (Humphries, 2010). But it was regulated by municipal authorities. These contracts were a way of overcoming a fundamental problem in the market for human capital. How can talented but poor individuals acquire training in a profession if they lack the means to pay for it? The apprentice contract sought to overcome this problem by locking an apprentice in for a certain number of years, usually seven, during which time he would provide labor services for the master in return for bed, board, education, and training. As the apprentice became more skilled, his labor would become much more valuable than his costs of upkeep and training, allowing the master to recoup the outlay of the earlier years.

Apprenticeship was not unique to Britain, but it was not tied to the guilds as it was in the rest of Europe. Wallis (2008, p. 854) notes that apprenticeships in early modern England "thrived despite, not because of, the guilds." In practice, apprentices often left their contracts early (Minns and Wallis, 2012). Journeymen would take their skills from one town to another. This was important because the type of skills they transferred were best transferred in person (de la Croix, Doepke, and Mokyr, 2017). As a result of the movement of labor and a fluid and mobile labor market for apprentices in London, craft skills were diffused widely both in London and beyond. This can help explain Britain's relatively high level of human capital. It can also help explain why the difference in wages between skilled and unskilled workers was relatively low (van Zanden, 2009).

In short, Britain had many of the prerequisites for industrial expansion – at least, those prerequisites we can now see with the benefit of hindsight. It had political institutions that protected property rights, while also allowing their adjustment and renegotiation. It was open to innovation and invention (despite the downsides associated with too rigorous an enforcement of intellectual property). It had access to the Atlantic and its slave economies, while avoiding the perils of the resource curse. Its political elites, while mercantilist, encouraged domestic trade and, despite tariffs and other restrictions, did not repress international trade. It had labor market institutions that avoided the costs associated with guild privileges, but provided skills and training on a large enough scale.

Britain was not the only place with at least one of these traits. The free cities of the Holy Roman Empire had many of the best-skilled laborers on the continent. The Dutch had secure property rights and access to international markets. The Spanish and Portuguese had worldwide colonial empires. Perhaps the difference was that the British had *all* of these factors? Take any one away and it is unlikely that Britain would have industrialized the way it did. But how did Britain industrialize? We turn to this crucial issue next.

An Innovative Economy

The Industrial Revolution saw a range of innovations concentrated in certain sectors of the British economy. To illustrate the cumulative nature of the major breakthroughs, we focus on one of those sectors: the cotton textile industry.

For centuries, the productivity of spinners had been constrained by the use of a single spinning wheel. In 14th-century China, there were experiments with multiple spindles. In Europe, this development did not occur until the mid-18th century. The first successful machine using this technique was the spinning jenny, invented by James Hargreaves in 1764 or 1765 (see Figure 8.3). Prior to Hargreaves's invention, spinning was a labor-intensive activity, usually performed by women working from their own homes. In both Europe and Asia, spinning was produced through a decentralized system of household production, often in the countryside. Merchants or "putter-outers" would distribute raw cotton fiber to spinners and then return a week or so later to collect the

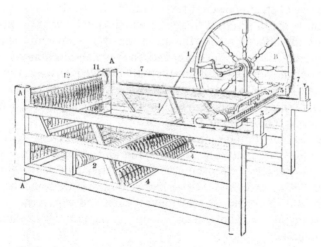

Figure 8.3 The spinning jenny

Source: Figure in the public domain, available at https://en.wikipedia.org/wiki/Spinning_jenny #/media/File:Spinning_Jenny_improved_203_Marsden.png.

spun cotton thread. Weaving – also a labor-intensive activity – tended to be the prerogative of men and was typically better paid than spinning.

Hargreaves was able to solve the problem of operating multiple spindles at once by placing the spinning wheel (which powered the spindles) on its side, while placing the spindles themselves in a vertical position. It took several years for him to iron out problems in the design, but once he had done so, spinning jennies began selling across the northwest of England. As Allen (2009a) documents, the spinning jenny reduced the costs of spinning by more than half. It also changed the way work was organized. Individuals working in their homes could not afford such an expensive piece of machinery and it only made sense to employ it in a larger enterprise. Thus, spinning jennies facilitated the rise of factories in which capitalist entrepreneurs owned the capital-intensive machinery and the spinners earned a wage. This development also enabled longer working hours and was a precondition for the replacement of human labor by machine labor.

While the spinning jenny was an important breakthrough, its impact was limited by the fact that it could only spin weft yarn (Styles, 2021) and its spinning wheel was still powered by hand. In 1769, Richard Arkwright developed a machine that could be powered by water: the water frame (see Figure 8.4). Critical to this development were rollers which drew out the fiber so that it could be twisted by the spindle. Arkwright built on earlier innovations and designs, and his use of rollers was borrowed from techniques used in metallurgy. The water frame represented a significant advance and led to the establishment of large cotton mills, often close to rivers.

The next development was Samuel Crompton's spinning mule (see Figure 8.5). The mule combined the spinning jenny and the water frame and subsequently enabled the rise of steam-powered textile mills. Unlike the jenny or the water frame, the mule could produce fine yarn which could rival that produced by hand-spinners in India. Alongside the invention of these machines, many other processes were mechanized and improved. The result was a dramatic fall in the real price of cotton yarn. Overall productivity doubled between the 1760s and the 1830s, by which time British cotton textiles were more competitive than Indian cotton textiles, even though British wages were four to five times higher in nominal terms (Allen, 2009a, pp. 151–5).

Cotton textiles saw remarkable productivity growth. It was the largest of a number of industries, including iron-making and watches, that experienced continuous productivity improvements in the latter half of the 18th century (Mokyr, 1990; Kelly and Ó Gráda, 2016). More change would come in subsequent decades. Why did these changes take place when and where they did? This is the key question, and it is hotly debated among economic historians. We turn now to this debate.

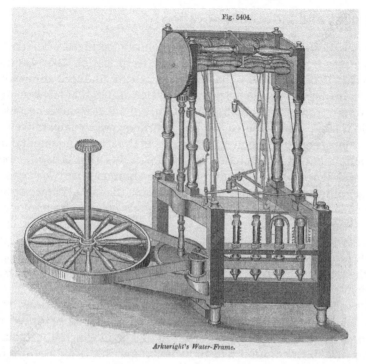

Figure 8.4 Arkwright's water frame

Source: Figure in the public domain, available at https://en.wikipedia.org/wiki/Spinning_frame #/media/File:Spinning_frame01.jpg.

Figure 8.5 Crompton's spinning mule

Source: Figure in the public domain, available at https://en.wikipedia.org/wiki/Spinning_mule #/media/File:Mule-jenny.jpg.

High Wages and Induced Innovation

Allen (2009a) argued that the Industrial Revolution occurred when and where it did because it was a response to the relative prices of labor, capital, and energy. This is an argument that economists call "induced innovation" or "biased technological change." Specifically, Allen argues that labor-saving technologies were profitable to develop in Britain, but not elsewhere, because labor in Britain was expensive whereas capital and energy were comparatively cheap.

Allen compares two economies with access to the same fundamental production function, but with different factor endowments (that is, land, labor, and capital), and hence different factor prices. The argument has two stages. In the first stage, initial relative factor prices determine the initial choice of technology. When labor is relatively expensive, producers choose a technology which is labor-saving and capital-intensive. On the contrary, when labor is cheap, producers will choose labor-intensive production. In the second stage, there is relatively rapid technological progress in the capital-intensive technology. This makes the capital-intensive technology profitable even in locations where labor costs are low and capital and energy are relatively more expensive.

Allen's model is best suited to explain the pattern of innovations in cotton textiles. The spinning jenny did not require knowledge of advanced mathematics or science. It was an engineering challenge in which numerous small problems of implementation had to be overcome. But it did require capital. Hargreaves was supported by Robert Peel, a local putting-out merchant and farmer. Similarly, Arkwright's water frame solved an engineering problem: "[T]he originality was not in thinking up the roller, rather the challenges were the practical issues of making the roller work in application" (Allen, 2009a, pp. 200–1).

The steam engine was different. Here, prior scientific advances were crucial. Particularly important were an understanding of atmospheric pressure and the realization that as water evaporates it produces a vacuum. Otto von Guericke's demonstration of this point, through his air pump of 1657, was critical. Christopher Huygens experimented with the idea of a "gunpowder engine" in which he pioneered the development of a piston-based engine. Using this knowledge, Denis Papin built several experimental steam engines in the late 17th century. While none of these were close to being commercially viable, Thomas Newcomen drew on these early models when he developed his atmospheric engine (see Figure 8.6) (Wooton, 2015).

One of the earliest uses of the steam engine was in coal mining. Coal mines suffered from frequent and dangerous flooding. Engines could pump out the water, making mining safer. As Allen (2009a, p. 161) puts it: "Scientific curiosity and court patronage may have been reason enough for Torricelli, Boyle, Huygens and other scientists to devote their time and money to studying air pressure, but Newcomen was motivated by prospective commercial gain." After Newcomen's invention, it was possible to incrementally improve the

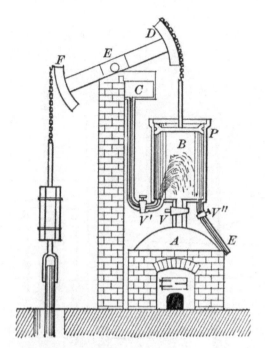

Figure 8.6 Schematic of the Newcomen steam engine

Source: Figure in the public domain, available at https://en.wikipedia.org/wiki/Newcomen_atmos
pheric_engine#/media/File:Newcomen6325.png.

design. The coal consumption needed to run a steam engine fell from around 45 to 30 pounds per horsepower hour between 1712 and the 1760s to around 17 pounds by the 1770s due to improvements made by John Smeaton (Allen, 2009a, pp. 165–6).

The big breakthrough in steam technology came from James Watt in combination with his business partner Matthew Boulton. Watt's engine improved efficiency by introducing a separate condenser (see Figure 8.7). Allen (2009a) characterizes Watt's efforts as epitomizing the private R&D model of technological change. Major improvements in pumping had to await the expiration of Watt's patent, but after 1800 there were dramatic improvements in steam technology. Although it took decades for steam engines to be widely adopted, they ended up revolutionizing many industries, including transport. Steam locomotives and steamships would become the predominant form of transport in the 19th century.

According to Allen (2009a), inventions like the steam engine, and improvements upon those inventions, were driven by high British wages. Entrepreneurs sought labor-saving methods to avoid paying those high wages. But why were they so high? Part of the answer has to do with the developments we outlined in the previous section. Allen accounts for high British wages in the context of

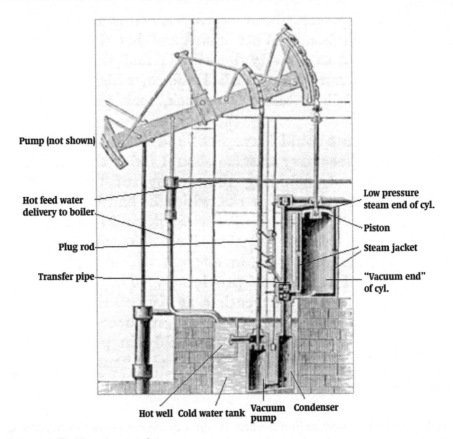

Pump (not shown)

Hot feed water delivery to boiler

Plug rod

Transfer pipe

Low pressure steam end of cyl.

Piston

Steam jacket

"Vacuum end" of cyl.

Hot well Cold water tank Vacuum pump Condenser

Figure 8.7 The Watt steam engine

Source: Figure in the public domain, available at https://en.wikipedia.org/wiki/Watt_steam_engine#/media/File:Watt_steam_pumping_engine.JPG.

the comparative commercial success achieved during the 17th and 18th centuries, in which overseas trade played a particularly important role.

Cheap energy is another part of Allen's story. Cheap energy was partly the result of prior developments. The coal industry developed in England in response to a shortage of timber in the 16th century. In particular, the growth of London exhausted nearby sources of timber and induced a switch to coal-burning. This was a drawn-out process that required innovations like improvements to the chimney. It also provided incentives for the expansion of the mining industry. Cheap coal was a particularly important spur to the development of steam engines (see Figure 2.10).

Allen's argument has come under critical scrutiny. First, technological change does not always economize on the most expensive factor. For profit-maximizing entrepreneurs, all costs are economized. The conditions under which directed technological change seeks to economize on the most expensive factor depend on the degree of substitutability between labor and capital. We do not yet have a good estimate of whether these conditions were met in Industrial Revolution Britain.

Second, more detailed studies have refined Allen's account in the specific context of the Lancashire cotton industry in the mid-18th century. Styles (2021), for instance, argues that it was not the overall level of wages in the British economy that mattered for the incentive to adopt a new technology. It was the specific cost of labor in regional textile centers like Lancashire. Humphries and Schneider (2019) provide counter-evidence suggesting that female spinners did not in fact earn as high wages as Allen claimed.

Third, Allen infers that labor was expensive in Britain because wages were high. However, high real wages reflected high levels of human capital and not just the cost of labor. British workers were better fed, taller, capable of working longer, and more skilled and numerate than their equivalents elsewhere (Kelly and Ó Gráda, 2014). The higher wages they commanded may therefore not be an accurate measure of labor costs.

Finally, Allen's explanation does not address one key aspect of Britain's industrialization: its large supply of highly skilled workers. It was these workers who drove the Industrial Revolution. Allen's explanation also does not account for the role that scientific advancements played in revolutionizing many key industries. Sure, science was not important for some of the advances in cotton textile machinery. But it was for the steam engine and metallurgy. A satisfying explanation of the Industrial Revolution needs to account for these factors while also accounting for why it began in Britain. We turn next to such an explanation.

An Enlightened Economy

Thus far, we have noted numerous preconditions for industrialization. All were apparent in Britain on the eve of industrialization. These include a large supply of highly skilled workers, a large domestic economy, limited and stable governance, and access to the growing Atlantic economy. Yet, none of these explanations can account for why British innovators were so adept at taking advantage of recent advances in *science*. This is the last part of the puzzle in need of explanation.

Mokyr (2009, 2016) offers a theory addressing precisely this puzzle. He emphasizes the role that cultural elites of the Enlightenment played in propelling European – and particularly British – technological innovation. Specifically, Mokyr (2016) emphasizes the role played by the Republic of Letters in producing a culture that rewarded and encouraged innovation. The Republic of Letters was a Europe-wide forum in which Enlightenment elites disseminated and disputed the cutting-edge scientific findings and philosophical insights of the day. It provided a setting for ideas to be tested and norms of good behavior and scientific standards to develop. In previous eras and in other societies, innovators were often siloed. Brilliant individuals often worked in isolation (like Renaissance polymath Leonardo de Vinci). Or they were dependent on the patronage of a single individual, often a monarch whom they might offend or displease. But individual genius was not enough to produce a culture of innovation. And the patronage systems of most pre-modern societies were not conducive to the pursuit of innovative new ideas.

The Republic of Letters crossed national and religious borders and followed strict rules of intellectual engagement. Networks of elite minds were formed that would have been impossible without this forum. For instance, the famous French philosopher Voltaire corresponded with cultural elites far away from his home in Paris – in England, Spain, Italy, Portugal, Germany, the Netherlands, and beyond (see Figure 8.8). The Republic of Letters was remarkably open to new scholars advancing ideas that overturned existing orthodoxies, while also succeeding at vetting for quacks and charlatans. Participants in the Republic of Letters created a hierarchy of merit wherein individuals were judged on the basis of their ideas and not their social pedigree. The Republic of Letters was successful because it weeded out bad ideas and enabled good ideas to diffuse and spread.

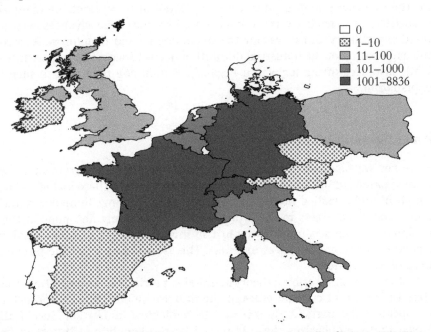

Figure 8.8 Number of letters in Voltaire's correspondence in the Republic of Letters, 1755–76

Figure does not include 100 letters with Russia, three with Sweden, one with Ecuador, one with Haiti, three with India, one with Kazakhstan, one with Panama, one with Turkey, and one with the US. *Data source*: Edelstein et al. (2010).

According to Mokyr (2016), great individuals and scientists mattered, but they did not act on their own. Mokyr depicts in vivid detail the followers and secondary figures who played a crucial role in disseminating the new ideology of progress. For instance, individuals such as Samuel Hartlib played a central role in the establishment of the Royal Society (the world's oldest surviving scientific academy, founded in 1660 in Great Britain). So did John Wilkins, Warden of Wadham College Oxford, who was another founder of the Royal Society. It was these lesser known scientists, along with the more famous thinkers of the day such as Isaac Newton, who helped build a marketplace for ideas. This was not a deliberate or planned process. The actions of various writers, intellectuals, and scientists across Europe built a shared community of thinkers and innovators from which emerged the Republic of Letters.

This culture of growth cannot be assessed in isolation from other developments. For example, Mokyr (2016) emphasizes that the emergence of a Europe-wide postal service was key to scholarly communication. This began in the 15th century as the de Tasso family began organizing a postal system in Italy before expanding into the Holy Roman Empire a century later. By the 17th century, a postal network linked all of Europe and made feasible a continuous and reliable correspondence between scholars living in different countries.

Political fragmentation was also important. What made Europe unique, according to Mokyr, was the combination of cultural unity with political fragmentation. Fragmentation per se imposes numerous costs, some of which we discussed in Chapter 7. Any benefits from fragmentation could only be obtained because it coincided with a thriving intellectual culture that spanned political borders. The political divisions of Europe meant that innovative and heretical thinkers had an avenue of escape from heavy-handed political authorities. This escape valve prevented the ideas and innovations of the Renaissance and Reformation from being suppressed or lost once the Counter-Reformation became ascendant in Southern Europe after 1600. Fragmentation and polycentricism allowed Descartes and Pierre Bayle to flee France, and Hobbes and Locke to flee England.

The political divisions of Europe also meant that there was a host of potential patrons and protectors. No writer or scientist was dependent on the favor of a single, all-powerful monarch. Furthermore, the cultural unity of Europe meant that the inventors, innovators, and tinkerers in England and the Dutch Republic could build on the advances of the European-wide Scientific Revolution. Europe's interconnectivity due to the Republic of Letters helped to give rise to a continent-wide Enlightenment Culture.

But how did the Republic of Letters contribute to the onset of industrialization? More to the point, why did a pan-European institution help facilitate industrialization in *Britain* (and not elsewhere)? This is where the presence of other preconditions is important. Mokyr (2009) argues that it was not just the ideas of the Enlightenment that mattered, but also the capacity of certain people to take those ideas and put them into practice. This required a large group of people with practical skills: craftsman, artisans, and tinkerers. On the eve of industrialization, England had these people in abundance. The new spirit of scientific inquiry met a response from this large group of apprentice-trained and skilled craftsmen. Most other parts of the world did not have such a large group of highly skilled mechanical workers. Those that did, like the independent cities of the Holy Roman Empire, lacked a number of the other preconditions for growth. In the rest of the world, other important preconditions did not materialize. Political fragmentation in the medieval Middle East and pre-modern India does not seem to have promoted innovation. Meanwhile, the political unity of Qing China produced an elite culture that was conservative and stifled free thinking.

According to Mokyr (2009), it was British skilled workers who internalized key Enlightenment cultural ideas. Among the most important of these ideas was that the world could be transformed for the betterment of humankind. The mentality that the world could be improved upon was key to increasing the rate at which technological change occurred (Howes, 2017). This was why so many innovators of the period contributed new ideas to areas outside of their specialization or technical background (Mokyr, 2009). Edmund Cartwright, best known for his invention of the power loom, exemplified this mentality. It was not just textile spinning that he attempted to improve. He also "developed agricultural machinery, designed fireproof building materials, made medical discoveries, contrived a crank-operated, horse-less 'centaur carriage', and experimented with manures and potatoes as the superintendent of the Duke of Bedford's model farm" (Howes, 2017, pp. 3–4). Cartwright was hardly unique in this regard. Many of the best-known innovators of the period contributed to a wide spectrum of fields. These ideals culminated in what Mokyr (2009) calls an "Industrial Enlightenment," with its locus in Britain.

As Crafts (2011) notes, Allen's and Mokyr's views of the origins of the Industrial Revolution can be reconciled. Technological change in the Industrial Revolution could have been labor-saving and a response to high labor costs. At that same time, a cultural transformation along the lines Mokyr envisions could have been critical in increasing the supply of would-be inventors, tinkerers, and entrepreneurs. Although we side with the latter as being more critical, both arguments shed significant light on why Britain industrialized.

Chapter Summary

This chapter addresses one of the most important questions regarding how the world became rich: why did the Industrial Revolution take place when and where it did? We first identified the many preconditions that Britain had on the eve of industrialization (around 1750). These included relatively limited and representative governance, a large domestic economy, access to the Atlantic economies, and a large base of highly skilled mechanical workers. Other places in Europe (and around the world) had some of these prerequisites, but only Britain had all of them. We argued in this chapter that they were all necessary, at least for British industrialization to proceed the way it did. In fact, many of these preconditions interacted with others so that one mattered only in the presence of another.

Having identified the preconditions for industrialization, we proceeded to examine two of the primary recent theories on why Britain industrialized first. One, by Allen, emphasizes Britain's high wages and relatively cheap energy. This combination incentivized producers to innovate the types of labor-saving technologies that were the hallmark of the Industrial Revolution. However, this explanation does not account for why Britain had so many highly skilled mechanical workers on the eve of industrialization. It was these workers who were so important to creating, implementing, and repairing the inventions of the Industrial Revolution. Nor does Allen's argument account for the use of science in many of the key inventions of the Industrial Revolution. Although some inventions in cotton spinning did not require scientific knowledge, other inventions did. Most famously, advances in steam engines and metal-lurgy used cutting-edge scientific principles. These facts are accounted for in the second major theory, proposed by Mokyr. Mokyr argues that an "Industrial Enlightenment" pervaded Britain in the late 18th and 19th centuries. This movement drew upon the newest scientific principles from across Europe. Unlike other parts of Europe, Britain was able to complement scientific pro-duction with mechanical skill. It was this combination that enabled the many innovations of the Industrial Revolution and ensured that Britain's industrial-ization was not just a blip. If anything, the rate of innovation has continued to increase ever since.

Clearly, Britain no longer has a monopoly on innovation. Nor is it the richest economy in the world. It was overtaken in the early 20th century. In any case, Britain's industrialization did not immediately result in large gains in per capita income. That would have to wait for the middle decades of the 19th century. It was only then that modern, sustained economic growth began. How did this happen? How did Britain become rich? How did other parts of the world become rich? Understanding what happened in Britain is important, because that is where modern economic growth first emerged. But if we care about the processes through which billions have been lifted out of poverty and billions more have somewhat comfortable lifestyles, we need to leave Britain and address how (parts of) the rest of the world became rich. This is the focus of the next chapter.

9

The Rise of the Modern Economy

The Industrial Revolution was a technological revolution. Over time, it would bear economic fruit. But it did not do so immediately. Modern economic growth, characterized by sustained increases in per capita income without major reversals, did not begin until the middle decades of the 19th century. How did this happen? How do we connect the dots from industrialization to modern economic growth? After all, Britain's industrial period was not the first time in world history that economic growth occurred. But previous episodes of growth were overwhelmed by negative shocks or Malthusian forces. Why did this episode of innovation and expansion become self-sustaining? How did this episode ultimately impact the wider population? How did it spread? Why did it spread rapidly to some parts of the world but it took centuries to spread elsewhere? These are the questions we answer in these concluding chapters. When we are done, we will have a pretty good idea of how the world became rich.

The Fruits of Industrialization

The Industrial Revolution is sometimes conceived as a "take-off" (for example, by Rostow, 1960). This metaphor suggests an ever-accelerating rate of economic growth. But this is a little misleading. Overall economic growth during the Industrial Revolution was modest by 20th-century standards. British growth during industrialization was much slower than in 21st-century China, post-World War II West Germany or Japan, or the US around the turn of the 20th century.

But the Industrial Revolution *was* a revolution. What made it so revolutionary was that Britain was ultimately the first economy to achieve *sustained and permanent* per capita GDP growth over a long period. It was also the first large economy to transform the basis of the economy away from agriculture to industry. Crafts (2018, p. 11) describes the achievements of the Industrial Revolution in the following terms: "[T]he economy of the mid-nineteenth century was established on a different trajectory from that of a hundred years earlier. In particular, sustained labour productivity growth based on steady technological progress and higher levels of investment had become the basis of significant growth in real income per person notwithstanding rapid population growth." In other words, this was a period of *economic development* for the British economy.

It is these changes that are responsible for the economy we know today. But how did this revolution affect the common person? Per capita GDP only tells part of the story. Wealth need not be distributed to the masses. Clearly, at some point the lot of most became better. As we noted in Chapter 1, people living in wealthy countries who are at the bottom of today's income distribution are better off on most fronts than almost everyone who ever lived prior to 300 years ago. This is an immense accomplishment. But how did it happen?

Possibly the most important economic change brought on by the Industrial Revolution was that the *structure* of the economy changed. Since the Neolithic Revolution some 6,000–10,000 years ago, most people in every settled society in the world were engaged in agriculture. While there were a few smaller states built on trade (such as the medieval Italian city-states or early modern Holland), never before was a large state anything but overwhelmingly agricultural. This changed with industrialization, first in Britain and then elsewhere.

In fact, this transformation began prior to the Industrial Revolution. Labor left agriculture and traditional industries and moved into manufacturing and industry (Taylor and Wrigley, 2014). The proportion of English workers in agriculture was less than 40% in 1700, testifying to the sophistication of the English urban economy. By 1851, the share of workers in agriculture had fallen to 23.5%. In contrast, 45% of the labor force were in industrial employment (Crafts, 2018, p. 28).

Were the fruits of industrialization widely distributed? In the short run, the answer is no. Figure 9.1 reveals that while GDP per capita took off in the late 18th and early 19th centuries, wages stagnated until the 1830s. Real wages even fell slightly in the second half of the 18th century, just as Britain was industrializing. Afterwards, "some slight progress was made in the mid-1830s ... [but] it was not until the mid-1840s that they at last started to ascend to a new height" (Feinstein, 1998, p. 649).

It is possible that movements in real wages reflect differences between the industrializing north of Britain and the rest of the country. According to Kelly, Mokyr, and Ó Gráda (2020), areas which traditionally had lower wages such as Manchester and Liverpool experienced rapid wage growth between 1770 and 1840, while the south of England experienced deindustrialization and falling wages. The apparent puzzle of stagnant real wages in the Industrial Revolution may thus be an artifact of economic historians looking at the average of the two phenomena.

Be that as it may, between the 1780s and 1850s, real wages rose less than 15% for working-class families despite significant economic growth. Why did real wages stagnate during the Industrial Revolution? Several explanations have

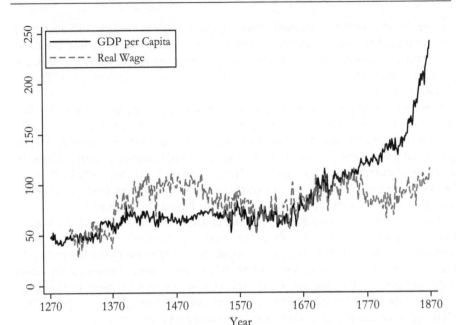

Figure 9.1 GDP per capita and real wages in England/Great Britain, 1270–1870 (1700 = 100)

Data sources: Broadberry, Campbell, Klein, Overton, and van Leeuwen (2015) for GDP data, Allen (2001) for real wage data. Data refer to England between 1270 and 1700 and Great Britain from 1700 to 1870.

been proposed. First, Malthusian forces remained relevant. The population of England and Wales increased from 6.1 million in 1750 to 17.9 million in 1851. A Malthusian framework suggests that such rapid population growth should have exerted severe downward pressure on real wages.

A second factor was war. Britain was engaged in a nearly continuous twenty-five-year struggle with Revolutionary and then Napoleonic France during the middle years of the Industrial Revolution. Population growth meant that Britain had become a net importer of food. War, blockages, and disruption meant that food prices soared, eating into workers' disposable incomes. Protection, in the form of the Corn Laws, ensured high food prices until their repeal in 1841. The period following the end of the Napoleonic Wars was one of depression and crisis as the British government strove to return to the Gold Standard and to restructure finances strained by years of conflict.

Third, technological change in this period was generally labor-saving. In a period before labor unions, this entailed a fall in labor's share of GDP during the early years of the Industrial Revolution. In contrast, the share of profit in national income rose. The consequence was that inequality rose. The majority of the gains in income went to the owners of land and capital rather than to workers. Allen (2009*b*) calls this "Engels' Pause" after Friedrich Engels,

Karl Marx's co-author of the *Communist Manifesto* (1848) and the author of *The Conditions of the Working Class in England in 1844* (1845).

These conditions gave rise to a pessimistic view of the promise of industrialization. Poets like William Blake and Robert Southey condemned the smoke and smog of mills and textile factories. They likewise railed against the dehumanizing nature of industrial work. Blake made famous the phrase "dark satanic mills," likely in reference to a steam-powered flour mill built by Boulton and Watt that was close to where he lived. The pessimistic view was most famously expressed by Marx and Engels in their *Communist Manifesto*, in which they saw no gain in living standards accruing from industrialization and mechanization. It continued to be expressed by left-leaning historians such as Eric Hobsbawm and E.P. Thompson, the latter of whom remained certain of "the truly catastrophic nature of the Industrial Revolution," a period marked by "intensified exploitation, greater insecurity and increasing human misery" (Thompson, 1965, p. 198).

The pessimistic view received apparent support from many classical economists. David Ricardo envisioned an "iron law of wages" that would in the long run push the wages of workers back down to subsistence. Malthus believed that only sexual restraint was capable of maintaining living standards above subsistence. Even John Stuart Mill, writing in 1848, was skeptical of the ability of machines and mechanization to achieve a sustained increase in living standards (Berg, 1980, pp. 332–42).

In contrast, there were those who appreciated that something unique was occurring. Thomas Macaulay (1830, pp. 560–1) painted this optimistic view of the economic conditions of ordinary people in 1830s Britain in response to Southey:

> When this island was thinly peopled, it was barbarous; there was little capital; and that little was insecure. It is now the richest and the most highly civilized spot in the world; but the population is dense. Thus we have never known that golden age which the lower orders in the United States are now enjoying. We have never known an age of liberty, of order, and of education, an age in which the mechanical sciences were carried to a great height, yet in which the people were not sufficiently numerous to cultivate even the most fertile valleys. But, when we compare our own condition with that of our ancestors, we think it clear that the advantages arising from the progress of civilization have far more than counterbalanced the disadvantages arising from the progress of population. While our numbers have increased tenfold, our wealth has increased a hundredfold.

Macaulay's assessment was certainly rose-tinted. However, it was Macaulay, and not Southey, Smith, or Malthus, who correctly envisioned the consequences of sustained economic growth:

> If we were to prophesy that in the year 1930 a population of fifty millions, better fed, clad, and lodged than the English of our time, will cover these islands ... that machines constructed on principles yet undiscovered, will be in every

house, that there will be no highways but railroads, no travelling but by steam, that our debt, vast as it seems to us, will appear to our great-grandchildren a trifling incumbrance, which might easily be paid off in a year or two, many people would think us insane. We prophesy nothing; but this we say: If any person had told the Parliament which met in perplexity and terror after the crash in 1720 that in 1830 the wealth of England would surpass all their wildest dreams, that the annual revenue would equal the principal of that debt which they considered as an intolerable burden, that for one man of ten thousand pounds then living there would be five men of fifty thousand pounds, that London would be twice as large and twice as populous, and that nevertheless the rate of mortality would have diminished to one half of what it then was ... our ancestors would have given as much credit to the prediction as they gave to Gulliver's Travels. Yet the prediction would have been true. (Macaulay, 1830, pp. 563–4)

While economic historians have debated whether the pessimists or optimists had the truth of it since the early 19th century, it is evident that in the long run the optimists were correct. Macaulay's predictions were remarkably prescient.

The same forces responsible for the initial increase in inequality and wage stagnation produced after 1840 an economy in which living standards rose in a sustained fashion for all. Why did this change occur, and how did it lead to greater living standards for most of the population? How did it spread beyond Britain? We turn to these issues next.

The Second Industrial Revolution

When most of us think about world-changing technologies today, we tend to think of "high-tech" technologies that have their basis in scientific knowledge, such as robotics, computing, semiconductors, rocketry, aeronautics, space flight, and nuclear technology. But this was not always the case. As discussed in Chapter 8, many of the dominant technologies of the First Industrial Revolution (c. 1750–1830) were not science-based. Most of the breakthroughs in textile production, for instance, were mechanizations of previously known methods.

In contrast, since the 1870s, most major technological advances have been built on the scientific knowledge-base of humanity (Mokyr, 1990, 2002). North (1981) called this seismic shift in the rate of technological change the "marriage of science and technology." It is often known as the Second Industrial Revolution.

The Second Industrial Revolution, generally dated from 1870 to 1914, differed from the first in its use of science. This was important because it accelerated the rate of technological change. New inventions in medicine, chemicals, and energy paved the way for more inventions as well as improvements upon those inventions. They also enabled more scientific discoveries. This period saw a feedback from science to technology that is still the dominant paradigm today (Mokyr, 1998).

A number of world-changing technologies emerged in this period. They are summarized in Table 9.1. A distinguishing feature of all of these technologies is that they required what Mokyr (2002) calls "useful knowledge." This is knowledge about the deeper (generally scientific) processes that make the invention work. Without a broad base of applicable, useful knowledge, scientific advances are likely to peter out. Once the base of useful knowledge is large enough, it can be applied with direct application in mind. Although much discovery will always be done via trial and error, directed trial and error using scientific principles makes success much more likely.

The technologies of the Second Industrial Revolution affected nearly all industries. They revolutionized transportation. Rail became much more efficient and less costly due to cheaper and more durable steel. Bicycles, automobiles, and airplanes came on the scene. Harnessing electricity allowed for an improved telegraph, railway, and indoor lighting. Health improved. Modern sewerage systems, disinfectants, and medicines like aspirin became widespread.

Unlike the First Industrial Revolution, the onset of the Second Industrial Revolution was *not* confined to Britain. Numerous other countries were at the forefront of this movement. Germany led the way in chemistry. France and the US were also leaders. Why did some countries catch up with Britain, and in some cases take the lead? Why did other countries fail to do so? What was different about the Second Industrial Revolution?

Table 9.1 Major inventions of the Second Industrial Revolution

Invented	Massively expanded or improved
Cheap steel	Electricity
– Used in construction, ships, railroad tracks	– Used in telegraph, railway, light bulb
Automobile	Railroads and diesel engine
Airplane	Telegraph (and networks)
Telephone	Vulcanized rubber
Typewriter	Anesthetics and antiseptics
Chemical dyes	Sewerage systems
Internal combustion engine	Sewing machine
Chemical fertilizers	Food canning
Synthetic plastic	Clean water supply
Dynamite	Soda-making
Sulphuric acid	Disinfectants
Aspirin	
Bicycle	
Barbed wire	
Fungicides	

Data source: Mokyr (1998).

Because science was so crucial to advancements in the Second Industrial Revolution, *education* was key to its spread (Galor, 2005). To quote a classic paper by Nelson and Phelps (1966, p. 70), "[E]ducated people make good innovators, ... [and] education speeds the process of technological diffusion." This had not been the case in the First Industrial Revolution (Mitch, 1999), during which Britain had no lead in formal education (Mokyr, 1990, p. 240). Rather, the First Industrial Revolution occurred in Britain because of the preconditions noted in Chapters 7 and 8.

There is a difference between having a large proportion of the population capable of reading and writing and having a small proportion of the population educated at a high level. Mokyr (2009) refers to the latter as upper-tail human capital and notes that this may have been more important in accelerating the rate of innovation in the late 18th and early 19th centuries. In fact, upper-tail human capital in France predicts both city growth and industrial innovation after the Industrial Revolution (Squicciarini and Voigtländer, 2015). Yet, during the Second Industrial Revolution, having a higher fraction of the population with at least basic education also became increasingly economically valuable. Workers with basic literacy and numeracy were better suited for working with machinery and submitting to factory discipline.

The Second Industrial Revolution was the first period in which "capital–skill complementarity" drove economic and technological development (Goldin and Katz, 1998; Galor and Moav, 2006). It was not just that some places had more scientists and inventors. The types of goods produced in this period, such as those highlighted in Table 9.1, required *highly educated* workers for their manufacture. Technology alone does not cause economic growth. It must be transformed into something economically productive. The more highly educated workers a society has – engineers, clerks, pharmacists, and so on – the more these new technologies can be put to productive use.

Places that led in education were therefore the most capable of taking advantage of the new economic opportunities afforded by the second wave of industrialization. Prussia provides an important example. It was a relatively late industrializer, but when it did industrialize in the 19th century, it caught up fast and even surpassed the world's leaders on many fronts. This was in large part due to its initial lead in education (Becker, Hornung, and Woessmann, 2011). After its defeat to Napoleon in the first decade of the 19th century, Prussia imposed a series of reforms emphasizing education. This had the unforeseeable consequence of setting up Prussia to later adopt and improve upon technologies flowing in from Britain and elsewhere. Within Prussia, those places that were more highly educated in the early 19th century ended up taking the industrial lead. Ultimately, Germany (which unified in 1871) was a leader of the Second Industrial Revolution.

The proximate cause of success during the second wave of industrialization was education. Places with a more highly educated workforce were more likely to adopt and implement new technologies. Ultimately, they created the technologies themselves. Those areas with lower rates of education – particularly the type of "useful" education complementary to the new types of capital – were not ready to adapt to the new world. But this is only part of the story. Why did some parts of the world invest in education in the first place? There are many answers to this question. They are all related to the features discussed in the first six chapters.

The Demographic Transition

The Second Industrial Revolution was responsible for a sustained rise in living standards wherever it took hold. We noted before that this was not the case for the First Industrial Revolution. British living standards changed remarkably little between 1750 and 1830 despite overall economic growth. What made the Second Industrial Revolution different?

One of the most important factors holding back living standards during the First Industrial Revolution was demography. Fertility, in particular, increased in the first few decades of the First Industrial Revolution (see Figure 9.2). This was largely due to better economic opportunities and urbanization. Illegitimacy rates soared. The average age at first marriage fell. The result was that the British population increased from around 6 million in 1750 to 10.5 million

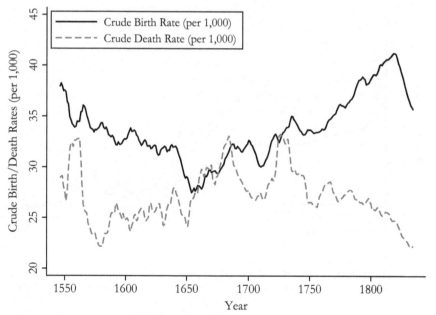

Figure 9.2 Fertility and mortality in England, 1541–1839

Data source: Wrigley and Schofield (1981).

in 1801 and 27 million in 1851. The growing population put downward pressure on wages, which did not rise despite increases in productivity. For this reason, Malthus, writing in the early years of industrialization, predicted that economic growth was incapable of staving off demographic disaster.

Malthus turned out to be wrong. In particular, he did not fully anticipate the extent to which married couples would seek to limit their number of children. This demographic transition was a critical turning point in economic history. Families began to deliberately choose family size within marriage. It began in France in the late 18th and early 19th centuries before spreading across Northern Europe and the US in the late 19th century during the second Industrial Revolution (see Figure 9.3). Prior to this transition, married women might have eight or more births (Guinnane, 2011). Whether or not a society was close to the feasible maximum birth rate of around forty to fifty births per 1,000 people largely depended on practices that limited marriage or involved infanticide.

The timing and nature of the fertility transition remain subject to debate. Certain populations began restricting fertility earlier, including Jews in Western and Central (though not Eastern) Europe. The first country to experience the demographic transition was France (see Figure 9.3), where the birth rate began falling even before the Revolution. The reasons for this decline are not well understood. Spolaore and Wacziarg (2021) view the demographic

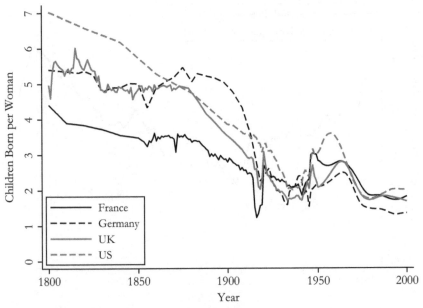

Figure 9.3 Children born per woman in Western Europe and the US, 1800–2000
Data source: Roser (2021a).

transition as being spread by cultural contact. They note that specific parts of France experienced the demographic transition first, and that it only spread to more culturally remote regions such as Brittany more slowly. One point emphasized by Spolaore and Wacziarg is that modern fertility norms diffused from France, the originator of European cultural modernity, and not from England, the source of economic modernity.

In Britain, the demographic transition only occurred in the 1880s. Although marital fertility among the upper classes began to decline earlier before spreading to the middle and working classes (Clark and Cummins, 2015), this leaves the precise timing of the fertility transition unexplained. Regardless of its timing, how should we think about the demographic transition? From the perspective of the Malthusian model, it represents a reversal of the birth rate–income relationship (see Chapter 5). After the mid-19th century, higher incomes no longer resulted in more surviving children.

The demographic transition had various consequences for economic growth. Most directly, it relieved Malthusian population pressure. But this is perhaps less important than the accompanying increase in investment in human capital.

The demographic transition and increased investment in human capital were related. According to unified growth theory, which we introduced in Chapter 5, the latter *caused* the former. Technological progress caused the return to human capital to rise. This induced parents to invest in human capital for their children (see Galor, 2011). Hence, parents began to invest in the "quality" of their children (that is, their education) instead of the quantity of children. In England, this shift began in the mid-19th century (see Figure 9.4).

The Uneven Diffusion of Modern Economic Growth

In this short book, we cannot examine how each part of the world became rich. (If you are interested in the – mostly European – countries that followed Britain's path to industrialization in the 19th century, Cameron [1993] gives a great overview.) But if we want to know how the world became rich, we should know *something* about how other parts of the world prospered. This includes the US – the world's leading economy in the 20th century. We also need to know something about how parts of the world outside of Europe and its former colonies became rich. The next chapter covers the spread of riches to East Asia's first industrial nation, Japan, and ultimately to the Asian Tigers and China.

Britain was the first industrial economy. By the end of the 19th century, sustained economic growth had spread to other parts of the world. Most notably, as we will shortly see, it spread to the US. Industrialization also diffused throughout Western Europe, first to Belgium and then to Germany. It did not, however, spread to all parts of the world. The question is why not?

The standard model which economists use to study modern economic growth is the Solow model, named after Nobel laureate Robert Solow (1956). In

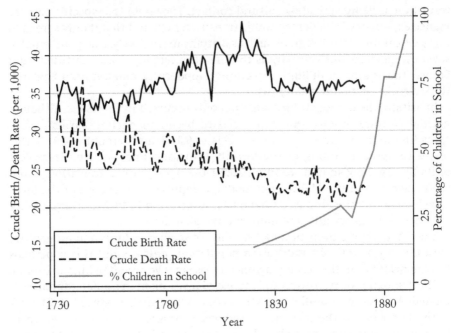

Figure 9.4 Human capital and the demographic transition in England, 1730–1890
Data sources: Wrigley and Schofield (1981), Galor (2005), and Roser (2021b).

the Solow model, the ultimate driver of long-run economic growth is innovation. While the model has little to say about the origins of sustained economic growth, it provides insight for understanding the *diffusion* of economic growth.

In the Solow model, so long as innovations in leading economies become available to less developed economies, poorer countries will grow faster than richer countries. This is called *catch-up growth* or *convergence*. The intuition is simple. For countries far away from the economic and technological frontiers, the marginal productivity of capital is high. These economies should attract high levels of investment and grow more rapidly than those that are already capital-abundant.

Catch-up growth can help explain why from the late 19th century onwards many European economies began to experience accelerated growth. Those that caught up imported the technologies of the First and Second Industrial Revolutions. Germany is a good example. Economic growth was exceptionally fast from the 1840s onwards. Germany even became a leading innovator in many technologies of the Second Industrial Revolution.

A different version of "catching up" was put forth in a classic work by Gerschenkron (1962). He argued that there were certain economic advantages for countries that embarked upon industrialization from a more primitive starting point. Countries like Germany and later Japan and Russia could move fairly quickly to the technological frontier in certain sectors of the economy. They could skip intermediary steps, particularly in capital-intensive sectors. Late industrializers often mobilized capital through investment banks or state investment rather than relying on private capital markets.

Many of the factors considered in previous chapters can account for why some countries converged whereas others did not. Consider institutions. Where there are few checks on autocratic political power, technology adoption may not occur (Scheidel, 2019, ch. 12). As we will see in the next chapter, inward turns in Tokugawa Japan and Ming and Qing China delayed the adoption of Western technology by centuries. The Ottomans delayed the adoption of the printing press by 250 years (Coşgel, Miceli, and Rubin, 2012). The benefits of these technologies were widespread. But the potential downsides were narrowly targeted to the elite. Unconstrained rulers can prevent the spread of such technologies. Constrained rulers have a much harder time doing so.

Institutions were likewise critical to both convergence and divergence with the rest of the world in the late 19th and early 20th centuries. In places that converged with the world's economic leaders, most notably Western Europe and North America, the quality of political institutions improved dramatically. An important reason why the economic growth that began in the 19th century did not peter out was therefore institutional. Existing elites or those who gained from the status quo were unable to block innovation. As economic growth transformed societies, the political systems of the leading economies were, in general, able to meet the challenge by introducing new reforms and policies.

There were many paths of institutional development in the converging countries. In 1800, the newly independent US was among the most democratic societies on earth, as measured by the rights it granted white men. But it was marred by the institution of slavery, which denied the most basic rights to 17% of the population. As we saw in Chapter 8, Britain entered the 19th century with a constitutional arrangement that protected property rights, encouraged innovation, and was capable of heading off revolutionary pressures. But it was also a deeply unequal society, where the right to vote belonged to a minority, child labor was common, and the law was highly inequitable in its implementation and effects. Needless to say, in all these societies, the rights of women were highly restricted. Until the French Revolution, most of continental Europe was governed by absolutist monarchies that retarded economic growth via complex regulations, diverse and confusing tax systems, and local monopolies.

Over the course of the 19th century, these societies moved in both a liberal and democratic direction. In the terminology of North, Wallis, and Weingast (2009), they became fully "open-access orders." In continental Europe, the French Revolution played an important role in dismantling feudal institutions (Acemoglu, Cantoni, Johnson, and Robinson, 2011). In Britain, revolutionary violence was largely avoided as elites pre-emptively democratized in order to head off unrest (Acemoglu and Robinson, 2006). Importantly, these moves towards more inclusive political institutions were accompanied by the reform of various economic institutions. By the end of the century, freedom of contract had been expanded in most Western European countries, usury laws were abolished, child labor was increasingly limited, workers gained the right to organize, and working men had the right to vote.

Culture also played a role in shaping patterns of convergence and divergence. In Chapter 4, we defined culture as the "lens" through which people view the world. When this lens views Western industrial technologies as inconsistent with long-held beliefs about Western inferiority, adoption is unlikely. Cultural factors also *interact* with institutional factors. This may help explain the slow uptake of industrial technologies in the Ottoman Empire and China (Iyigun, Rubin, and Seror, 2021). Both were at one point ahead of Europe on many dimensions. Accepting the (temporary) superiority of Europe's industrial technologies required a change in worldview. Such a change does not happen overnight.

Yet, even when foreign technologies are desired, many conditions need to be just right. Importantly, while the extent to which "war is the mother of invention" is disputed, war can certainly be bad for the spread of technology. Countries tend to not want their rival combatants acquiring cutting-edge industrial technologies. During the Napoleonic Wars, British engineers were prohibited from leaving the country and the export of machinery was banned. The general European peace after 1815 was one reason why technology spread as rapidly as it did. Relative to most of European history, the period between the Napoleonic Wars and World War I was *peaceful*. This was particularly true after 1870. The onset of a prolonged period of peace between the Great Powers was favorable to the diffusion of economic growth. This period is often called the First Era of Globalization. World trade grew by more than 400%. The share of trade in world GDP would not recover until the 21st century.

It was not just manufacturing technology that spread in this period. New transportation and communication technologies diffused as well. As we noted in Chapter 2, investments in these types of technologies can help overcome the problems of "bad geography." International freight rates declined. Cheaper freight rates and improved transportation technologies made it possible for land-abundant North America to export grain to Europe (O'Rourke and Williamson, 1999). This grain invasion greatly benefited workers in European cities, who saw their real wages rise. Investments such as the Suez Canal were also crucial. Supply and demand expanded together. Although maritime freight rates declined by 50%, the fall in freight costs alone cannot explain the scale of the trade expansion (Jacks, Meissner, and Novy, 2011). Transportation investments were driven by increased demand for traded goods and by institutional improvements across the world.

Among the most important transportation improvements in this period was the steamship. Prior to its invention, the costs of trade depended on how accessible a given location was for sailing ships. After the invention of the steamship, however, this was no longer the case. The new technology helped spur a trade boom. But the benefits of increased trade and greater integration into the global economy were dependent on institutions. It was only in countries with strong constraints on executive power that increased exposure to international trade led to economic development (Pascali, 2017).

Not all countries took the same path towards modern economic growth. It is mistaken to suppose the *only* way a country can grow rich is through industrialization. While this was true of Britain, the US, and Germany, there were also countries that grew rich *without* industrializing. Foremost among them were Denmark, the Netherlands, Australia, and New Zealand. These economies were able to specialize in commercial food production or processing, usually for export markets. This required international markets and some degree of globalization.

For instance, Denmark developed a butter industry. This involved the application of scientific ideas, but to food production rather than manufacturing. The success of Denmark was predicated on particular institutional and cultural developments. As documented by Lampe and Sharp (2018), educated elites played a critical role in the introduction of new scientific techniques and in providing capital; these techniques were then adopted by smaller farmers and by the development of cooperative dairies. These innovations, however, proved difficult to transfer to other countries. In Ireland, for instance, political conflict limited the diffusion of both the cooperative organizational form and new innovations (O'Rourke, 2007a, 2007b).

Globalization was also central for Australia's economic development. Initially founded as a penal colony, the country experienced rapid immigration and rising real wages after the discovery of gold in the 1840s and 1850s. Like that of other smaller economies, Australia's prosperity hinged on global trade and stable international conditions (McLean, 2013). The first major Australian export was merino wool from New South Wales, which became an important input into the British textile industry. The Australian economy was correspondingly vulnerable to any downturn in the international economy, as occurred in 1890 and during World War I. But overall Australia prospered. As was the case with Denmark, the first wave of globalization in the late 19th century was crucial to Australia becoming rich.

The First Era of Globalization saw the spread of sustained economic growth. But it also saw tremendous economic divergence. While economies in Western Europe and North America grew, per capita incomes stagnated elsewhere, particularly in China, India, and the Middle East. There are many reasons for this. Colonial institutions, as discussed in Chapter 6, provide one reason. Rapid population growth, as discussed in Chapter 5, provide another. Additionally, as the expansion of global trade knitted different parts of the world together, poorer countries increasingly specialized in exporting primary products. This could be a source of growth. Cash crops played an important role in the economic development of West Africa in the early 20th century. Yet, there were downsides. Above all, the prices of primary products tended to be highly volatile

(Williamson, 2006). This led to crashes in countries dependent on the export of goods whose prices fell.

We will now turn to how the modern economy spread to what would become the world's largest economy: the US. This is not to ignore diffusion to other follower countries, some of which we highlight above. Rather, we wish to keep the book concise, and the US case is too central to the "world becoming rich" for us to ignore.

How the US Became Rich

In the second half of the 19th century, the US became the fastest growing major economy in the world. By the early 20th century, it had both the largest economy and the highest standard of living in the world. Understanding how economic growth and industrialization spread to the US is therefore paramount for understanding how the world became rich. Why did the US first catch up and then eventually overtake the UK as the world's economic leader?

America was initially a technological follower. Yet, it grew rapidly. Between 1790 and 1860, growth was not driven by efficiency so much as enormous increases in effective land and natural resources per worker. Population growth was rapid, but extra land and natural resources were added to the economy at an even faster rate.

By the mid-19th century, American manufacturing achieved very high levels of productivity (Broadberry, 1994, 1998). Yet, at that point, manufacturing was only a small part of the economy. It was not until at least the 1880s that it became the driving force behind American economic growth (see Figure 9.5). In what follows, we examine these developments. Where applicable, we link them to the preconditions discussed in Chapters 7 and 8 that were crucial for Britain's industrial rise.

Following independence, US international trade grew considerably. There was rapid population growth, and the population expanded westward. Two aspects of this development deserve attention. The first was the emergence of the US South as a major cotton exporter. The second was the rise of the Northeast as a manufacturing center.

The invention of the cotton gin by Eli Whitney in 1793 enabled the Southern states to specialize in this highly lucrative export crop. Prior to this, the expansion of cotton had been limited by the fact that the cotton that grew in inland areas – so-called "short-staple cotton" – required painstaking cleaning. On average, a cotton picker might be able to clean only a pound of short-staple cotton a day. The gin – an old-fashioned term for engine – was a machine that passed cotton through a wooden drum to clean it, catching the fibers in a mesh. Cotton gins were initially powered by hand or horse-power, but over time they became mechanized. As North (1966, p. 68) noted, "It was cotton which was the most important influence in the growth of market size and the consequent

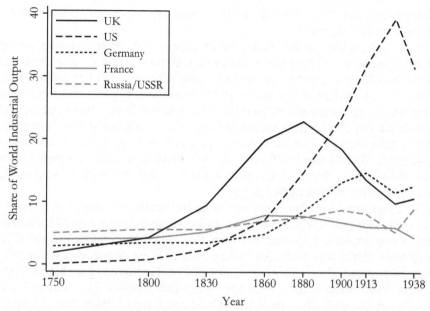

Figure 9.5 Shares of world industrial output, 1750–1938

Data source: Kennedy (1987, Tables 6, 18).

expansion of the economy." It also led to the spread of slavery. Cotton picking was exhausting but easy to supervise work and hence suited for coerced labor.

The rise of cotton impacted not only the economy of the US but also its political economy. Demand for slaves rose. The booming cotton trade drove the center of slavery south and west, away from Virginia and North Carolina towards the "black belt" of Louisiana, Mississippi, and Alabama.

Slave-produced cotton was highly profitable and it made the fortunes of many a planter in the South. It was an utterly brutal system, and it played a central role in Southern society. Nevertheless, it is important to recognize that cotton exports represented less than 6% of the economy. While this is far from a trivial number, exaggerated claims have been made of the pivotal importance of slavery and cotton to American economic growth.

In fact, the existence of slavery slowed Southern industrialization and urbanization. Southern elites held their wealth primarily in the form of slaves. Investing in slaves was profitable, and it took resources away from other, industrial, pursuits (Ransom and Sutch, 1988). This limited local market size, making industrial production all the less attractive. As Majewski (2009, p. 17) notes, "[S]lavery severely limited the size of markets for southern manufacturers. Cities such as Richmond, Norfolk, and Charleston, serving sparsely populated hinterlands, lagged behind northern rivals. The southern economy certainly generated substantial profits for the region's many planters and farmers, but the slower growth of cities, industry, and population created a sense of relative decline."

In any case, removing slavery did not mean no cotton. Absent slavery, cotton manufacturers would have had to purchase cotton from non-slave sources. And in the medium-run, cotton production could have expanded through small-scale farming (Wright, 2020). Southern elites certainly would have been poorer without slavery. Cotton prices would have been higher in the absence of coerced slave labor. But there is little reason to suppose that this would have been more than a temporary disruption to textile production. Clegg (2015, p. 296) notes that when "Britain was briefly cut off from American cotton imports by the War of 1812, the price of cotton rose less than it did in the 1860s, suggesting less dependence in this earlier period."

The other important development was in the Northeast, where the technologies of the First Industrial Revolution spread earliest. The growth of industrial production expanded 100-fold between 1790 and 1850. Factors identified by both Allen and Mokyr in Chapter 8 help explain these developments. Initially, the rapid spread of new ideas from Britain was facilitated by a shared Anglo culture that linked Britain with the newly independent US. "Culture" was clearly not the only cause of New England's industrialization, but it helped. Those cultural attributes emphasized by Mokyr as crucial for Britain's rise did not exist in many parts of the world. This was a hurdle that likely delayed industrialization. This hurdle was minimal in New England, given its shared heritage with Britain.

Moreover, Allen's argument (centered on relative factor prices) has bite for the US. Real wages were high in America prior to the Revolution – by some estimates higher than in Britain (Lindert and Williamson, 2016). Energy was cheap. Water power and other natural resources such as timber were abundant. This created a strong incentive for labor-saving innovation. Examples include the first automatic flour mill invented by Oliver Evans in 1782 and Whitney's cotton gin. Allen (2011a, p. 83) writes: "[T]he success of the American economy depended on the application of inventive engineering across the full spectrum of industries. The incentive to mechanize was provided by the high cost of labour. The successful response required a large pool of potential inventors. The interplay between challenge and response made the USA the world's productivity leader." Until 1880, the relative price of unskilled labor compared to energy and capital was not higher in the US than in Britain. However, after 1880, "the incentives to invent higher productivity technology led to an American lead. The incentives to use more power per worker in America increased significantly in this period – without a corresponding change in Britain" (Allen, 2014, p. 332).

Another precondition highlighted in Chapter 7 was limited and representative government. Like Britain, the US had this, although not for everyone. In Britain, this mattered for public good provision, particularly transport networks. This was also the case in the US, even if the circumstances were different.

Of particular importance was the Interstate Commerce Clause, which prevented individual states from passing laws that impeded inter-regional trade and prohibited the granting of transport monopolies. For instance, this clause struck down New York State's attempt in 1824 to grant a steamboat monopoly to Robert Fulton.

Improvements in transport infrastructure began in earnest in the early 19th century. Probably the most famous improvement was the Erie Canal, completed in 1825, which connected New York City to the Great Lakes. Improvements like this helped knit together different regions and different markets. Inter-regional trade resulted, permitting greater specialization and the rise of an integrated domestic market for manufactured goods (North, 1966). Such large domestic markets were another precondition found in Chapter 7. Only after the US was connected was such a market available.

The largest investments were in railroads, which were funded with both public and private funds. Chapter 2 reviewed the debate over the importance of the railroads. Recent findings suggest that they had an enormous impact on US economic growth, mainly because they improved market access (Donaldson and Hornbeck, 2016). By 1890, US aggregate productivity would have been some 25% lower had there been no railroads (Hornbeck and Rotemberg, 2021). In short, the railroad contributed to integrating the US into a large and homogeneous market, one of the preconditions for the rise of American manufacturing.

A second way in which US political institutions played an important role was through investment in education. Unlike Britain, whose human capital advantage was based primarily on mechanical skills, the US invested in formal public education. Most of this investment was at the local, municipal level. Engerman and Sokoloff (2012) claim this was a consequence of its political institutions. Local government in Colonial America was highly decentralized, egalitarian, and democratic, particularly in the Northeast. Meanwhile, in the South, large-scale landlords had incentive to keep their labor force uneducated. Literacy was of little value in farming. Keeping the masses (both slaves and poor whites) uneducated limited their outside options, allowing the elite to keep wages low (Galor, Moav, and Vollrath, 2009). This was not the case in the North, where industrialists could gain from a more productive workforce. As a result, Northern states had relatively high literacy rates and basic education.

Literacy rates stagnated in the mid-19th century with industrialization and rapid immigration. However, in the early 20th century, the high school movement brought a dramatic expansion in secondary education (Goldin and Katz, 2008). This rise in human capital was so central to American growth in the 20th century that Goldin (2001) calls it the "human capital century."

Other factors were distinct to the American experience. Some were important for why the US became rich, others not. For instance, the US employed protective tariffs. Proponents of tariffs saw them as protecting "infant industries" from foreign competition. But was the tariff essential for American industrialization? The answer given by most economic historians is a qualified no. The tariff did speed the growth of manufacturing, particularly in the New England textile industry (Harley, 1992*a*, 1992*b*; Rosenbloom, 2004), but tariffs likely just sped up a process that would have happened anyway (Irwin, 2000, 2002).

American culture was also unique. But it is hard to discern which aspects of American culture were important for the acceleration of economic growth that occurred in the 19th century. Recall our discussion of the Weber hypothesis in Chapter 4. For Weber, the archetypical example of how Calvinism could mutate into a set of values suitable for economic growth was an American: Benjamin Franklin. But as we also saw in that chapter, the evidence for a specific Protestant work ethic – independent of the effects that operated via education and human capital – is weak. Perhaps more important than Calvinism per se was the general attitude that commerce was a means to social advancement (Appleby, 2010). As the US lacked a hereditary aristocracy, it lacked the inhibiting social norms that penalized commerce and encouraged successful merchants and entrepreneurs from buying land and entering the nobility.

A long tradition, dating at least back to Frederick Jackson Turner (1893), locates a unique American individualism in the frontier. While American individualism has had a significant effect on the country's politics, taxation, and welfare state (Bazzi, Fiszbein, and Gebresilasse, 2020), it is unclear whether this frontier culture played an important role in its industrialization. Early industrialization tended to be far from the frontier: first in the Northeast and later in the Midwest. Rather, it is more likely that the willingness of Americans to move to the frontier – something that was commented upon by 19th-century European observers such as Alexis de Tocqueville (1958) – reflected a broader American cultural belief in the possibility of economic improvement.

Another important feature of America's growth experience was immigration. The population of the US grew from less than 4 million in 1790 to more than 76 million by 1900. While much of this was due to natural growth (that is, births exceeding deaths), immigration played a key role (see Figure 9.6). This had multiple implications for economic growth and industrialization. First, it contributed to the growth of domestic markets. Even by the 1850s, outside experts commented on America's large and deep domestic market for manufactured goods. Second, it provided the large workforce needed for the US to become a major manufacturing center. Third, immigrants brought with them human capital. This contributed to American inventiveness – a large share of US inventors were immigrants or second-generation immigrants. In fact, counties with more immigration in this period had more and larger manufacturing establishments, greater agricultural productivity, and higher rates of innovation (Sequeira, Nunn, and Qian, 2020). Those counties that had high levels of historical immigration *still* have significantly higher incomes, less poverty, less unemployment, more urbanization, and higher educational attainment *today*.

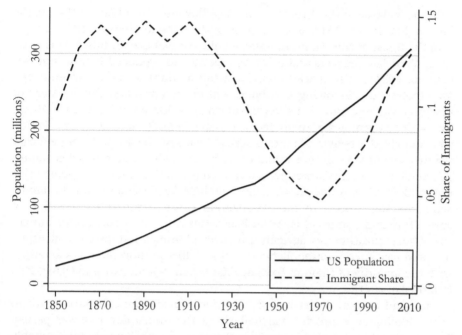

Figure 9.6 US population and immigrant share, 1850–2010

Data sources: Various US Censuses and Migration Policy Institute (https://www.migrationpolicy.org /programs/data-hub/charts/immigrant-population-over-time).

The Soviet Detour

Another path to industrialization was pioneered in Russia. This path was based on command and control rather than on markets. Why did this take place? And why did it ultimately result in failure?

Recent empirical research has overturned conventional views about the pre-Soviet Russian economy. In the mid-19th century, Imperial Russia was a closed, backwards agrarian economy. But following a series of modernizing reforms by the end of the 19th century, Russia had, with Meiji Japan, joined the group of late industrializing economies. By the early 20th century, it was one of the fastest growing economies in the world (Gregory, 1994).

Despite its rapid growth, Russia remained agrarian. Agriculture made up almost 60% of the economy in 1913 (Gregory, 2004b, p. 185). Inefficient serf-based agriculture had been a major drag on productivity in the Russian economy during much of the 19th century, even after the formal abolition of serfdom in 1861 (Markevich and Zhuravskaya, 2018). But agrarian reforms, notably the Stolypin Reforms of 1906 and 1911, made peasants residual claimants. This had the potential to unlock agricultural productivity (Castañeda Dower and Markevich, 2018). This period of rapid growth, however, ended with the collapse of the Russian economy following World War I (1914–18), the Russian Revolution (1917), and the onset of the Russian Civil War (1917–22).

In the midst of this, Lenin imposed a policy of War Communism. This effectively abolished markets and private property and produced famine and destitution. We lack the space to provide a full account of the Communist era. Nonetheless, the following bare-bones outline is important for the story of modern economic growth. From this catastrophic low point in the early 1920s, the Soviet economy began to recover under Lenin's New Economic Policy, which enabled a revival of market activity. Marxist theory had assumed that the first socialist revolution would occur in a heavily industrialized economy. The Russian economy, however, even though it had been rapidly growing prior to World War I, was not industrialized. Stalin's "achievement" was to rapidly accelerate the process of industrialization through the collectivization of agriculture and a series of Five-Year Plans. This came at a catastrophic human cost. Collectivization saw agricultural yields plummet and forced requisitioning produced mass famine. Between 5.5 and 10.8 million died of starvation, with the majority of them in Ukraine (Markevich, Naumenko, and Qian, 2021; Naumenko, 2021).

The rapid pace of Soviet industrialization provided an alternative path to other developing countries, particularly in the immediate post-war period. The Soviet state succeeded in providing many basic public goods, most notably excellent technical education and essential healthcare. The Soviet Union also eradicated smallpox and other diseases earlier than the US (Troesken, 2015).

This accelerated pace of industrialization could not be sustained, however. Even during the early phase of rapid growth, inefficiencies and wastage were legendary (Gregory and Harrison, 2005). Many problems were initially disguised by the sheer amount of labor (much of it slave labor), physical capital, and natural resources the Soviet economy could mobilize. Ultimately, though, the centralization of all economic decisions in the hands of a dictator produced chaos. Stalin spent his time making seemingly trivial decisions, including setting the price of metro tickets and making detailed managerial appointments (Gregory, 2004a, pp. 112–14). Corruption and rent-seeking were endemic (Anderson and Boettke, 1997; Boettke, 2001). There were reforms after the death of Stalin, but as the Soviet economy developed in the 1950s and 1960s, it struggled to provide basic consumer goods that people wished to purchase.

Economic growth is ultimately about producing economic value. Here, the Soviet economy failed. Soviet elites had access to special stores where Western products were available but to which ordinary Soviet citizens were denied access. The Soviet economy came to depend more and more heavily on exports of oil and natural gas. When the price of oil collapsed in the 1980s, pressure to reform the Soviet economy became impossible to stop. And when Mikhail Gorbachev began the process of reform, this soon led to the collapse of the Soviet economy and the Communist system (Boettke, 1993).

The story of Soviet industrialization has two lessons. First, Communism is incompatible with long-run growth. The Soviet Union was unable to implement its original economic blueprint. The actual Soviet economy relied on black markets and was unable to suppress the profit motive. Over time, it became more and more sclerotic. A second lesson is that autocratic government can stifle growth in the long run. This certainly does not mean that economic growth cannot happen under autocracy – we will discuss recent Chinese economic growth in the next chapter. Nor is limited governance sufficient to bring about modern, sustained growth. Yet, the Soviet case remains an important reminder of the potentially devastating economic consequences of unchecked political power.

Chapter Summary

While the modern economy first arose in Britain, it was not confined there. We have seen in this chapter how it spread to parts of Western Europe and to the US.

The US had several advantages in this respect. It shared a common language and culture with Great Britain so that intellectual developments in one country were rapidly transmitted to the other, even after the Revolutionary War. It had high wages, abundant land, and natural resources. This made it well suited to adopt labor-saving technologies. Similarly, while Britain had a comparatively large internal market for a pre-industrial economy, the US had a huge domestic market. This was particularly true as its population expanded and spread west and its internal transport networks improved. All of these factors worked in favor of the US becoming an industrial giant by the late 19th century. Although many other factors contributed to the continued economic growth of the US in the 20th century, that is material for another book.

But what about the rest of the world? In the 20th century, the fruits of the modern economy expanded well beyond Western Europe and its offshoots. How did this happen? Were the factors highlighted in previous chapters crucial? We turn to these issues next.

10

Industrialization and the World It Created

This book is titled "How the World Became Rich." So far, we have discussed why parts of Western Europe and the US became rich. But that is only around 10–15% of the world's population! To understand how the *world* became rich, we need to understand how parts of the *rest of the world* obtained the fruits of the modern economy.

Before proceeding, let us circle back to something we said in the first chapter. We are well aware that the entire world is not actually rich. Over a billion people still live in abject poverty. Eradicating such poverty should be among the chief goals of civilization. We believe humanity is well on the way to achieving this daunting task.

The world as a whole has certainly become much richer in the last 200 years. In the last century or so, the fruits of these riches have finally spread well beyond Europe and the US. They have also spread well beyond small groups of elites. This is seen most starkly in Asia. As recently as 1960, most of the continent was extremely poor – though no poorer than most civilizations have been in world history (see Figure 10.1). After all, the condition for nearly every human being living before 1800 was poverty or near-poverty. This changed over the course of the 20th century, and it continues to change in the present. Asia is becoming richer, and as such the world is becoming richer. This chapter is dedicated to how this happened.

Sure, there is a long way to go. And sure, the path is even more fraught in sub-Saharan Africa, parts of Latin America, and parts of Central and South Asia. But this is real, tangible progress. The world is becoming richer.

Delayed Catch-up: The Shadow of Colonization (and Other Factors)

One important reason that some countries have taken so long to catch up is the shadow cast by colonization. It is highly unlikely, as we discussed in Chapter 6, that colonization explains why the colonized world did not industrialize *first*.

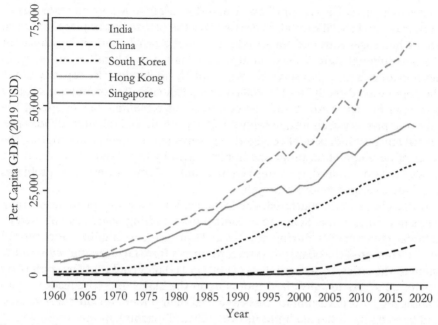

Figure 10.1 Per capita GDP in select Asian countries, 1960–2019

Data source: World Bank (2019).

However, in many parts of the world, colonization undoubtedly played a role in delayed convergence.

As we discussed in Chapter 6, the kinds of institutions that colonial rulers established had persistent effects on subsequent development. Labor-scarce, land-abundant colonies in North America, Australia, New Zealand, and, to a degree, Argentina flourished in the late 19th century. Their institutional development followed that of their parent countries, and they attracted large amounts of migrants and capital. Australia, for instance, though founded as a penal colony in which convicts were treated harshly, developed a system of regional self-government that culminated in the establishment of the country as a constitutional monarchy in 1900. Elsewhere, however, much more extractive economic and political institutions were put in place.

Many parts of the formerly colonized world that were subject to extractive institutions still languished behind the world's leading economies. This includes much of sub-Saharan Africa, South Asia, and parts of Latin America. In some of these countries, the extractive institutions put in place by colonizers remained after independence.

But the institutions put in place by colonial rulers were not the only relevant factor. Prior conditions also mattered. Pre-colonial Nigeria, for example, was highly fragmented, and most people lived close to subsistence. A large-scale, centralized state never emerged. Nigeria was also heavily affected by the slave trades, which, as we saw in Chapter 6, left a negative legacy on state formation, trust, and social capital. The structures the British put in place to govern such a heterogeneous and fractured society left a problematic inheritance for the post-colonial state. The colonial regime "failed to centralize authority, to develop an effective civil service, and, relatedly, to develop the capacity to tax the population directly" (Kohli, 2004, p. 292). Following independence, Nigeria was beset by civil conflict and the economy has remained dependent on the export of primary products, notably oil. Sharp ethnic and religious divides prevented any post-independence Nigerian government from even attempting the types of developmental programs implemented by East Asian states from the 1960s onwards. Indeed, ongoing violence and endemic governance problems continue to limit economic growth.

Policy choices also mattered. For instance, following independence, urban elites in countries like Kenya took control of marketing boards established by colonial governments during the Great Depression to stabilize agricultural prices. They used the boards to extract resources from farmers and redistribute them to the cities. In Senegal, Bates (1981, p. 111) observed that "by conferring privileged access to subsidized inputs upon the Makebouts [the leaders of an Islamic sect], the government thus enhanced their power over the rural masses, and by so doing, it helped build its own political machine in the countryside." These policies were politically expedient but costly economically.

India, the largest of the former colonies (British India also included modern-day Pakistan and Bangladesh), likewise remained poor, though its growth has improved in recent decades. This is hardly something inherent in the region. Historically, India was a major textile producer, and at the height of its prosperity around 1600, per capita incomes were around 60% of British per capita incomes. During the 17th and 18th centuries, however, the Indian economy declined. The urban share of the population was perhaps 15% in 1600. It fell during the subsequent centuries to only 8.7% by 1870. Per capita GDP fell by about 30% in the same period (Broadberry, Custodis, and Gupta, 2015, p. 67). Broadberry, Custodis and Gupta (2015, p. 71) conclude that India was relatively "prosperous . . . at the height of the Mughal Empire during the time of Akbar [but] much of this prosperity had disappeared by the eighteenth century."

A confluence of factors were responsible for India's economic decline. These factors included worsening climatic conditions, multiple invasions, and endemic warfare (Clingingsmith and Williamson, 2008). The sack of Delhi by Nadir Shah of Persia (1739) ravaged the capital of the Mughal Empire, leaving tens of thousands dead. The subsequent conquest of much of the sub-continent by the British East India Company also involved protracted warfare and pillaging that furthered economic dislocation and decline. Following decades of decline, the Indian textile industry, which was reliant on skilled labor and low wages, was then hit hard by the introduction of manufactured cotton exports from industrializing Britain. This was largely the consequence of technological innovation, not British commercial policy (Gupta, 2019, p. 808).

The establishment of the British Raj (after the brutal suppression of the Indian Mutiny) could have brought an opportunity for growth. Total GDP did in fact increase, but per capita incomes stagnated. There are many reasons for this. While there was capital investment from Britain, it was concentrated on the construction of the railway system. Other infrastructure was largely neglected, although the early 20th century did see large-scale improvements in irrigation and fertilizers. Attempts to institute a system of property rights had the unintended consequence of creating a class of absentee landlords. Factor markets, particularly credit markets, remained undeveloped and local farmers remained reliant on moneylenders.

Demography also mattered. The Indian economy remained Malthusian. Increases in productivity translated into faster population growth rather than rising living standards. This was partly a reflection of the trading regime imposed by the British. India remained a producer of primary products and an importer of British manufactured goods (Galor and Mountford, 2008). Investment in agriculture stalled. And there was very little improvement in education. At independence, only 17% of the population had basic literacy (Gupta, 2019, p. 805). On this front, India lagged far behind countries like Brazil or Japan.

Upon independence in 1947, opportunities for economic growth in India were thus circumscribed. As was the case elsewhere in the developing world, Indian economic policy was influenced by the example of the Soviet Union and the popularity of economic planning. Indian politicians such as Jawaharlal Nehru (Prime Minister, 1947–64) pursued state-led industrialization and aimed at industrial self-sufficiency. For critics of this system such as Lal (2005, pp. 263–4), the technocratic appeal of planning was combined with a deep distrust of commerce rooted in the caste system. These policies were loudly supported by Western economic advisors such as John Kenneth Galbraith and Joan Robinson and backed by generous developmental aid (White, 2012, pp. 250–9). Galbraith advised that "what is not in doubt is the need for planning by the less developed country. . . . [T]he market cannot reach forward to take great strides when these are necessary" (quoted in White, 2012, p. 253).

These policies had very disappointing results. There was some catch-up growth, but overall performance lagged. India's per capita GDP growth averaged 1.2% per year between 1950 and 1980, falling far short of the leading East Asian economies. As we will see, this was largely because those East Asian countries remained more open to international trade and were less protectionist. The "License Raj" created incentives for endemic rent-seeking and corruption. By the 1980s, the consequences of import substitution and central planning were evident for all to see. In response, the government began to deregulate the economy in the 1990s. Only after this happened did India finally turn a corner.

Along with China, which we will discuss shortly, alleviating poverty in South Asia is of utmost importance for eliminating abject poverty worldwide. As of 2015, 731 million people in the world were living in extreme poverty (less

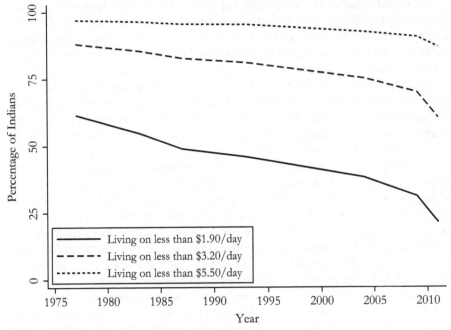

Figure 10.2 Percentage of Indians living in extreme poverty, 1977–2011

Data source: World Bank (2019).

than $1.90/day). Of these, 216 million live in South Asia (another 413 million live in sub-Saharan Africa) (World Bank, 2020a). The trends are encouraging, though. The liberalizing reforms that began in the 1990s have brought economic growth to India.

Growth has brought with it increased inequality and environmental degradation. According to the World Health Organization, ten of the eleven most polluted cities in the world are in India (WHO, 2018). But growth has also delivered on poverty reduction. And the future holds hope. The percentage of Indians living in abject poverty declined from 61.6% in 1977 to 21.2% in 2011 (see Figure 10.2). The number of Indians making a slightly higher income ($5.50/day) also increased from 3% in 1977 to 13.2% in 2011. While there is a long way to go for India to become rich, the trends are pointing in the right direction.

How Japan Became Rich

The first non-Western country to achieve sustained economic growth was Japan. Following the Meiji Restoration in 1868, which deposed the Shogun, Japan implemented a rapid program of state-building and industrialization. These reforms focused on creating a modern army and navy that could resist Western imperialism. But they went beyond military affairs and ended up reshaping the whole of Japanese society. The success of these efforts was confirmed when the Japanese defeated China in the First Sino-Japanese War of 1894–5 and then Russia in 1904–5. What enabled Japan to successfully pursue this policy of industrialization and state-building?

Many observers at the time of the Meiji Restoration viewed Japan as a backwards and highly repressive society. This description had some merit. Tokugawa Japanese (1603–1868) society was organized into four rigid and hereditary classes comprising samurai, farmers, artisans, and merchants. There was no unified state. The shogun, the most powerful lord in Japan, ruled only 15% of the country. The remaining territory was divided into some 260 domains, each headed by a local lord (*daimyo*), which maintained their own armed forces (Koyama, Moriguchi, and Sng, 2018). As a result, currencies and taxes varied from place to place. Trade with the outside world was highly restricted. The Dutch trading post at Dejima in Nagasaki harbor was the sole point of contact permitted with the West.

The latest estimates of per capita GDP and real wages suggest that the average Japanese person was considerably poorer than his or her counterparts in 19th-century Europe or North America (Figure 10.3). Nonetheless, recent research suggests that in many respects Tokugawa Japan was a successful pre-industrial economy.

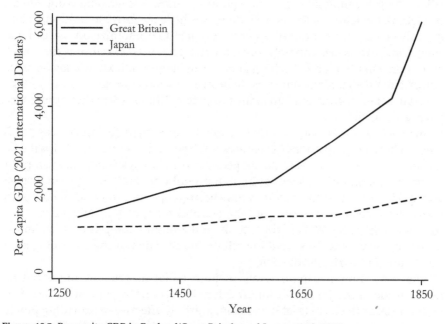

Figure 10.3 Per capita GDP in England/Great Britain and Japan, 1280–1850

Data source: Broadberry, Guan, and Li (2018): 2021 international dollars converted from 1990 international dollars at a rate of $2.03:1.

Several aspects of economic development in the Tokugawa period stand out. First, urbanization levels were comparatively high. In 1800, 13% of the population lived in towns of more than 10,000 inhabitants compared to 3–4% in China (Vries, 2020, p. 68). Second, over the course of the Tokugawa period, Japan experienced Smithian growth based on the expansion of markets and internal trade (Sugihara, 2004). Peasants became increasingly engaged with, and connected to, markets. Pressure on scarce land led to an intensification of labor inputs in agriculture, evident in the practice of double cropping (Saito, 2005). Peasants often worked in handicraft production for the market. This process of proto-industrialization paralleled developments in parts of early modern Europe.

We saw in Chapter 7 that functioning factor markets were a likely precondition for sustained economic growth in Europe. They were also present in Tokugawa Japan. Even though formal property rights were not granted, peasants had de facto rights over their land. Permanent sales of land were forbidden in theory, but in practice a market for land existed and functioned through mortgage contracts that enabled peasants to transfer property for limited periods (Saito, 2009).

Relative factor prices were, however, different than those in northwestern Europe. Japanese real wages were low by European standards. As a result, the Japanese path of development was not favorable to the development of labor-saving technologies like the spinning jenny. Rather, following Allen's framework (reviewed in Chapter 8), there was little incentive to innovate labor-intensive technological improvements designed to economize on scarce land, energy, and capital. Fortunately for Japan, it did not need to reinvent the wheel. As we noted in Chapter 9, catch-up growth can happen quickly by *adopting* technology from the leading countries. To be in a position to do so, a country needs a certain set of institutional and cultural preconditions. Were these present in Tokugawa Japan?

One such precondition is human capital. Investment in human capital is affected both by institutions (it requires funding) and by culture (it helps if education is valued). These were not impediments in Tokugawa Japan. Even prior to the Meiji Restoration, levels of human capital were high for a pre-industrial society. Literacy and numeracy may have been comparable to Western European levels. Platt (2004, p. 4) writes of "the establishment of tens of thousands of commoner schools, 276 domain schools, and around 1,500 private academies" in the Tokugawa era. This would facilitate the adoption of the technologies of the Second Industrial Revolution.

Why were human capital levels so high in Japan prior to industrialization? Although the Japanese state was highly decentralized prior to the Meiji Restoration, at the local level it was comparatively effective in providing public goods. Per capita tax revenues were higher in the lands ruled by the Shogun than in Qing China, and this difference grew over time (Sng and Moriguchi, 2014). Local lords in Tokugawa Japan invested in local public goods such as road infrastructure and drainage projects. Local civil engineering projects also enabled new land to be brought into cultivation (Kanzaka, 2019).

Overall, the Tokugawa legacy was one of relatively high taxes and involvement of the local government in economic life. These institutional and cultural factors meant that the coalition that replaced the Tokugawa Shogunate in 1868 was in a relatively strong position to implement a program of successful state-building. However, this required a political revolution at the national level (Koyama, Moriguchi, and Sng, 2018).

The reforms implemented in the wake of the Meiji Restoration were radical. The Japanese state reforged itself in a matter of decades. It was one of the most remarkable examples of state modernization. The Meiji government established a system of compulsory education and raised taxes significantly, prompting revolts and uprisings which were suppressed with considerable violence. The new regime also abolished the samurai class, but was able to do so without resistance in the vast majority of cases by granting them bonds in lieu of their previous legal privileges.

Vries (2020) describes the Meiji regime "a capitalist state." By this he means a state in which guilds and local monopolies were abolished so as to create a single, unified labor market. It was also a state that favored business in both its fiscal policy and its regulatory policies. This included supporting the formation of large industrial conglomerates known as *zabatsu*.

Even though it was pro-business, the Meiji government was not protectionist. Indeed, it could not have protected industry had it wanted to. Owing to treaties signed in the late Tokugawa period, Meiji Japan could not impose high tariffs on foreign imports (tariffs averaged less than 4%). It became highly integrated into the world economy, moving from producing a wide range of products domestically to importing what was expensive to produce and exporting what could be produced cheaply. This brought about sizable benefits to Japanese consumers. Bernhofen and Brown (2005) estimate that relative to the counterfactual world in which Japan remained autarkic, free trade raised GDP by 8–9%.

This export-led growth was predicated on the growth of a manufacturing sector. By the beginning of the 20th century, the structure of the Japanese economy already resembled that of the industrial leaders. The share of manufacturing in total output matched the US, even though Japan was far poorer (Perkins and Tang, 2017, p. 173).

This creation of an industrial economy required both high levels of investment and the mobilization of an industrial workforce. As in Industrial Revolution Britain, workers from the countryside were subjected to factory discipline and long working hours. Large numbers of women entered the labor force to work in textile factories, often living and working in harsh conditions (Hunter, 2003).

Another factor was education. As we have seen, education is an important factor in labor productivity. Japan already had relatively high levels of literacy prior to the Meiji Restoration, but tertiary education was lacking. As early as 1864, the Shogunate had sent students to study at Western universities, including University College London and the University of Cambridge. This continued during the Meiji period (Koyama, 2004), which saw the introduction of a three-tier educational system based on Western models. Vries (2020, p. 212) notes that "between 1880 and 1940, there was a fortyfold increase in the number of students enrolled in higher scientific and technical education and an eighty-fold increase in the number of students in further technical and commercial education."

The Japanese educational advantage ultimately contributed to its convergence with the world leaders. One important challenge that Japan had to overcome, like other late developers, was that factor prices remained different from those in the leading Western economies. Wages were much higher in Europe than in Japan. This was an obstacle for Japanese industrialization, because it meant that Western technology was often not worth adopting. Cheaper labor could just do what expensive Western technology could do. But this is where the Japanese educational advantage mattered. Allen (2011a, p. 122) notes: "Some [low wage] countries limped along with inappropriate technology, but the Japanese response was far more creative: they redesigned Western technology to make it cost-effective in their low-wage economy." Over time, the Japanese modified Western technologies to make them more appropriate for Japanese factor prices. This made Japan become the lowest-cost cotton producer in the world by the early 20th century. Similar developments occurred in other industries, as Ma (2004) demonstrates for the silk industry.

While growth was impressive in the post-1867 period, it was not fast enough to fully catch up with the leading economies of Western Europe and North America. The Japanese economy that emerged in the Meiji period was shaped by the global economy that developed in the late 19th century. That economy, as we have seen, was based on the free-flowing movement of goods, capital, and people. Japan lacked natural resources – in particular it lacked coal, oil, and gas. In order for its manufacturing to develop, it needed access to international markets. Japanese textile exports did well during World War I, driving British producers out of many traditional markets. But they were severely hit by the Great Depression and the worldwide movement towards protectionism that rapidly followed.

This economic crisis fueled Japanese hardliners who sought to insulate the country from global economic shocks through the pursuit of empire in mainland Asia. This strategy bore catastrophic results in World War II and it was only in the 1950s and 1960s that the Japanese economy began to grow again.

Initially, post-war growth seemed to follow the path laid out in the Meiji period. Over time, the Japanese economy was able to enter new high-tech industries, where it had a comparative advantage due to its skilled workforce. By the 1980s, Japan was one of the world's leading economies. It had truly become rich.

How the East Asian Tigers Became Rich

Many other parts of the world became rich in the 20th century. Chief among these were the "East Asian Tigers": Hong Kong, Singapore, South Korea, and Taiwan. Figures 10.4 and 10.5 put East Asian growth in context. Figure 10.4 compares per capita GDP in South Korea to Nigeria. Both countries had similarly low levels of income in the early 1960s. The divergence began in the late 1960s and early 1970s when Nigeria, like many countries in sub-Saharan Africa, entered into a period of civil war and military rule. Nigeria was also adversely affected by the general growth slowdown that occurred following the Oil Shock of 1973. In contrast, South Korea continued to register high rates of economic growth throughout the 1970s and 1980s. And as we discussed in Chapter 1, the secret to modern economic growth is that it is *sustained*.

Figure 10.5 paints a more general picture. It compares the growth of the tiger economies to growth in sub-Saharan Africa and Latin America. While sub-Saharan Africa as a whole experienced stagnation, many countries within the region actually experienced growth reversals in the 1970s and 1980s. Growth only resumed (slowly) in the 1990s. Latin American countries began the period richer than East Asian societies but they grew more slowly. As a result, by 2019, per capita incomes in Latin America and the Caribbean were only 28.6% of those in South Korea, Singapore, and Hong Kong ($10,826 vs. $37,841).

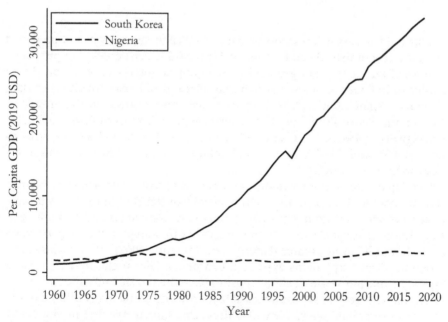

Figure 10.4 Per capita GDP in South Korea and Nigeria, 1960–2019

Data source: World Bank (2019)

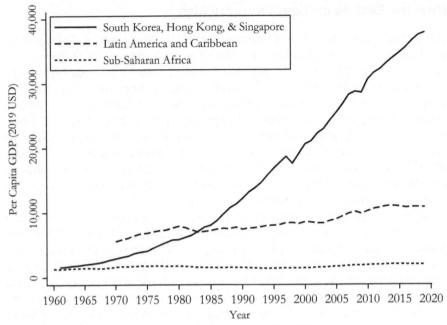

Figure 10.5 Per capita GDP in various parts of the world, 1960–2019
Data source: World Bank (2019).

Why did the East Asian Tigers become rich? Their success was not predicted by many economists ahead of time. In 1961, Paul Rosenstein-Rodan published a series of forecasts about growth in developing countries. He envisioned that countries in South Asia and sub-Saharan Africa would grow much faster than their East Asian counterparts. He particularly underestimated the growth of Taiwan and South Korea, predicting average growth rates of 0.96% and 1.4%, respectively, between 1961 and 1976 as compared to actual average growth rates of 4.8% and 7.3% (Acemoglu and Robinson, 2012a). Why was this success story so hard to foretell?

Like Japan, these countries did not need to reinvent the wheel. Countries that are poor and far from the technological frontier should in theory be able to achieve rapid economic growth by importing new ideas and technologies. As technology advances in rich countries, the catch-up potential of poor countries should be even greater (Parente and Prescott, 2002). In one sense, this economic "catch-up" helps explain much of the rise of the four East Asian Tigers. In another sense, it simply pushes back the puzzle and raises a further question: why were these countries able to catch up while many other parts of the world remained poor? We will address this shortly. We first need a better understanding of why some countries have the prerequisites for catch-up growth.

In general, "catch-up" is not simply a matter of poor countries importing technologies from rich countries. This of course does happen to some extent. Cellular phones and later smartphones spread rapidly across the developing world in the early 2000s. But in many cases, this is insufficient to ensure catch-up growth. Pritchett (1997) characterized the dominant trend between 1950 and the 1990s as "divergence big time" between the wealthy and poor world.

Given the dominant themes of this book, it should come as no surprise that catch-up is not simply a matter of importing technology. Institutions matter. So does culture. So do geography, demography, and a society's colonial past. Which of these were important in allowing East Asia to buck the trend?

In many respects, the geography of East Asia was not promising for modern economic growth. Taiwan, Singapore, and South Korea lack natural resources, especially oil and gas. But as we discussed in Chapter 2, it is often *economic geography* that matters more than the presence of natural resources. By economic geography we mean the presence of manmade economic hubs and agglomerations. One of the most robust findings in economics is that countries close to one another are more likely to trade with one another (the so-called "gravity model" of trade).

Geographic features were hardly the only critical factors. But the emergence of a cluster of densely populated manufacturing and consumption hubs in East Asia was an important precondition for both the initial and continuing successes of the economies of the region. Had Taiwan been located off the coast of West Africa, it is hard to imagine it being as successful.

As we just saw, Japan was the first country to industrialize in Asia. South Korea, Taiwan, Singapore, and Hong Kong are not only geographically proximate to Japan, but had also been ruled or occupied by it (the former two for a substantial period of time earlier in the 20th century). As a result, these East Asian economies were well placed to follow the path pioneered by Japan. Moreover, as the East Asian economies began their rapid growth later than Japan, they were further from the economic frontier and had a larger "backlog" of modern technologies to import. This gave them greater potential for rapid growth.

Geography mattered in another way. The East Asian economies were all relatively small. They were therefore forced to rely on international markets. They did not fall into the trap that many larger developing countries did of relying on protective tariffs and subsidies to support domestic manufacturing firms. It also helped that the world moved towards freer trade after 1945 with the establishment of GATT (the General Agreement on Tariffs and Trade). Protective tariffs and subsidies appeared plausible in countries with large domestic markets like Brazil and India. Such policies could work (as in 19th-century America), but in practice they often freed domestic manufacturers from the threat of international competition and encouraged rent-seeking and corruption.

The poster child for these failures was Hindustan Motors, based in Kolkata, India. From 1957 onwards, protected by a complex system of import permits and government subsidies, Hindustan Motors produced the Ambassador motor car. There was nothing wrong per se with this car. Yet, trade protections allowed Hindustan Motors to keep producing and selling the same, largely unchanged, vehicle for decades. It was not until the liberalization of the Indian economy in the 1980s, which allowed Japanese cars to be sold in India, that it became evident how far behind Indian automobiles had fallen. Small and medium-sized countries like Hong Kong, Singapore, South Korea, and Taiwan were insulated from making such mistakes. Simply by virtue of their size, they had to rely on international markets.

What role did institutions play in East Asian development? In Chapters 3 and 9, we noted that institutions which *constrain executive power* have been important in the story of economic growth. In Western Europe, the US, Canada, and Australia, constraints on executive power tended to come through democratic institutions. Yet, the East Asian Tigers were not initially democratic. South Korea and Taiwan remained dictatorships until the 1980s. Democratization followed economic growth rather than preceding it. Does this speak against the "preconditions" we highlighted in earlier chapters?

As we discussed in Chapter 3, institutions are context-specific. A range of different institutional arrangements can evolve to constrain rulers, solve collective action problems, or enable credible commitments. Democracy is one solution. Others exist. As Haggard (2004, p. 53) writes, "[T]he search for a single institutional 'taproot' of growth is likely to be a misguided exercise." In fact, there was no single set of policies pursued by all of the tiger economies, nor did they share the same institutions.

As each country had different political constituencies to satisfy and different traditions and histories, they pursued a range of different policies. Hong Kong, as a British colony, was the most reliant on markets and the most open to trade – though even here there was a substantial role for government in the provision of public housing. Singapore, also an ex-British colony, relied on a pragmatic combination of the market and government.

In South Korea, formal constraints on executive power were weak at best in the early years of industrialization. As a result, industrial policy was more heavily directed by the government. But the South Korean economy was also subject to discipline by worldwide markets. The key players were *chaebols*, large industrial conglomerates that obtained government support and guaranteed bank loans. The success of the *chaebols* rested ultimately on their ability to enter export markets. The South Korean economy at the time was simply too small and poor to provide a sufficiently large consumer base to support large-scale manufacturing. These factors allowed South Korean industrialization to succeed, perhaps *in spite of* the heavy role played by the state. Export reliance provided much-needed market discipline and mitigated some of the problems of corruption and non-transparency that otherwise afflicted large firms. Reliance on exports is thus one feature that unifies the experiences of the four Asian tiger economies.

In the absence of democratic institutions, the East Asian Tigers found ways to constrain executive power. They did this by working in conjunction with business elites in the private sector. In the post-war period, Haggard (2004, p. 60) notes that "political leaderships in all of these countries faced the problem of how to mobilize resources under political circumstances that were highly uncertain." Institutions like *chaebols* can be viewed as resolving commitment problems between the state and the private sector. These institutions diverged from those in the West and opened the tiger economies up to charges of cronyism and corruption. But they also served an important function by restraining predatory instincts of rulers.

To appreciate the importance of institutions in the East Asian success story, it is informative to contrast it with the ultimate failure of the Eastern Bloc economies in the same period. Eastern Bloc economies were able to achieve fairly rapid growth initially. The state played a key role in mobilizing resources; it forced savings to rise rapidly and encouraged industrialization. The problems began once this initial period of recovery from World War II passed (Eichengreen, 2007). Without a developed market, producers lacked the incentives to produce goods that consumers wanted to buy. Inefficiencies within the system accumulated. Incentive problems within firms' bureaucracies grew worse over time, creating more opportunities for rent-seeking.

Other factors mattered as well. In East Asia, cultural norms influenced by the Chinese Confucian ideal of an educated ruling class favored investment in human capital. Demographic factors also mattered. As they invested heavily in human capital, East Asian societies rapidly underwent a demographic transition. Average annual population growth in South Korea slowed from 2.6% in the 1960s to 1.1% in the 1980s. In Hong Kong it fell from 2.5% to 1.4% in the same period. This gave a one-off boost to recorded growth rates – though it also means that these societies may run into adverse demographic headwinds in the future. Meanwhile, population growth was stable in South America and growing rapidly in sub-Saharan Africa. In the Asian tiger economies, family sizes shrank as households moved from large families to small households with highly educated children.

To what extent is the East Asian Tigers' success replicable? China was able to replicate many aspects of the East Asian economic model after its disastrous experience with Communism, albeit on a much larger scale. However, for countries in other parts of the world with different histories, cultures, and geographies, the lessons from the East Asian miracle may be more limited.

How China Is Becoming Rich

One enduring puzzle in the history of economic growth is why China did not industrialize first. During the height of the Song dynasty (960–1279), China was much richer than even the wealthiest parts of Europe. Yet by 1850, Chinese per capita GDP was one-fifth that of England (Broadberry, Guan, and Li, 2018). This gap would greatly expand over the subsequent century. What happened? Why did China not undergo an Industrial Revolution first?

These are not the only questions that must be answered. In the past forty years, the Chinese economy has grown at a break-neck speed. After decades of mismanagement, famine, and persecution by Communist rule produced mass impoverishment, the growth of the last four decades has lifted around *one billion* Chinese citizens out of dire poverty. As recently as 1990, 66.2% of Chinese were earning less than $1.90 per day, and 98.3% of the population made less than $5.50 per day (World Bank, 2020b). In a country of around 1.5 billion people, these numbers are staggering.

China has become much wealthier in the last few decades. As of 2016, only 0.5% of the population made less than $1.90 per day and 23.9% made less than $5.50 per day (World Bank, 2020b). Per capita GDP has risen from $71 in 1962 (around $0.20 per day) to $10,262 in 2019 (see Figure 10.6). This is one of the great human triumphs of our lifetime. Over one billion people have been lifted out of the most extreme poverty in China alone. There is still work to be done, of course. But this should not make us lose sight of what an achievement this is. How did it happen?

First, we need to tackle the mystery of why China did not become rich first. While there is much evidence that the economic peak of the pre-modern

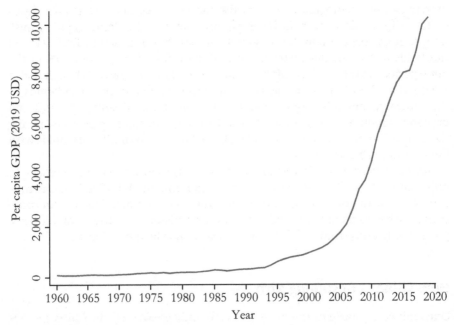

Figure 10.6 Chinese per capita GDP, 1960–2019

Data source: World Bank (2020b).

Chinese empire was in the Song dynasty, recent scholarship focuses on the last imperial Chinese dynasty – the Qing dynasty – who ruled China from 1644 to 1912. During the first 150 years of Qing rule, China reached its greatest geographic extent and experienced a remarkable boom in population. According to Glahn (2016, p. 322) this "boom of the eighteenth century rested on a foundation of steady growth in population and agricultural output" and represented "the maturation of the market economy."

Pomeranz (2000) suggested that around 1750 there was little to distinguish the economy of Europe from that of China. According to this argument, the divergence between China and the West has to be explained in terms of factors that became relevant *after* 1750. Subsequent scholarship does not support this claim, as we shall see, but it was indeed the case that in many respects Qing China had institutions that looked favorable for economic growth.

Consider Adam Smith's statement that little else is required for economic growth "but peace, easy taxes, and a tolerable administration of justice; all the rest being brought about by the natural course of things" (Stewart, 1793/1980, p. 322). China in the 18th century certainly had the first two ingredients for growth and arguably had the third ingredient too.

First, China was a large unified state. Though it has been divided on many occasions, its longevity as a centralized state is in fact unique (Ko and Sng, 2013; Ko, Koyama, and Sng, 2018). From 1683 to 1796, Qing China enjoyed a long period of internal peace. The only wars were on the frontiers against nomadic peoples. In contrast, European states were frequently at war, as we discussed in Chapter 3. The sheer size of China and high degree of political centralization also facilitated market integration. As we noted in Chapter 2, Northern and Southern China were connected via the Grand Canal over 1,000 years ago. This connected markets for grain and other goods. By the 18th century, the Grand Canal was supplying Beijing with almost 1 million tonnes of rice annually (Glahn, 2016, p. 332). And as we saw in Chapter 8, China and parts of Western Europe had comparable levels of market integration around 1750 (Shiue and Keller, 2007), although Chinese market integration appears to have declined thereafter (Bernhofen, Li, Eberhardt, and Morgan, 2020).

Second, taxes were low in Qing China. In contrast to Europe, which saw a dramatic rise in fiscal extractions by the state between 1500 and 1800, in China the tax burden fell over time. The Qing imposed lower taxes than previous Chinese dynasties, and the per capita tax rate fell further during the 18th century (Sng, 2014). The central state did not regulate the economy. Merchants, organized through guilds, regulated commercial affairs at a local level.

On Smith's final point (the importance of a tolerable administration of justice), China was governed by a large, meritocratic bureaucracy. Contemporaries in 18th- and early 19th-century Europe saw this institution as ensuring fair and impartial government. They contrasted it to European governments, which were staffed with individuals appointed through patronage or through the sale of offices. Voltaire, for instance, celebrated the examination system as a form of impartial and benign government (yü Têng, 1943). In fact, the Chinese examination system was the model for the introduction of professional bureaucracies in England and later the US. Overall, the Chinese state provided more public goods and was less intrusive than its European counterparts (Wong, 1997, 2012). Certainly, by pre-modern standards, Chinese institutions provided something approximating a tolerable administration of justice. Over time, however, there is evidence of increasing corruption (Sng, 2014).

Despite these apparent advantages, rather than experiencing sustained economic growth after 1750, China went into decline. A series of peasant rebellions, culminating in the Taiping Rebellion of 1850–64, left millions dead. Defeated by Britain in the Opium Wars (1839–42 and 1856–60), China was forced to cede Hong Kong and to allow Western colonial powers to establish trading posts within the empire.

There are numerous proximate causes of this collapse. These include political failure by Qing elites and a Malthusian crisis brought about by a rapidly growing population and limited ecological resources. But the deeper cause was the absence of sustained innovation. The reasons for this were institutional and cultural. As documented by Needham (1995), China had been the most technologically innovative part of the world for centuries prior to 1500. But this was no longer the case by the 18th century.

One reason for this was China's political institutions. The emperor was relatively unconstrained in contrast to Western Europe, where cities had autonomy and parliaments contested the sovereign's rule. More important still was Europe's fragmentation. Although it meant costly barriers to trade and frequent conflict, fragmentation ensured that there was a considerable degree of competition in the system (Scheidel, 2019). As we discussed in Chapter 8, it was this fragmentation that allowed goods and people to relocate to more favorable environments. Such freedoms were absent in imperial China.

Moreover, while the imperial bureaucracy was meritocratic, it was subject to imperial discretion (Brandt, Ma, and Rawski, 2014, p. 74). This meant that bureaucratic agents were disincentivized to do their jobs "too well." If they did, the central government could crack down on them at any moment. It would be all the more likely to do so if the bureaucrat were wealthy or independent (Ma and Rubin, 2019). China was governed by a centralized, hierarchical, hub-and-spoke network with the emperor at the center. This hub-and-spoke structure was an efficient way of organizing a large and far-flung empire, but it impeded the flow of information between different nodes, discouraged innovation, and made the entire empire vulnerable to system-wide collapse (Root, 2020).

These centralizing and autocratic tendencies were strengthened in the 17th and 18th centuries, at a time when representative institutions were on the rise in Western Europe. Unsure of their own political legitimacy, the Qing rulers of China governed more autocratically. One particularly pernicious set of policies they implemented were the "literary inquisitions," which cracked down on possible sources of dissent while promoting a narrow and traditional understanding of China's intellectual history (Xue, 2021).

For these reasons, the Qing institutional and cultural environment was not conducive to innovation. While the imperial examination system encouraged investment in human capital, it tended to reproduce existing knowledge. The brightest students had an incentive to pursue Confucian education, which had little practical application to science or technology (Huff, 1993; Lin, 1995). Such cultural norms may not have been as big of an issue under the Song, who actively encouraged innovation, but they became a binding constraint under the Qing dynasty. The importance of these norms meant that even when the central government attempted reforms akin to the Meiji Reforms – the so-called Self-Strengthening Movement (1860–94) – they did so in a Confucian context. Practical education was largely eschewed in favor of the old classics. This is summarized by the famous formula: "Chinese learning as the basis; Western learning for practical use" (Wright, 1957, p. 1).

The lack of competition or a forum that encouraged innovation ultimately impeded anything like the Scientific Revolution or Enlightenment from occurring in China. As Mokyr (2016, p. 318) puts it, despite being highly centralized and sharing a single written language and literary culture, "China paradoxically lacked a single unifying coordinating mechanism such as a competitive market in which new ideas were tested." Hence, a combination of centralized political institutions and a culture favoring the Confucian classics over what Mokyr (2002) calls "useful knowledge" were jointly responsible for stifling Chinese innovation in the centuries prior to the Industrial Revolution. Nevertheless, to speak of a Chinese failure here is misguided. As Mokyr (2016, p. 338) notes, "[W]hat is exceptional, indeed unique, is what happened in eighteenth-century Europe."

It is important to recognize that these factors did not act in isolation. They interacted with one another. For instance, consider the clan-based nature of Chinese families. As we discussed in Chapter 4, kin-based cultures have certain advantages and disadvantages over individualistic cultures. On the one hand, kin-based cultures have a larger safety net. The "clan" tends to provide such insurance. However, this comes at the cost of institutional development. In medieval Western Europe, societies were forced to form corporations that provided mutual aid. These included guilds, communes, and business associations. Such institutions were unnecessary in China, where the clan provided mutual aid (Greif and Tabellini, 2017). A similar logic explains why banking and finance first emerged in the West. In the absence of the clan, there was a greater need for interpersonal risk sharing and resource pooling. Such needs were much less pronounced in China, since the clan mitigated these risks. As a result, there was less need for banking and finance (Chen, Ma, and Sinclair, forthcoming).

The clan-based nature of Chinese families also played a role in the country's demography. Until the one-child policy was introduced in 1979, China had a high birth rate. Early marriage and a multi-generational family system in which newly married couples moved into the paternal home allowed women to marry early and kept fertility rates high. Much of Chinese history is consistent with a Malthusian perspective, as discussed in Chapter 5. The dominant features were high birth rates, high death rates, and little long-run change in per capita income. This framework helps explain why China remained poor despite being a world technological leader for most of the medieval period. All of those advancements resulted in more people, not more wealth per person. For instance, while the total amount of cultivated land more than tripled between 1400 and 1913, the total population more than *quintupled* from 65 to 80 million in 1400 to 430 million in 1913 (Brandt, Ma, and Rawski, 2014, p. 52).

If institutions, culture, and demography are in part responsible for China never fulfilling its technological promise, what role did these factors play in explaining why the country has been able to grow rapidly in the past four decades? It is this important question we turn to next. The Chinese miracle is remarkable: nearly one billion people have been taken out of extreme poverty within the span of our lifetime. How did this happen? Do the factors highlighted in this book shed any light on China's rise?

China has remained an autocracy despite the vicissitudes that it experienced following its defeat in the Opium Wars and the fall of the Qing dynasty. The Republican period (1912–49) saw the first sustained local efforts at statebuilding and industrialization. Between 1912 and 1936, Chinese industrial output grew at a faster rate than Japan, India, or Russia/the USSR (Brandt, Ma, and Rawski, 2017, p. 198). One achievement of the Communist period (1949–) was to build on this and to successfully construct a modern centralized state. But this came at a tremendous human cost. The Communist period saw forced collectivization of agriculture and a series of Five-Year Plans culminating in the disastrous Great Leap Forward (1958–62). The resulting famine was the direct consequence of Communist policies.

What happened next illustrates one of the costs of moving away from a market economy. In a market economy, the pace of industrialization was constrained by the productivity of agriculture. If too many workers were drawn into the cities to work in factories, demand for foodstuffs would increase and grain in the fields would go unharvested. The scissors of supply and demand would drive prices up, slowing the pace of industrialization.

Mao and his advisors believed they could accelerate this process by bypassing the market mechanism. Specifically, they thought that peasants were inefficiently cultivating small plots of land or not using the latest fertilizers. They also suspected that peasants were hoarding grain in the hope of profit. Collectivization was thus seen as a means both to greatly increase production and to render the resulting food surplus legible to the state, which could easily collect and transport it to feed the urban population. The Great Leap Forward was thus a misguided attempt to jump-start industrialization.

Regardless of the personal culpability of Mao, it was the broader political system, one characterized by a lack of checks and balances, that was crucial in magnifying the scale of the tragedy. At the heart of the famine were over-optimistic estimates of grain production. This was in large part due to local bureaucrats having a systematic incentive to inflate estimates. On top of this, highly inflexible procurement and an unwillingness of political elites to recognize the problem led to disaster. Local cadres used extreme violence to enforce their quotas. Peasants accused of hiding food or of shirking were beaten and sometimes killed. Collectivization saw productivity plummet as the tacit knowledge peasant farmers had of their local soils was lost when they were herded into collective farms. In fact, the famine was most severe in areas where agricultural productivity had been the highest (Meng, Qian, and Yared, 2015). Meanwhile, news of mass starvation was covered up. The numbers who died during the Great Famine are debated. Plausible estimates range from around 15 to 45 million (Ó Gráda, 2015, pp. 130–73). Even at the more conservative estimates of 20–30 million dead, this manmade famine ranks among the most destructive episodes in human history.

An important lesson of this book is that political institutions are a key reason why economically beneficial policies are often ignored while economically destructive policies are pursued. The fact that China was ruled by an autocratic and highly centralized state made these policy disasters not only possible but also likely. The disasters of the Great Leap Forward and the Great Famine were followed by the Cultural Revolution, during which (according to conservative estimates) 750,000–1,500,000 people died. While the Chinese Communist Party had been successful in unifying the country and investing in basic education and healthcare, the result of the Great Leap Forward and the Great Famine was that by the 1970s China was one of the poorest places on the earth. Yet, the autocratic and highly centralized nature of Communist rule also enabled the country to successfully reverse course under Deng Xiaoping, the Chinese leader who initiated market-oriented reforms in 1979.

We have highlighted in this book the importance of constraints on executive power in promoting growth. In the case of the East Asian Tigers, constraints were not formally part of the political system. The Tigers benefited from being small. This meant that private enterprise was able to constrain the government's autocratic tendencies. But this was not the case for China. The Chinese central government remained exceedingly powerful relative to other important organizations and people. Yet, China still modernized its economy and escaped poverty. Can the features we have highlighted in this book account for this feat?

Much like Japan and the East Asian Tigers, China did not need to reinvent the wheel of industrialization or the modern economy. It could borrow industrial inputs and managerial know-how from abroad via opening up to foreign direct investment. Tremendous under-utilized economic potential had clearly been there for decades prior to the reforms of the late 1970s. With over one billion people languishing in subsistence farming, China was an obvious source of low-wage labor. But a large labor force was hardly the only or most important factor in Chinese growth. After all, such a labor force existed prior to the 1980s, and surplus labor has long been a characteristic of developing economies.

China's economic reforms can be divided into two periods: early reforms between 1978 and 1995 and post-1995 reforms (Brandt, Ma, and Rawski, 2017). The first set of reforms dismantled many aspects of the command economy. Agriculture had been gravely damaged by collectivization and the misguided attempt to industrialize rural areas. In the late 1970s, these policies began to be reversed. Among the first reforms was the revival of household farming. Grain output rose by nearly one-third between 1978 and 1984 (Brandt, Ma, and Rawski, 2014, p. 96). Importantly, these increases in agricultural productivity freed up hundreds of millions of workers to move into industrial labor.

The post-1995 reforms involved widespread privatization. The state's share of industrial output declined from almost 50% in 1995 to 24% in 2008. There was also an expansion in legal protection for private enterprise. There was no rule of law in pre-reform China. As a market economy was introduced, a corresponding legal system had to be developed. One important development was the adoption of elements of German civil law such as the right for private citizens to sue the government (Fukuyama, 2014, p. 364). Despite Communist opposition to private property rights, reforms were able to create

> a set of usufructuary (usage) rights that could be bought, sold, mortgaged, or transferred, in which the state nonetheless retained formal ownership. Thus, in China's booming real estate market, no one technically "owns" an apartment or house. One owns the equivalent of a lease whose term extends up to seventy years, which is acquired in exchange for land-use fees. (Fukuyama, 2014, p. 366)

China did not adopt Western institutions wholesale. Rather, relatively minor moves towards greater rule of law were sufficient to induce a radical transformation of its economy and society.

As with other East Asian economies, another aspect of China's rise was its increased openness to global trade. The establishment of economic zones encouraged foreign direct investment into the country. Given how far behind China was from the world's economic frontier and how low its wages were, there were tremendous opportunities for catch-up growth. Once China rejoined the global economy, its trade ratio rose from 9.7% to 31.9% between 1978 and 1993 (Brandt, Ma, and Rawski, 2014, p. 98). Foreign investment poured in and state enterprises were made more efficient. Growth accelerated in the 1990s and 2000s, driven by reforms that restructured the bloated public sector. Chinese growth has slowed since the early 2000s (when growth was around 10% per year; it is now around 6–7%), but this is precisely what a model of catch-up growth would predict.

That is what happened. But how did it happen? How did such rapid growth occur under an autocratic government? Two features of China's history are important for understanding its modern growth. The first is institutional.

Although the Chinese emperor historically faced few constraints, one difference between the way that the Chinese and Europeans legitimated political rule was that, for the Chinese, good rule meant legitimate rule. A good Chinese emperor was viewed as having the "Mandate of Heaven." If he were overthrown or responded poorly to a crisis, it was a sign that he did not have the Mandate.

This principle continues to hold influence for legitimating Communist rule today, even if in a different guise. After the death of Mao in 1976, whose legitimacy was tied to his role as the founding father of the People's Republic of China, the Chinese leadership faced a legitimacy deficit. Not only did none of the potential successors to Mao have a personal history like his, but there was internal turmoil over who would lead. Given this legitimacy deficit, Deng Xiaoping, who led China from 1978 to 1989, turned to "good rule means legitimate rule." This helped solve many of the issues associated with unconstrained governance. Even though the state could have infringed on the rights of its citizens at any time – and it certainly did, and continues to today, especially its ethnic and religious minorities – doing so in a way that would have undermined economic growth would have also undermined the legitimacy of the ruling Communist Party. As China has remained highly centralized and autocratic, there is always a possibility of the current economic policies being reversed. And indeed, under Xi Jinping's presidency since 2013 there has been both a strengthening of autocracy and a move away from the market. China has not escaped from the "bad emperor problem."

Another historical feature that has contributed to China's growth has to do with its culture. Like Japan and other East Asian countries, literacy was relatively high in pre-modern China. This was a product of a culture that viewed education as a means of rising economically and socially. Although historically education was confined to the Confucian classics, this type of education became less important after the dismantling of the old Chinese bureaucracy in 1905. But the emphasis on education remained, especially in those places where it was important in the past. In fact, places that produced more top-level bureaucrats in the imperial period still have much higher levels of educational attainment today (Chen, Kung, and Ma, 2020). This legacy of high educational attainment is likely one reason that Chinese economic success has not petered out (Brandt, Ma, and Rawski, 2014).

This section glosses over numerous aspects of Chinese history and its recent rise. Yet, much like the other cases considered in this chapter, it reveals both the potential and the limits of using lessons from history to understand why poor parts of the world can become rich. China has become relatively rich without having many of the attributes of 18th-century England or the 19th-century US. Above all, it has had few constraints on governance. Yet, those histories point us to what might matter for economic growth to occur. Institutions are of critical importance. But we also are limited in our knowledge of which institutions matter. When China abandoned command and control, it also defied the policy consensus of the 1990s (known as the Washington Consensus) which emphasized privatization and deregulation (Weber, 2021). Yet, China's pace of economic growth was faster than those countries that adopted what were perceived to be best-practice policies.

The appropriate institutional reforms will always be context-dependent and politically constrained. This is one of the key takeaways from this book. What worked to make some parts of the world rich worked in a certain cultural, historical, and institutional context. We can learn from this past, but we should not be wedded to it.

Chapter Summary

The advent of modern economic growth created tremendous opportunities for catch-up growth. But these opportunities were difficult to grasp. Not all societies were able to benefit from them.

Some were colonies and hence unable to implement independent economic policies. Others had factor endowments that were unsuited for the labor-saving, capital-intensive technologies produced by countries on the technological frontier. Still others had institutions that repressed entrepreneurship and markets. The kinds of political institutions that had for centuries governed the agrarian empires of Eurasia were not suited for the new environment in which rapid technological change was possible.

For these reasons, while the global economy greatly expanded after 1800 and technological innovations diffused across the world, the pace of growth was uneven. India and much of Africa remained Malthusian economies. Total GDP increased tremendously in these countries, but it was almost all absorbed into population growth. Per capita income remained close to subsistence.

Outside Europe or settler colonies like Argentina, Australia, and New Zealand that were land- and resource-abundant and underpopulated, in the middle of the 19th century there was little sign of sustained growth in per capita income. The first non-Western country to achieve rapid economic growth was Japan. This was predicated on a change in political institutions and, in the absence of natural resources or abundant farmland, was initially based on Japan's successful entry into international textile markets. Later, Japanese firms moved into iron, steel, and manufacturing. The path pioneered by Japan could be followed by other East Asian countries with similar factor endowments such as South Korea, Taiwan, Singapore, and Hong Kong. Later, following an experiment with Communist central planning, a version of it could implemented on a much larger scale (and with a much greater role of government and state-owned firms) by China.

In many respects, these developments have contributed more to the world becoming rich than anything that happened in England or the US. The countries that became rich first hold a relatively small share of the world's population. For the world to become rich, it was necessary for those riches to spread to more populated places. First and foremost this meant Asia, which holds around 60% of the world's population. There is still a long way to go. But the developments summarized in this chapter give reason for optimism that soon the whole world will indeed be rich.

11

The World Is Rich

The world is richer than it has ever been. It is likely to continue to become richer for the foreseeable future. The world becoming richer means that more and more of humanity can be lifted from dire poverty. Riches free human minds to concentrate on pursuits besides acquiring the basic necessities of life. Riches allow us to live longer and healthier lives and provide us with material comforts that our ancestors could have only dreamed of. In the 2020s, we will reach a point where basic comforts are available to a large fraction of the world's population – although certainly not everyone. This achievement deserves to both be celebrated and understood.

We still have a long way to go. While over a billion people have been lifted out of poverty just in our lifetime, around a billion people still live in abject poverty. Many of these people live in sub-Saharan Africa, although many others live in Latin America, Central Asia, South Asia, and Southeast Asia. Lifting these people out of poverty is one of the most important things the next generation of humans can do. But how can this be achieved?

Understanding where wealth comes from helps us lift more people out of poverty. This is why we wrote this book. The literature in economics and economic history has provided many answers to these questions in recent years, but until now there has not been one place where interested readers could go to get an understanding of these various theories. Nor do most existing accounts seriously consider the interactions between their proposed explanation and other theories. The goal of this book is to do both. In the first part of the book, we provided an overview of the primary explanations for "how the world became rich." We discussed theories focusing on geography, institutions, culture, demography, and colonization. As we were writing these chapters, we realized just how hard it is to discuss these theories in isolation. How do you talk about institutions without considering the effect of culture, or how they are shaped by geography? Is demography really independent of institutions? Can we really silo off colonization as if it existed independent of the various attributes of the colonizing and colonized countries?

This is why, in the second part of the book, we drew these theories together to explain why the first place to achieve sustained economic growth – Britain – did so. Of course, this required explaining some of the peculiarities of British history. But we were also able to use this history to understand *what* preconditions mattered for Britain's industrialization and *why* they mattered. Both of these are important. The "what" matters because it provides insights into the preconditions that might generally be necessary for sustained economic growth. The "why" matters because it gives insight into what might have been particular about Britain and thus not necessary in other contexts.

Going beyond Britain, as we do in Chapters 9 and 10, has led us to a few key insights. Once the initial breakthrough to sustained economic growth had taken place, the path was open for other countries to achieve catch-up growth. Certain institutions, particularly those that encouraged innovation and entrepreneurship and allowed for the free-flowing of ideas, may have been less important for countries catching up to the frontier (as opposed to those on the frontier).

Markets are also crucial for sustained economic growth. Textbook economics often focuses on the efficiency properties of markets: the principle that in a competitive market, prices will be bid down to marginal cost so that there is no deadweight loss. But from a long-run perspective, what matters more is that markets provide incentives for innovation. Growth episodes like the Industrial Revolution were not planned by policy-makers. They resulted from an untold number of decisions by private individuals to experiment with new production methods or to build new factories or to mechanize production. Command economies are also capable of growth. In the short run, they can grow faster than market economies because policy-makers can use coercion to mobilize resources. This occurred in the Soviet Union under Stalin and in Eastern Europe after World War II. But sheer labor power and investment eventually run into diminishing returns if there is no innovation and there are no markets to coordinate investment decisions. And while command economies like the Soviet Union excelled at military innovation, they were abysmal at providing new goods that consumers actually wanted to buy.

Market do not operate in a vacuum. As Adam Smith understood, the proposition that self-interest or market forces have beneficial outcomes is conditional on the appropriate institutional environment. For this reason, we have placed considerable emphasis on institutions throughout this book. But institutions cannot be viewed in isolation. A society's institutional environment *interacts* with other variables. This means that the outcomes associated with certain institutional environments will be context-specific. For example, the institutional reforms that led China to escape extreme poverty in the 1980s were quite minor: they involved restoring private production in agriculture, the creation of special economic zones, and the abandonment of central planning. At no time did the Chinese Communist Party contemplate the introduction of genuine representative institutions or formal constraints on the state. The important point is that this liberalization occurred at a point in time when rapid convergence to the economic frontier was possible. Even relatively minor institutional changes had huge payoffs as China was able to become the world's low-cost producer of manufactured goods.

Institutions also interact with culture. By culture, recall that we mean the conceptual lens or heuristics individuals in a society use to interpret the world. Sustained economic growth may have been possible in the ancient world. Certainly, the Roman Empire at its height had an integrated and sophisticated market economy. Yet, one reason it never achieved anything close to an "industrial revolution" appears to have been cultural. Successful individuals in the Roman Empire aspired to a life of leisure. In contrast, consider the case of Britain that we surveyed in Chapters 7 and 8. Britain had many of the institutional prerequisites needed for take-off by the mid-18th century: relatively limited government, an apprenticeship system that honed the skills of craftsmen, and institutions favoring investment in public goods. But it also had cultural attributes that complemented these institutions. Hard work did not place someone at the bottom of the social scale. Among the intellectual elite, the idea of continued progress seemed like a realistic and worthwhile goal. These cultural attributes were not unique to Britain. They were shared with parts of continental Europe, and many non-European societies had some of these attributes at some point in their history. But no society, at least prior to the mid-18th century, had the combination of these cultural attributes and institutional characteristics.

Once the key elements of sustained growth emerged, first during Britain's Industrial Revolution, and then more decisively after 1850, elements of the blueprint provided by the early developers could be used elsewhere, even if it looked a bit different depending on the location. In Chapter 10, we showed how different parts of the world took pieces of that blueprint and adapted them to their own institutional and cultural characteristics. In some cases, such as Meiji Japan, this required a wholesale institutional change. In other cases, such as late 20th-century China, pieces of the blueprint were adapted to the local institutional and cultural context.

This is what makes the problem of economic development in the poorest parts of the world so vexing. There is no silver bullet. We know what has worked in various historical contexts. But merely transplanting what worked elsewhere to poverty-stricken societies isn't the solution. Context matters. Culture and the historical past matter. So do demography and geography.

Of course, this does not mean that bringing wealth to the world's poorest is a lost cause. Knowing what did work and why it worked matters precisely because it allows us to build a cumulative body of knowledge. This, in turn, helps provide a framework for understanding what economic policies are likely to succeed. It will take substantial local knowledge to know how to apply this framework to a given society. Which parts can be used and which can be discarded? While the answer is always "it depends," this knowledge is still vital to even know where to begin.

Although this book has almost exclusively focused on the positive side of the world becoming rich (with the obvious exception of colonization), we are aware of the downsides. Foremost among these is climate change. Industrialization saw a massive rise in the use of fossil fuels, which polluted many parts of the world and contributed to the heating of the earth. If the current pace of global warming continues (or even continues to rise at a slower pace), all of the economic advancements highlighted in this book might have been for naught. We cannot enjoy the fruits of prosperity if we have killed the ecosystems necessary for human life on earth.

But there is reason for hope on this front too, and it is related to global prosperity. On the one hand, as countries industrialize and consumption rises, they initially tend to pollute more. Not only do these countries have more factories, but people drive more automobiles and eat more meat (which contributes much more to environmental degradation than plant agriculture). On the other hand, they also have more resources to combat deforestation and to invest in mitigation. Many of the richest countries today have reduced their levels of pollution in recent decades.

Moreover, if humanity is going to survive a changing climate, the answer will likely lie in technological progress. Whether this means technologies that allow for clean energy production, carbon capture, or something else, we cannot say. And it is not just that we are not experts. In reality, it is likely that nobody knows what yet-to-be discovered technologies will help alleviate climate change. But this is one of the most important reasons why prosperity is so important. When human brain power can be used for solving the most pressing issues of the day rather than focusing on where one's next meal is coming from, the odds of technological progress are much greater. Freeing up a few billion minds to help solve these problems is probably our best hope. So, while modern economic growth may have been a leading cause of climate change, it is also at the center of the solution.

We hope this book has given you some insight into how the world became rich. We also hope it gives you a better appreciation of just how important understanding history is for modern problems. It is not so much that history repeats itself. It is that we can learn so much from history – what worked, why it worked, and in what context it worked. The blueprints of the past contain much valuable information. While it is not always obvious how to use that information – if it can be used at all – it is one of the most valuable resources we have for making the world a better place.

References

Acemoglu, Daron, Davide Cantoni, Simon Johnson, and James A. Robinson. 2011. "The Consequences of Radical Reform: The French Revolution." *American Economic Review* 101(7): 3286–307.

Acemoglu, Daron and Simon Johnson. 2007. "Disease and Development: The Effect of Life Expectancy on Economic Growth." *Journal of Political Economy* 115(6): 925–85.

Acemoglu, Daron, Simon Johnson, and James A. Robinson. 2001. "The Colonial Origins of Comparative Development: An Empirical Investigation." *American Economic Review* 91(5): 1369–401.

Acemoglu, Daron, Simon Johnson, and James A. Robinson. 2002. "Reversal of Fortune: Geography and Institutions in the Making of the Modern World Income Distribution." *Quarterly Journal of Economics* 117(4): 1231–94.

Acemoglu, Daron, Simon Johnson, and James A. Robinson. 2005a. "Institutions as a Fundamental Cause of Long-run Growth." In *Handbook of Economic Growth*, Vol. 1, ed. Philippe Aghion and Steven Durlauf. Amsterdam: Elsevier, pp. 385–472.

Acemoglu, Daron, Simon Johnson, and James A. Robinson. 2005b. "The Rise of Europe: Atlantic Trade, Institutional Change, and Economic Growth." *American Economic Review* 95(3): 546–79.

Acemoglu, Daron and James A. Robinson. 2006. *The Economic Origins of Dictatorship and Democracy*. New York: Cambridge University Press.

Acemoglu, Daron and James A. Robinson. 2012a. "The Big Mis-forecast." http://whynations fail.com/blog/2012/4/6/the-big-mis-forecast.html.

Acemoglu, Daron and James A. Robinson. 2012b. *Why Nations Fail*. New York: Crown Business.

Acemoglu, Daron and James A. Robinson. 2019. *The Narrow Corridor: States, Society, and the Fate of Liberty*. New York: Penguin.

Acemoglu, Daron and Alexander Wolitzky. 2011. "The Economics of Labor Coercion." *Econometrica* 79(2): 555–601.

Akçomak, İ Semih, Dinand Webbink, and Bas ter Weel. 2016. "Why did the Netherlands Develop So Early? The Legacy of the Brethren of the Common Life." *Economic Journal* 126(593): 821–60.

Alesina, Alberto and Paola Giuliano. 2015. "Culture and Institutions." *Journal of Economic Literature* 53(4): 898–944.

Alesina, Alberto, Paola Giuliano, and Nathan Nunn. 2013. "On the Origins of Gender Roles: Women and the Plough." *Quarterly Journal of Economics* 128(2): 469–530.

Allen, Robert C. 1992. *Enclosure and the Yeoman*. Oxford: Clarendon Press.

Allen, Robert C. 1994. "Agriculture during the Industrial Revolution." In *The Economic History of Britain since 1700*, ed. Roderick Floud and Donald McCloskey. Cambridge: Cambridge University Press, pp. 96–122.

Allen, Robert C. 2001. "The Great Divergence in European Wages and Prices from the Middle Ages to the First World War." *Explorations in Economic History* 38(4): 411–47.

Allen, Robert C. 2009a. *The British Industrial Revolution in Global Perspective*. Cambridge: Cambridge University Press.

Allen, Robert C. 2009b. "Engels' Pause: Technical Change, Capital Accumulation, and Inequality in the British Industrial Revolution." *Explorations in Economic History* 46(4): 418–35.

Allen, Robert C. 2011a. *Global Economic History: A Very Short Introduction*. Oxford: Oxford University Press.

Allen, Robert C. 2011b. "Why the Industrial Revolution Was British: Commerce, Induced Invention, and the Scientific Revolution." *Economic History Review* 64(2): 357–84.

Allen, Robert C. 2014. "American Exceptionalism as a Problem in Global History." *Journal of Economic History* 74(2): 309–50.

Allen, Robert C., Jean-Pascal Bassino, Debin Ma, Christine Moll-Murata, and Jan Luiten van Zanden. 2011. "Wages, Prices, and Living Standards in China, 1738-1925: In Comparison with Europe, Japan, and India." *Economic History Review* 64(1): 8–38.

Allen, Robert C. and Jacob Louis Weisdorf. 2011. "Was There an 'Industrious Revolution' before the Industrial Revolution? An Empirical Exercise for England, c. 1300–1830." *Economic History Review* 64(3): 715–29.

Alsan, Marcella. 2015. "The Effect of the TseTse Fly on African Development." *American Economic Review* 105(1): 382–410.

Andersen, Thomas Barnebeck, Jeanet Bentzen, Carl-Johan Dalgaard, and Paul Sharp. 2017. "Pre-Reformation Roots of the Protestant Ethic." *Economic Journal* 127(604): 1756–93.

Anderson, Gary M. and Peter J. Boettke. 1997. "Soviet Venality: A Rent-seeking Model of the Communist State." *Public Choice* 93(1–2): 37–53.

Anderson, R. Warren, Noel D. Johnson, and Mark Koyama. 2017. "Jewish Persecutions and Weather Shocks, 1100–1800." *Economic Journal* 127(602): 924–58.

Appleby, Joyce. 2010. *The Relentless Revolution: A History of Capitalism*. New York: W.W. Norton & Company.

Arrow, Kenneth J. 1972. "Gifts and Exchanges." *Philosophy and Public Affairs* 1(4): 343–62.

Arruñada, Benito. 2016. "How Rome Enabled Impersonal Markets." *Explorations in Economic History* 61(1): 68–84.

Arteaga, Fernando, Desiree A. Desierto, and Mark Koyama. 2020. "Shipwrecked by Rents." CEPR Discussion Paper 15300.

Ashraf, Quamrul and Oded Galor. 2011. "Dynamics and Stagnation in the Malthusian Epoch." *American Economic Review* 101(5): 2003–41.

Bai, Ying and James Kai-sing Kung. 2011. "Climate Shocks and Sino-nomadic Conflict." *Review of Economics and Statistics* 93(3): 970–81.

Bai, Ying and James Kai-sing Kung. 2015. "Diffusing Knowledge while Spreading God's Message: Protestantism and Economic Prosperity in China, 1840–1920." *Journal of the European Economic Association* 13(4): 669–98.

Bailey, Mark. 2014. *The Decline of Serfdom in Late Medieval England: From Bondage to Freedom*. Woodbridge: Boydell & Brewer.

Ball, Philip. 2017. *The Water Kingdom: A Secret History of China*. Chicago: University of Chicago Press.

Balla, Eliana and Noel D. Johnson. 2009. "Fiscal Crisis and Institutional Change in the Ottoman Empire and France." *Journal of Economic History* 69(3): 809–45.

Banerjee, Abhijit and Lakshmi Iyer. 2005. "History, Institutions, and Economic Performance: The Legacy of Colonial Land Tenure Systems in India." *American Economic Review* 95(4): 1190–213.

Banfield, Edward C. 1958. *The Moral Basis of a Backward Society*. New York: Free Press.

Bateman, Victoria N. 2011. "The Evolution of Markets in Early Modern Europe, 1350–1800: A Study of Wheat Prices." *Economic History Review* 64(2): 447–71.

Bateman, Victoria N. 2012. *Markets and Growth in Early Modern Europe*. London: Pickering & Chatto.

Bates, Robert H. 1981. *Markets and States in Tropical Africa*. Berkeley: University of California Press.

Bazzi, Samuel, Martin Fiszbein, and Mesay Gebresilasse. 2020. "Frontier Culture: The Roots and Persistence of 'Rugged Individualism' in the United States." *Econometrica* 88(6): 2329–68.

Becker, Gary S. and H. Gregg Lewis. 1973. "On the Interaction between the Quantity and Quality of Children." *Journal of Political Economy* 81(2, Part 2): S279–88.

Becker, Gary S., Tomas J. Philipson, and Rodrigo R. Soares. 2005. "The Quantity and Quality of Life and the Evolution of World Inequality." *American Economic Review* 95(1): 277–91.

Becker, Sascha O., Katrin Boeckh, Christa Hainz, and Ludger Woessmann. 2016. "The Empire Is Dead, Long Live the Empire! Long-run Persistence of Trust and Corruption in the Bureaucracy." *Economic Journal* 126(590): 40–74.

Becker, Sascha O., Erik Hornung, and Ludger Woessmann. 2011. "Education and Catch-up in the Industrial Revolution." *American Economic Journal: Macroeconomics* 3(3): 92–126.

Becker, Sascha O. and Ludger Woessmann. 2008. "Luther and the Girls: Religious Denomination and the Female Education Gap in Nineteenth-century Prussia." *Scandinavian Journal of Economics* 110(4): 777–805.

Becker, Sascha O. and Ludger Woessmann. 2009. "Was Weber Wrong? A Human Capital Theory of Protestant Economic History." *Quarterly Journal of Economics* 124(2): 531–96.

Beckert, Sven. 2014. *Empire of Cotton: A Global History*. New York: Vintage Books.

Belloc, Marianna, Francesco Drago, Mattia Fochesato, and Roberto Galbiati. 2021. "Wealth Accumulation and Institutional Capture: The Rise of the Medici and the Fall of the Florentine Republic." Unpublished manuscript.

Benedictow, Ole J. 2005. *The Black Death 1346–1353: The Complete History*. Woodbridge: The Boydell Press.

Berg, Maxine. 1980. *The Machinery Question and the Making of Political Economy, 1815–1848*. Cambridge: Cambridge University Press.

Berg, Maxine. 2004. "Consumption in Eighteenth- and Early Nineteenth-century Britain." In *Cambridge Economic History of Modern Britain*, Vol. 1, *Industrialisation, 1700–1860*, ed. Roderick Floud and Paul Johnson. Cambridge: Cambridge University Press, pp. 357–87.

Berkowitz, Daniel, Katharina Pistor, and Jean-François Richard. 2003. "Economic Development, Legality, and the Transplant Effect." *European Economic Review* 47(1): 165–95.

Berman, Harold J. 1983. *Law and Revolution: The Formation of the Western Legal Tradition*. Cambridge, MA: Harvard University Press.

Berman, Harold J. 2003. *Law and Revolution, II: The Impact of the Protestant Reformations on the Western Legal Tradition*. Cambridge, MA: Harvard University Press.

Bernhofen, Daniel M. and John C. Brown. 2005. "An Empirical Assessment of the Comparative Advantage Gains from Trade: Evidence from Japan." *American Economic Review* 95(1): 208–25.

Bernhofen, Daniel M., Jianan Li, Markus Eberhardt, and Stephen L. Morgan. 2020. "The Secular Decline of Market Integration during Qing China's Golden Age." Working Paper.

Besley, Timothy and Maitreesh Ghatak. 2010. "Property Rights and Economic Development." In *Handbook of Development Economics*, Vol. 5, ed. Dani Rodrik and Mark Rosenzweig. Amsterdam: Elsevier, pp. 4525–95.

Bisin, Alberto and Thierry Verdier. 2017. "On the Joint Evolution of Culture and Institutions." NBER Working Paper 23375.

Blaydes, Lisa and Eric Chaney. 2013. "The Feudal Revolution and Europe's Rise: Political Divergence of the Christian West and the Muslim World before 1500 CE." *American Political Science Review* 107(1): 16–34.

Blaydes, Lisa and Christopher Paik. 2021. "Muslim Trade and City Growth before the Nineteenth Century: Comparative Urbanization in Europe, the Middle East and Central Asia." *British Journal of Political Science* 51(2): 845–68.

Boettke, Peter. 1993. *Why Perestroika Failed: The Politics and Economics of Socialist Transformation.* London: Routledge.

Boettke, Peter. 2001. *Calculation and Coordination.* London: Routledge.

Bogart, Dan. 2012. "A Small Price to Pay: A Historical Perspective on Infrastructure Regulation during Britain's Industrialization." Mimeo.

Bogart, Dan. 2014. "The Transport Revolution in Industrialising Britain." In *The Cambridge Economic History of Modern Britain* (new edn.), Vol. 1, *1700–1870,* ed. Roderick Floud, Jane Humphries, and Paul Johnson. Cambridge: Cambridge University Press, pp. 368–91.

Bogart, Dan, Eduard J. Alvarez-Palau, Oliver Dunn, Max Satchell, and Leigh Shaw Taylor. 2017. "Market Access and Urban Growth in England and Wales during the Pre-steam Era." Working Paper.

Bogart, Dan and Gary Richardson. 2009. "Making Property Productive: Reorganizing Rights to Real and Equitable Estates in Britain, 1660–1830." *European Review of Economic History* 13(1): 3–30.

Bogart, Dan and Gary Richardson. 2011. "Property Rights and Parliament in Industrializing Britain." *Journal of Law and Economics* 54(2): 241–74.

Bogart, Dan, Max Satchell, Eduard J. Alvarez-Palau, Xuesheng You, and Leigh Shaw Taylor. 2017. "Turnpikes, Canals, and Economic Growth in England and Wales, 1800–1850." Working Paper.

Bolt, Jutta, Robert Inklaar, Herman de Jong, and Jan Luiten van Zanden. 2018. "Rebasing 'Maddison': New Income Comparisons and the Shape of Long-run Economic Development." GGDC Research Memorandum no. 174.

Bolt, Jutta and Jan Luiten van Zanden. 2020. "Maddison Project Database, version 2020." *Maddison Style Estimates of the Evolution of the World Economy: A New 2020 Update.*

Boserup, Ester. 1970. *Woman's Role in Economic Development.* London: George Allen and Unwin Ltd.

Bosker, Maarten, Eltjo Buringh, and Jan Luiten van Zanden. 2013. "From Baghdad to London: Unraveling Urban Development in Europe, the Middle East, and North Africa, 800–1800." *Review of Economics and Statistics* 95(4): 1418–37.

Botticini, Maristella and Zvi Eckstein. 2012. *The Chosen Few: How Education Shaped Jewish History, 70–1492.* Princeton, NJ: Princeton University Press.

Boyd, Robert and Peter J. Richerson. 1985. *Culture and the Evolutionary Process.* Chicago: University of Chicago Press.

Brandt, Loren, Debin Ma, and Thomas G. Rawski. 2014. "From Divergence to Convergence: Reevaluating the History behind China's Economic Boom." *Journal of Economic Literature* 52(1): 45–123.

Brandt, Loren, Debin Ma, and Thomas G. Rawski. 2017. "Industrialization in China." In *The Spread of Modern Industry to the Periphery since 1871,* ed. Kevin O'Rourke and Jeffrey Williamson. Oxford: Oxford University Press, pp. 197–228.

Braudel, Fernand. 1949/1973. *The Mediterranean, and the Mediterranean World in the Age of Phillip II,* Vol. 2. Translated by Siân Reynolds. Berkeley: University of California Press.

Brenner, Robert. 1976. "Agrarian Class Structure and Economic Development in Pre-industrial Europe." *Past & Present* 70(1): 30–75.

Brewer, John. 1988. *The Sinews of Power*. Cambridge, MA: Harvard University Press.

Brewer, John and Roy Porter, eds. 1993. *Consumption and the World of Goods*. London: Routledge.

Broadberry, Stephen. 1994. "Comparative Productivity in British and American Manufacturing during the Nineteenth Century." *Explorations in Economic History* 31(4): 521–48.

Broadberry, Stephen. 1998. "How Did the United States and Germany Overtake Britain? A Sectoral Analysis of Comparative Productivity Levels, 1870–1990." *Journal of Economic History* 58(2): 375–407.

Broadberry, Stephen, Bruce M.S. Campbell, Alexander Klein, Mark Overton, and Bas van Leeuwen. 2015. *British Economic Growth, 1270–1870*. Cambridge: Cambridge University Press.

Broadberry, Stephen, Johann Custodis, and Bishnupriya Gupta. 2015. "India and the Great Divergence: An Anglo-Indian Comparison of GDP per Capita, 1600–1871." *Explorations in Economic History* 55(1): 58–75.

Broadberry, Stephen, Hanhui Guan, and David Daokui Li. 2018. "China, Europe, and the Great Divergence: A Study in Historical National Accounting, 980–1850." *Journal of Economic History* 78(4): 955–1000.

Broadberry, Stephen and Bishnupriya Gupta. 2006. "The Early Modern Great Divergence: Wages, Prices and Economic Development in Europe and Asia, 1500–1800." *Economic History Review* 59(1): 2–31.

Broadberry, Stephen and John Joseph Wallis. 2017. "Growing, Shrinking, and Long-run Economic Performance: Historical Perspectives on Economic Development." NBER Working Paper 23343.

Bruhn, Miriam and Francisco A. Gallego. 2012. "Good, Bad, and Ugly Colonial Activities: Do They Matter for Economic Development?" *Review of Economics and Statistics* 94(2): 433–61.

Buringh, Eltjo and Jan Luiten van Zanden. 2009. "Charting the 'Rise of the West': Manuscripts and Printed Books in Europe, a Long-Term Perspective from the Sixth through Eighteenth Centuries." *Journal of Economic History* 69(2): 409–45.

Caferro, William P. 2008. "Warfare and Economy in Renaissance Italy, 1350–1450." *Journal of Interdisciplinary History* 39(2): 167–209.

Cagé, Julia and Valeria Rueda. 2016. "The Long-term Effects of the Printing Press in sub-Saharan Africa." *American Economic Journal: Applied Economics* 8(3): 69–99.

Cameron, Rondo E. 1993. *A Concise Economic History of the World: From Paleolithic Times to the Present*. New York: Oxford University Press.

Campbell, Bruce M.S. 2010. "Nature as Historical Protagonist." *Economic History Review* 63(2): 281–314.

Campbell, Cameron D., Wang Feng, and James Z. Lee. 2002. "Pretransitional Fertility in China." *Population and Development Review* 28(4): 735–50.

Cantoni, Davide, Jeremiah Dittmar, and Noam Yuchtman. 2018. "Religious Competition and Reallocation: The Political Economy of Secularization in the Protestant Reformation." *Quarterly Journal of Economics* 133(4): 2037–96.

Carmichael, Sarah G., Alexandra de Pleijt, Jan Luiten van Zanden, and Tine de Moor. 2016. "The European Marriage Pattern and Its Measurement." *Journal of Economic History* 76(1): 196–204.

Castañeda Dower, Paul and Andrei Markevich. 2018. "The Stolypin Reform and Agricultural Productivity in Late Imperial Russia." *European Review of Economic History* 23(3): 241–67.

Cavalli-Sforza, Luigi L. and Marcus W. Feldman. 1981. *Cultural Transmission and Evolution: A Quantitative Approach*. Princeton, NJ: Princeton University Press.

Centeno, Miguel Angel. 1997. "Blood and Debt: War and Taxation in Nineteenth-century Latin America." *American Journal of Sociology* 102(6): 1565–605.

Cervellati, Matteo and Uwe Sunde. 2005. "Human Capital Formation, Life Expectancy, and the Process of Development." *American Economic Review* 95(5): 1653–72.

Chaney, Eric. 2008. "Tolerance, Religious Competition and the Rise and Fall of Muslim Science." Unpublished paper.

Chaney, Eric. 2016. "Religion and the Rise and Fall of Islamic Science." Unpublished paper.

Chang, Ha-Joon. 2008. *Bad Samaritans: The Myth of Free Trade and the Secret History of Capitalism*. London: Bloomsbury Press.

Chaudhary, Latika and James Fenske. 2020. "Did Railways Affect Literacy? Evidence from India." CAGE Online Working Paper Series 529.

Chen, Ting, James Kai-sing Kung, and Chicheng Ma. 2020. "Long Live Keju! The Persistent Effects of China's Civil Examination System." *Economic Journal* 130(631): 2065–104.

Chen, Zhiwu, Chicheng Ma, and Andrew J. Sinclair. Forthcoming. "Banking on the Confucian Clan: Why Did China Miss the Financial Revolution?" *Economic Journal*. https://doi.org/10.1093/ej/ueab082.

Christian, Cornelius and Liam Elbourne. 2018. "Shocks to Military Support and Subsequent Assassinations in Ancient Rome." *Economics Letters* 171: 79–82.

CIA. 2019. "CIA World Fact Book." Data available at: https://www.cia.gov/the-world-factbook/.

Cipolla, Carlo M. 1952. "The Decline of Italy: The Case of a Fully Matured Economy." *Economic History Review* 5(2): 178–87.

Cipolla, Carol M. 1976. *Before the Industrial Revolution*. London: Methuen.

Clark, Gregory. 1994. "Factory Discipline." *Journal of Economic History* 54(1): 128–63.

Clark, Gregory. 2007. *A Farewell to Alms*. Princeton, NJ: Princeton University Press.

Clark, Gregory. 2010. "The Macroeconomic Aggregates for England, 1209–2008." *Research in Economic History* 27(1): 51–140.

Clark, Gregory and Neil Cummins. 2015. "Malthus to Modernity: Wealth, Status, and Fertility in England, 1500–1879." *Journal of Population Economics* 28(1): 3–29.

Clark, Gregory and David Jacks. 2007. "Coal and the Industrial Revolution, 1700–1869." *European Review of Economic History* 11(1): 39–72.

Clark, Peter, ed. 2001. *The Cambridge Urban History of Britain*, Vol. II. Cambridge: Cambridge University Press.

Clegg, John J. 2015. "Capitalism and Slavery." *Critical Historical Studies* 2(2): 281–304.

Clingingsmith, David and Jeffrey G. Williamson. 2008. "Deindustrialization in 18th- and 19th-century India: Mughal Decline, Climate Shocks and British Industrial Ascent." *Explorations in Economic History* 45(3): 209–234.

Cohn, Samuel. 2007. "After the Black Death: Labour Legislation and Attitudes towards Labour in Late-Medieval Western Europe." *Economic History Review* 60(3): 457–85.

Cooter, Robert D. 1997. "The Rule of State Law and the Rule-of-law State: Economic Analysis of the Legal Foundations of Development." *Annual World Bank Conference on Development Economics* 1996: 191–217.

Coşgel, Metin M., Thomas J. Miceli, and Jared Rubin. 2012. "The Political Economy of Mass Printing: Legitimacy and Technological Change in the Ottoman Empire." *Journal of Comparative Economics* 40(3): 357–71.

Cox, Gary W. 2016. *Marketing Sovereign Promises: Monopoly Brokerage and the Growth of the English State*. Cambridge: Cambridge University Press.

Crafts, Nicholas. 2011. "Explaining the First Industrial Revolution: Two Views." *European Review of Economic History* 15(1): 153–68.

Crafts, Nicholas. 2018. *Forging Ahead, Falling Behind and Fighting Back: British Economic Growth from the Industrial Revolution to the Financial Crisis.* Cambridge: Cambridge University Press.

Crosby, Alfred W. 1986. *Ecological Imperialism: The Biological Expansion of Europe, 900–1900.* Cambridge: Cambridge University Press.

Dalgaard, Carl-Johan, Anne Sofie B. Knudsen, and Pablo Selaya. 2020. "The Bounty of the Sea and Long-run Development." *Journal of Economic Growth* 25(3): 259–95.

Darity, William, Jr. 1992. "A Model of 'Original Sin': Rise of the West and Lag of the Rest." *American Economic Review* 82(2): 162–7.

David, A. Paul and Gavin Wright. 1997. "Increasing Returns and the Genesis of American Resource Abundance." *Industrial and Corporate Change* 6(2): 203–45.

Davis, Donald R. and David E. Weinstein. 2002. "Bones, Bombs, and Break Points: The Geography of Economic Activity." *American Economic Review* 92(5): 1269–89.

de la Croix, David, Matthias Doepke, and Joel Mokyr. 2017. "Clans, Guilds, and Markets: Apprenticeship Institutions and Growth in the Preindustrial Economy." *Quarterly Journal of Economics* 133(1): 1–70.

de Moor, Tine and Jan Luiten van Zanden. 2010. "Girl Power: The European Marriage Pattern and Labour Markets in the North Sea Region in the Late Medieval and Early Modern Period." *Economic History Review* 63(1): 1–33.

de Vries, Jan. 1993. "Between Purchasing Power and the World of Goods: Understanding the Household Economy in Early Modern Europe." In *Consumption and the World of Goods,* ed. John Brewer and Roy Porter. London: Routledge, pp. 85–132.

de Vries, Jan. 2003. "The Industrious Revolution and Economic Growth, 1650–1830." In *The Economic Future in a Historical Perspective,* ed. Paul A. David and Michael Thomas. Oxford: Oxford University Press, pp. 43–72.

de Vries, Jan. 2008. *The Industrious Revolution.* Cambridge: Cambridge University Press.

de Vries, Jan and Ad van der Woude. 1997. *The First Modern Economy: Success, Failure, and Perseverance of the Dutch Economy, 1500–1815.* Cambridge: Cambridge University Press.

Dell, Melissa. 2010. "The Persistent Effects of Peru's Mining Mita." *Econometrica* 78(6): 1863–903.

Dell, Melissa and Benjamin A. Olken. 2020. "The Development Effects of the Extractive Colonial Economy: The Dutch Cultivation System in Java." *Review of Economic Studies* 87(1): 164–203.

Dennison, Tracy and Sheilagh Ogilvie. 2014. "Does the European Marriage Pattern Explain Economic Growth?" *Journal of Economic History* 74(3): 651–93.

Derenoncourt, Ellora. 2019. "Atlantic Slavery's Impact on European and British Economic Development." Working Paper.

Desierto, Desiree A. 2018. "Formal Models of the Political Resource Curse." *Economics of Governance* 19(3): 225–59.

Desierto, Desiree A. and Mark Koyama. 2020. "The Political Economy of Status Competition: Sumptuary Laws in Preindustrial Europe." CEPR Discussion Papers 14407.

Desmet, Klaus and Stephen L. Parente. 2012. "The Evolution of Markets and the Revolution of Industry: A Unified Theory of Growth." *Journal of Economic Growth* 17(3): 205–34.

Diamond, Jared. 1997. *Guns, Germs, and Steel.* New York: W.W. Norton & Company.

Dicey, A.V. 1908. *Introduction to the Study of the Law of the Constitution.* London: Macmillan and Co. Ltd.

Dincecco, Mark. 2009. "Fiscal Centralization, Limited Government, and Public Revenues in Europe, 1650–1913." *Journal of Economic History* 69(1): 48–103.

Dincecco, Mark, James Fenske, Anil Menon, and Shivaji Mukherjee. 2019. "Pre-colonial Warfare and Long-run Development in India." University of Warwick Working Paper N. 426.

Dippel, Christian. 2014. "Forced Coexistence and Economic Development: Evidence from Native American Reservations." *Econometrica* 82(6): 2131–65.

Dittmar, Jeremiah E. and Ralf R. Meisenzahl. 2020. "Public Goods Institutions, Human Capital, and Growth: Evidence from German History." *Review of Economic Studies* 87(2): 959–96.

Dixit, Avinash. 2004. *Lawlessness and Economics.* Princeton, NJ: Princeton University Press.

Doepke, Matthias and Fabrizio Zilibotti. 2008. "Occupational Choice and the Spirit of Capitalism." *Quarterly Journal of Economics* 123(2): 747–93.

Donaldson, Dave. 2018. "Railroads of the Raj: Estimating the Impact of Transportation Infrastructure." *American Economic Review* 108(4–5): 899–934.

Donaldson, Dave and Richard Hornbeck. 2016. "Railroads and American Economic Growth: A 'Market Access' Approach." *Quarterly Journal of Economics* 131(2): 799–858.

Drelichman, Mauricio. 2005. "All That Glitters: Precious Metals, Rent Seeking and the Decline of Spain." *European Review of Economic History* 9(3): 313–36.

Drelichman, Mauricio and Hans-Joachim Voth. 2008. "Institutions and the Resource Curse in Early Modern Spain." In *Institutions and Economic Performance*, ed. Ethan Helpman. Cambridge, MA: Harvard University Press, pp. 120–47.

Drelichman, Mauricio and Hans-Joachim Voth. 2011. "Lending to the Borrower from Hell: Debt and Default in the Age of Philip II." *Economic Journal* 121(557): 1205–27.

Drelichman, Mauricio and Hans-Joachim Voth. 2016. *Lending to the Borrower from Hell: Debt, Taxes, and Default in the Age of Philip II.* Princeton, NJ: Princeton University Press.

Dyer, Christopher. 2005. *An Age of Transition? Economy and Society in England in the Later Middle Ages.* Oxford: Clarendon Press.

Easterly, William and Ross Levine. 1997. "Africa's Growth Tragedy: Policies and Ethnic Divisions." *Quarterly Journal of Economics* 112(4): 1203–50.

Edelstein, Dan, Maria Comsa, Melanie Conroy, Biliana Kassabova, Claude Willan, Chloe Edmundson, and Bugei Nyaosi. 2010. "Voltaire and the Enlightenment." Mapping the Republic of Letters, Stanford University. http://republicofletters.stanford.edu/casestudies/voltaire.html.

Eichengreen, Barry. 2007. *The European Economy since 1945: Coordinated Capitalism and Beyond.* Princeton, NJ: Princeton University Press.

Ekelund, Robert B., Robert Hébert, Robert Tollison, Gary Anderson, and Audrey Davidson. 1996. *Sacred Trust: The Medieval Church as an Economic Firm.* Oxford: Oxford University Press.

Ekelund, Robert B. and Robert D. Tollison. 1997. *Politicized Economies.* College Station, TX: Texas A & M University Press.

Eltis, David and Stanley L. Engerman. 2000. "The Importance of Slavery and the Slave Trade to Industrializing Britain." *Journal of Economic History* 60(1): 123–44.

Emson, H.E. 1992. "For the Want of an Heir: The Obstetrical History of Queen Anne." *BMJ: British Medical Journal* 304(6838): 1365–6.

Engerman, Stanley L. and Kenneth L. Sokoloff. 2012. *Economic Development in the Americas since 1500.* Cambridge: Cambridge University Press.

Enke, Benjamin. 2019. "Kinship, Cooperation, and the Evolution of Moral Systems." *Quarterly Journal of Economics* 134(2): 953–1019.

Epstein, S.R. 1991. "Cities, Regions and the Late Medieval Crisis: Sicily and Tuscany Compared." *Past & Present* 130: 3–50.

Epstein, S.R. 1998. "Craft Guilds, Apprenticeship, and Technological Change in Preindustrial Europe." *Journal of Economic History* 58(3): 684–713.

Epstein, S.R. 2000. *Freedom and Growth: The Rise of States and Markets in Europe, 1300–1700.* London: Routledge.

Federico, Giovanni, Max-Stephan Schulze, and Oliver Volckart. 2021. "European Goods Market Integration in the Very Long Run: From the Black Death to the First World War." *Journal of Economic History* 81(1): 276–308.

Feinstein, Charles H. 1998. "Pessimism Perpetuated: Real Wages and the Standard of Living in Britain during and after the Industrial Revolution." *Journal of Economic History* 58(3): 625–58.

Fernández, Raquel and Alessandra Fogli. 2009. "Culture: An Empirical Investigation of Beliefs, Work, and Fertility." *American Economic Journal: Macroeconomics* 1(1): 146–77.

Fernández-Armesto, Felipe. 2006. *Pathfinders: A Global History of Exploration.* New York: Norton.

Fernández-Villaverde, Jesús. 2022. *Global Economic History: Change and Continuity.* Princeton, NJ: Princeton University Press.

Fernández-Villaverde, Jesús, Mark Koyama, Youhong Lin, and Tuan-Hwee Sng. 2020. "Fractured-land and Political Fragmentation." Working Paper.

Feyrer, James and Bruce Sacerdote. 2009. "Colonialism and Modern Income: Islands as Natural Experiments." *Review of Economics and Statistics* 91(2): 245–62.

Finley, Moses I. 1973. *The Ancient Economy.* Berkeley: University of California Press.

Floud, Roderick, Robert W. Fogel, Bernard Harris, and Sok Chul Hong. 2011. *The Changing Body: Health, Nutrition, and Human Development in the Western World since 1700.* Cambridge: Cambridge University Press.

Flückiger, Matthias, Erik Hornung, Mario Larch, Markus Ludwig, and Allard Mees. Forthcoming. "Roman Transport Network Connectivity and Economic Integration." *Review of Economic Studies.* https://doi.org/10.1093/restud/rdab036.

Fogel, Robert W. 1964. *Railroads and American Economic Growth.* Baltimore: Johns Hopkins University Press.

Fogel, Robert W. 2004. *The Escape from Hunger and Premature Death, 1700–2000.* Cambridge: Cambridge University Press.

Foreman-Peck, James. 2011. "The Western European Marriage Pattern and Economic Development." *Explorations in Economic History* 48(2): 292–309.

Fouquet, Roger and Stephen Broadberry. 2015. "Seven Centuries of European Economic Growth and Decline." *Journal of Economic Perspectives* 29(4): 227–44.

Frankema, Ewout H.P. 2012. "The Origins of Formal Education in sub-Saharan Africa: Was British Rule More Benign?" *European Review of Economic History* 16(4): 335–55.

Frankema, Ewout H.P. and Marlous van Waijenburg. 2012. "Structural Impediments to African Growth? New Evidence from Real Wages in British Africa, 1880–1965." *Journal of Economic History* 72(4): 895–926.

Friedman, Benjamin M. 2005. *The Moral Consequences of Economic Growth.* New York: Vintage Books.

Fukuyama, Francis. 2011. *The Origins of Political Order.* London: Profile Books Ltd.

Fukuyama, Francis. 2014. *Political Order and Political Decay.* New York: Farrar, Straus and Giroux.

Fuller, Lon L. 1969. *The Morality of Law.* New Haven, CT: Yale University Press.

Galor, Oded. 2005. "From Stagnation to Growth: Unified Growth Theory." In *Handbook of Economic Growth*, Vol. 1, ed. Philippe Aghion and Steven Durlauf. Amsterdam: Elsevier, pp. 171–293.

Galor, Oded. 2011. *Unified Growth Theory*. Princeton, NJ: Princeton University Press.

Galor, Oded and Omer Moav. 2006. "Das Human-Kapital: A Theory of the Demise of the Class Structure." *Review of Economic Studies* 73(1): 85–117.

Galor, Oded, Omer Moav, and Dietrich Vollrath. 2009. "Inequality in Landownership, the Emergence of Human-Capital Promoting Institutions, and the Great Divergence." *Review of Economic Studies* 76(1): 143–79.

Galor, Oded and Andrew Mountford. 2008. "Trading Population for Productivity: Theory and Evidence." *Review of Economic Studies* 75(4): 1143–79.

Galor, Oded and David N. Weil. 2000. "Population, Technology, and Growth: From Malthusian Stagnation to the Demographic Transition and Beyond." *American Economic Review* 90(4): 806–28.

Gennaioli, Nicola and Hans-Joachim Voth. 2015. "State Capacity and Military Conflict." *Review of Economic Studies* 82(4): 1409–48.

Gerschenkron, Alexander. 1962. *Economic Backwardness in Historical Perspective*. Cambridge, MA: The Belknap Press.

Glahn, Richard von. 2016. *The Economic History of China*. Cambridge: Cambridge University Press.

Goldin, Claudia. 2001. "The Human-Capital Century and American Leadership: Virtues of the Past." *Journal of Economic History* 61(2): 263–92.

Goldin, Claudia and Lawrence F. Katz. 1998. "The Origins of Technology–Skill Complementarity." *Quarterly Journal of Economics* 113(3): 693–732.

Goldin, Claudia and Laurence F. Katz. 2008. *The Race between Education and Technology*. Cambridge, MA: Harvard University Press.

Goldstone, Jack A. 2002. "Efflorescences and Economic Growth in World History: Rethinking the 'Rise of the West' and the Industrial Revolution." *Journal of World History* 13(2): 323–89.

Gorodnichenko, Yuriy and Gerard Roland. 2011. "Individualism, Innovation, and Long-run Growth." *Proceedings of the National Academy of Sciences* 108(Supplement 4): 21316–19.

Gorodnichenko, Yuriy and Gerard Roland. 2017. "Culture, Institutions, and the Wealth of Nations." *Review of Economics and Statistics* 99(3): 402–16.

Gottfried, Robert S. 1983. *The Black Death: Natural and Human Disaster in Medieval Europe*. New York: The Free Press.

Grafe, Regina. 2012. *Distant Tyranny: Markets, Power, and Backwardness in Spain, 1650–1800*. Princeton, NJ: Princeton University Press.

Gregory, Paul R. 1994. *Before Command: The Russian Economy from Emancipation to Stalin*. Princeton, NJ: Princeton University Press.

Gregory, Paul R. 2004a. *The Political Economy of Stalinism*. Cambridge: Cambridge University Press.

Gregory, Paul R. 2004b. *Russian National Income, 1885–1913*. Cambridge: Cambridge University Press.

Gregory, Paul R. and Mark Harrison. 2005. "Allocation under Dictatorship: Research in Stalin's Archives." *Journal of Economic Literature* 43(3): 721–61.

Greif, Avner. 1989. "Reputation and Coalitions in Medieval Trade: Evidence on the Maghribi Traders." *Journal of Economic History* 49(4): 857–82.

Greif, Avner. 1993. "Contract Enforceability and Economic Institutions in Early Trade: The Maghribi Traders' Coalition." *American Economic Review* 83(3): 525–48.

Greif, Avner. 1994. "Cultural Beliefs and the Organization of Society: A Historical and Theoretical Reflection on Collectivist and Individualist Societies." *Journal of Political Economy* 102(5): 912–50.

Greif, Avner. 2000. "The Fundamental Problem of Exchange: A Research Agenda in Historical Institutional Analysis." *European Review of Economic History* 4(3): 251–84.

Greif, Avner. 2002. "Institutions and Impersonal Exchange: From Communal to Individual Responsibility." *Journal of Institutional and Theoretical Economics* 127(1): 168–204.

Greif, Avner. 2006. *Institutions and the Path to the Modern Economy: Lessons from Medieval Trade.* New York: Cambridge University Press.

Greif, Avner, Paul Milgrom, and Barry R. Weingast. 1994. "Coordination, Commitment, and Enforcement: The Case of the Merchant Guild." *Journal of Political Economy* 102(4): 745–76.

Greif, Avner and Jared Rubin. 2021. "Political Legitimacy and the Institutional Foundations of Constitutional Government: The Case of England." Working Paper.

Greif, Avner and Guido Tabellini. 2017. "The Clan and the Corporation: Sustaining Cooperation in China and Europe." *Journal of Comparative Economics* 45(1): 1–35.

Grier, Robin M. 1999. "Colonial Legacies and Economic Growth." *Public Choice* 98(3–4): 317–35.

Guinnane, Timothy W. 2011. "The Historical Fertility Transition: A Guide for Economists." *Journal of Economic Literature* 49(3): 589–614.

Guiso, Luigi, Paola Sapienza, and Luigi Zingales. 2006. "Does Culture Affect Economic Outcomes?" *Journal of Economic Perspectives* 20(2): 23–48.

Guiso, Luigi, Paola Sapienza, and Luigi Zingales. 2016. "Long-term Persistence." *Journal of the European Economic Association* 14(6): 1401–36.

Gupta, Bishnupriya. 2019. "Falling Behind and Catching Up: India's Transition from a Colonial Economy." *Economic History Review* 72(3): 803–27.

Gwartney, James D., Robert A. Lawson, Joshua Hall, and Ryan Murphy. 2019. *Economic Freedom of the World: 2019 Annual Report.* Vancouver: Fraser Institute.

Gwartney, James D., Robert A. Lawson, and Randall G. Holcombe. 1999. "Economic Freedom and the Environment for Economic Growth." *Journal of Institutional and Theoretical Economics* 155(4): 643–63.

Haggard, Stephan. 2004. "Institutions and Growth in East Asia." *Studies in Comparative International Development* 38(4): 53–81.

Hajnal, John. 1965. "European Marriage Patterns in Perspective." In *Population in History: Essays in Historical Demography,* ed. D.V. Glass and D.E.C. Eversley. London: Aldine, pp. 101–43.

Hajnal, John. 1982. "Two Kinds of Preindustrial Household Formation System." *Population and Development Review* 8(3): 449–94.

Hanley, Susan B. and Kozo Yamamura. 1977. *Economic and Demographic Change in Preindustrial Japan, 1600–1868.* Princeton, NJ: Princeton University Press.

Harley, C. Knick. 1992a. "The Antebellum American Tariff: Food Exports and Manufacturing." *Explorations in Economic History* 29(4): 375–400.

Harley, C. Knick. 1992b. "International Competitiveness of the Antebellum American Cotton Textile Industry." *Journal of Economic History* 52(3): 559–84.

Harley, C. Knick. 2004. "Trade: Discovery, Mercantilism and Technology." In *The Cambridge Economic History of Modern Britain,* Vol. 2, ed. Roderick Floud and Paul Johnson. Cambridge: Cambridge University Press, pp. 175–203.

Harper, Kyle. 2017. *The Fate of Rome.* Princeton, NJ: Princeton University Press.

Hart, Marjolen'T. 1991. "'The Devil of the Dutch': Holland's Impact on the Financial Revolution in England, 1643–1694." *Parliaments, Estates, and Representation* 11(1): 39–51.

Hausfather, Zeke. 2019. "Analysis: Why the UK's CO_2 Emissions have Fallen 38% since 1990." CarbonBrief. https://www.carbonbrief.org/analysis-why-the-uks-co2-emissions-have-fallen-38-since-1990.

Hausmann, Ricardo, Lant Pritchett, and Dani Rodrik. 2005. "Growth Accelerations." *Journal of Economic Growth* 10(4): 303–29.

Hay, Douglas, Peter Linebaugh, John G. Rule, E.P. Thompson, and Cal Winslow, eds. 1975. *Albion's Fatal Tree*. London: Allen Lane.

Hay, Simon I., Carlos A. Guerra, Peter W. Gething, Anand P. Patil, Andrew J. Tatem, Abdisalan M. Noor, et al. 2009. "A World Malaria Map: Plasmodium falciparum Endemicity in 2007." *PLoS Medicine* 6(3): e1000048.

Hayek, F.A. 1960. *The Constitution of Liberty*. London: Routledge.

Hayek, F.A. 1982. *Law, Legislation and Liberty: The Political Order of a Free People*, Vol. III. Chicago: University of Chicago Press.

Heldring, Leander, James A. Robinson, and Sebastian Vollmer. 2021. "The Economic Effects of the English Parliamentary Enclosures." Working Paper.

Henrich, Joseph. 2004. "Demography and Cultural Evolution: How Adaptive Cultural Processes Can Produce Maladaptive Losses: The Tasmanian Case." *American Antiquity* 69(2): 197–214.

Henrich, Joseph. 2015. *The Secret of Our Success: How Culture Is Driving Human Evolution, Domesticating our Species, and Making Us Smarter*. Princeton, NJ: Princeton University Press.

Henrich, Joseph. 2020. *The WEIRDest People in the World: How the West Became Psychologically Peculiar and Particularly Prosperous*. New York: Farrar, Straus and Giroux.

Henriques, Antonio and Nuno Palma. 2020. "Comparative European Institutions and the Little Divergence, 1385–1800." CEPR Discussion Paper 14124.

Herbst, Jeffrey. 2000. *States and Power in Africa: Comparative Lessons in Authority and Control*. Princeton, NJ: Princeton University Press.

Hobsbawm, Eric J. 1968. *Industry and Empire*. London: Weidenfeld & Nicolson.

Hoffman, Philip T. 2015. *Why Did Europe Conquer the World?* Princeton, NJ: Princeton University Press.

Hornbeck, Richard and Martin Rotemberg. 2021. "Railroads, Market Access, and Aggregate Productivity Growth." Working Paper.

Howes, Anton. 2017. "The Relevance of Skills to Innovation during the British Industrial Revolution, 1547–1851." Working Paper.

Huff, Toby. 1993. *The Rise of Early Modern Science*. Cambridge: Cambridge University Press.

Huillery, Elise. 2009. "History Matters: The Long-term Impact of Colonial Public Investments in French West Africa." *American Economic Journal: Applied Economics* 1(2): 176–215.

Hume, David. 1762. *The History of England*. Dublin: United Company of Booksellers.

Humphries, Jane. 2010. *Childhood and Child Labour in the British Industrial Revolution*. Cambridge: Cambridge University Press.

Humphries, Jane and Benjamin Schneider. 2019. "Spinning the Industrial Revolution." *Economic History Review* 72(1): 126–55.

Humphries, Jane and Jacob Weisdorf. 2019. "Unreal Wages? Real Income and Economic Growth in England, 1260–1850." *Economic Journal* 129(623): 2867–87.

Hunter, Janet. 2003. *Women and the Labour Market in Japan's Industrializing Economy: The Textile Industry before the Pacific War*. London: Routledge.

Inglehart, R., C. Haerpfer, A. Moreno, C. Welzel, K. Kizilova, J. Diez-Medrano, et al. 2018. *World Values Survey: All Rounds – Country-Pooled Datafile Version*. Madrid: JD Systems Institute. Data available at: http://www.worldvaluessurvey.org/WVSDocumentationWVL.jsp.

Inikori, Joseph E. 2002. *Africans and the Industrial Revolution in England*. Cambridge: Cambridge University Press.

Irwin, Douglas A. 2000. "Did Late-nineteenth-century US Tariffs Promote Infant Industries? Evidence from the Tinplate Industry." *Journal of Economic History* 60(2): 335–60.

Irwin, Douglas A. 2002. "Interpreting the Tariff–Growth Correlation of the Late 19th Century." *American Economic Review* 92(2): 165–9.

Iyer, Lakshmi. 2010. "Direct versus Indirect Colonial Rule in India: Long-term Consequences." *Review of Economics and Statistics* 92(4): 693–713.

Iyigun, Murat, Nathan Nunn, and Nancy Qian. 2017. "Winter Is Coming: The Long-run Effects of Climate Change on Conflict, 1400–1900." NBER Working Paper 23033.

Iyigun, Murat, Jared Rubin, and Avner Seror. 2021. "A Theory of Cultural Revivals." *European Economic Review* 135: art. 103734.

Jacks, David S., Christopher M. Meissner, and Dennis Novy. 2011. "Trade Booms, Trade Busts, and Trade Costs." *Journal of International Economics* 83(2): 185–201.

Jedwab, Rémi, Noel D. Johnson, and Mark Koyama. 2019. "Pandemics, Places, and Populations: Evidence from the Black Death." CEPR Discussion Paper.

Jedwab, Rémi and Alexander Moradi. 2016. "The Permanent Effects of Transportation Revolutions in Poor Countries: Evidence from Africa." *Review of Economics and Statistics* 98(2): 268–84.

Jha, Saumitra. 2015. "Financial Asset Holdings and Political Attitudes: Evidence from Revolutionary England." *Quarterly Journal of Economics* 130(3): 1485–545.

Johnson, Noel D. and Mark Koyama. 2017. "States and Economic Growth: Capacity and Constraints." *Explorations in Economic History* 64(1): 1–20.

Johnson, Noel D. and Mark Koyama. 2019. *Persecution and Toleration: The Long Road to Religious Freedom*. Cambridge: Cambridge University Press.

Jones, Eric. 2003. *The European Miracle* (3rd edn). Cambridge: Cambridge University Press.

Kamen, Henry. 1971. *The Iron Century: Social Change in Europe 1550–1660*. London: Weidenfeld & Nicolson.

Kandori, Michihiro. 1992. "Social Norms and Community Enforcement." *Review of Economic Studies* 59(1): 63–80.

Kanzaka, Junichi. 2019. "The Development of Civil Engineering Projects and Village Communities in Seventeenth- to Nineteenth-Century Japan." In *Public Goods Provision in the Early Modern Economy: Comparative Perspectives from Japan, China, and Europe*, ed. Masayuki Tanimoto and R. Bin Wong. Berkeley: University of California Press, pp. 150–71.

Karaman, Kivanc and Şevket Pamuk. 2013. "Different Paths to the Modern State in Europe: The Interaction between Warfare, Economic Structure and Political Regime." *American Political Science Review* 107(3): 603–26.

Kaufmann, Daniel, Aart Kraay, and Massimo Mastruzzi. 2011. "The Worldwide Governance Indicators: Methodology and Analytical Issues." *Hague Journal on the Rule of Law* 3(2): 220–46.

Kelly, Morgan, Joel Mokyr, and Cormac Ó Gráda. 2014. "Precocious Albion: A New Interpretation of the British Industrial Revolution." *Annual Review of Economics* 6(1): 363–89.

Kelly, Morgan, Joel Mokyr, and Cormac Ó Gráda. 2020. "The Mechanics of the Industrial Revolution." Working Paper.

Kelly, Morgan and Cormac Ó Gráda. 2014. "Ready for Revolution? The English Economy before 1800." Working Paper.

Kelly, Morgan and Cormac Ó Gráda. 2016. "Adam Smith, Watch Prices, and the Industrial Revolution." *Quarterly Journal of Economics* 131(4): 1727–52.

Kennedy, Paul. 1987. *The Rise and Fall of the Great Powers, 1500–1980*. New York: Vintatge Books.

Kitamura, Shuhei and Nils-Petter Lagerlöf. 2020. "Geography and State Fragmentation." *Journal of the European Economic Association* 18(4): 1726–69.

Ko, Chiu Yu, Mark Koyama, and Tuan-Hwee Sng. 2018. "Unified China; Divided Europe." *International Economic Review* 59(1): 285–327.

Ko, Chiu Yu and Tuan-Hwee Sng. 2013. "Regional Dependence and Political Centralization in Imperial China." *Eurasian Geography and Economics* 54(5–6): 470–83.

Kohli, Atul. 2004. *State-directed Development: Political Power and Industrialization in the Global Periphery*. Cambridge: Cambridge University Press.

Koyama, Mark. 2010a. "Evading the 'Taint of Usury': The Usury Prohibition as a Barrier to Entry." *Explorations in Economic History* 47(4): 420–42.

Koyama, Mark. 2010b. "The Political Economy of Expulsion: The Regulation of Jewish Moneylending in Medieval England." *Constitutional Political Economy* 21(4): 374–406.

Koyama, Mark. 2012. "The Transformation of Labor Supply in the Pre-industrial World." *Journal of Economic Behavior & Organization* 81(2): 505–23.

Koyama, Mark. 2016. "The Long Transition from a Natural State to a Liberal Economic Order." *International Review of Law and Economics* 47(1): 29–39.

Koyama, Mark, Chiaki Moriguchi, and Tuan-Hwee Sng. 2018. "Geopolitics and Asia's Little Divergence: State Building in China and Japan after 1850." *Journal of Economic Behavior & Organization* 155: 178–204.

Koyama, Noboru. 2004. *Japanese Students at Cambridge University in the Meiji Era, 1868–1912: Pioneers for the Modernization of Japan*. Translated by Ian Ruxton. Morrisville, NC: Lula Press.

Kremer, Michael. 1993. "Population Growth and Technological Change: One Million BC to 1990." *Quarterly Journal of Economics* 108(3): 681–716.

Kuran, Timur. 2011. *The Long Divergence: How Islamic Law Held Back the Middle East*. Princeton, NJ: Princeton University Press.

Kuran, Timur and Jared Rubin. 2018. "The Financial Power of the Powerless: Socio-economic Status and Interest Rates under Partial Rule of Law." *Economic Journal* 128(609): 758–96.

Kuru, Ahmet T. 2019. *Islam, Authoritarianism, and Underdevelopment: A Global and Historical Comparison*. New York: Cambridge University Press.

La Porta, Rafael, Florencio Lopez de Silanes, Andrei Shleifer, and Robert W. Vishny. 1998. "Law and Finance." *Journal of Political Economy* 106(6): 1113–55.

Lal, Deepak. 2005. *The Hindu Equilibrium, India c. 1500 BC–2000 A.D.* Oxford: Oxford University Press.

Lamb, H.H. 1982. *Climate, History, and the Modern World*. London: Methuen.

Lamoreaux, Naomi R. 2011. "The Mystery of Property Rights: A US Perspective." *Journal of Economic History* 71(2): 275–306.

Lampe, Markus and Paul Sharp. 2018. *A Land of Milk and Butter*. Chicago: University of Chicago Press.

Landes, David S. 1998. *The Wealth and Poverty of Nations: Why Some Are So Rich and Some So Poor*. New York: Norton.

Landes, David S. 2006. "Why Europe and the West? Why Not China?" *Journal of Economic Perspectives* 20(2): 3–22.

Lange, Matthew K. 2004. "British Colonial Legacies and Political Development." *World Development* 32(6): 905–22.

Lankina, Tomila and Lullit Getachew. 2012. "Mission or Empire, Word or Sword? The Human Capital Legacy in Postcolonial Democratic Development." *American Journal of Political Science* 56(2): 465–83.

Le Bris, David. 2019. "Testing Legal Origins Theory within France: Customary Laws versus Roman Code." *Journal of Comparative Economics* 47(1): 1–30.

Lee, James, Cameron Campbell, and Wang Feng. 2002. "Positive Check or Chinese Checks?" *Journal of Asian Studies* 61(2): 591–607.

Lemire, Beverly. 1991. *Fashion's Favourite: The Cotton Trade and the Consumer in Britain, 1660–1800*. Oxford: Oxford University Press.

Lewis, Bernard. 2002. *What Went Wrong? Western Impact and Middle Eastern Response*. Oxford: Oxford University Press.

Lin, Justin Yifu. 1995. "The Needham Puzzle: Why the Industrial Revolution Did Not Originate in China." *Economic Development and Cultural Change* 43(2): 269–92.

Lindert, Peter H. and Jeffrey G. Williamson. 2016. "American Colonial Incomes, 1650–1774." *Economic History Review* 69(1): 54–77.

Lowes, Sara and Eduardo Montero. Forthcoming. "Concessions, Violence, and Indirect Rule: Evidence from the Congo Free State." *Quarterly Journal of Economics*. https://doi.org/10.1093/qje/qjab021.

Lowes, Sara, Nathan Nunn, James A. Robinson, and Jonathan L. Weigel. 2017. "The Evolution of Culture and Institutions: Evidence from the Kuba Kingdom." *Econometrica* 85(4): 1065–91.

Ma, Debin. 2004. "Why Japan, Not China, Was the First to Develop in East Asia: Lessons from Sericulture, 1850–1937." *Economic Development and Cultural Change* 52(2): 369–94.

Ma, Debin and Jared Rubin. 2019. "The Paradox of Power: Principal–Agent Problems and Administrative Capacity in Imperial China (and Other Absolutist Regimes)." *Journal of Comparative Economics* 47(2): 277–94.

Macaulay, Thomas Babbington. 1830. "Sir Thomas More; or, Colloquies on the Progress and Prospects of Society by Robert Southey." *Edinburgh Review* 50: 528–65.

Maddison, Angus. 1983. "A Comparison of Levels of GDP per Capita in Developed and Developing Countries: 1700–1914." *Journal of Economic History* 43(1): 27–41.

Maddison, Angus. 1991. *Dynamic Forces in Capitalist Development: A Long-run Comparative View.* New York: Oxford University Press.

Maddison, Angus. 2001. *The World Economy: A Millennial Perspective*. OECD.

Maddison, Angus. 2007. *Contours of the World Economy, 1–2030 AD: Essays in Macro-economic History*. Oxford: Oxford University Press.

Majewski, John. 2009. *Modernizing a Slave Economy: The Economic Vision of the Confederate Nation*. Chapel Hill: University of North Carolina Press.

Malanima, Paolo. 2003. "Measuring the Italian Economy 1300–1861." *Rivista di Storia Economica* 21(1): 265–95.

Malanima, Paolo. 2005. "Urbanisation and the Italian Economy during the Last Millennium." *European Review of Economic History* 9(1): 97–122.

Malanima, Paolo. 2007. "Wages, Productivity and Working Time in Italy (1270–1913)." *Journal of European Economic History* 36(1): 127–71.

Malthus, T.R. 1798/2007. *An Essay on the Principle of Population*. New York: Dover.

Mann, Charles C. 2005. *1491: New Revelations of the Americas before Columbus*. New York: Alfred A. Knopf.

Manning, Patrick. 1990. *Slavery and African Life: Occidental, Oriental, and African Slave Trades*. Cambridge: Cambridge University Press.

Manning, Sturt. 2013. "The Roman World and Climate: Context, Relevance of Climate Change, and Some Issues." In *The Ancient Mediterranean Environment between Science and History*, ed. W.V. Harris. Leiden: Brill, pp. 103–72.

Markevich, Andrei, Natalya Naumenko, and Nancy Qian. 2021. "The Soviet Great Famine, 1932–1933." Working Paper.

Markevich, Andrei and Ekaterina Zhuravskaya. 2018. "The Economic Effects of the Abolition of Serfdom: Evidence from the Russian Empire." *American Economic Review* 108(4–5): 1074–117.

Marshall, Monty G. and Gabrielle Elzinga-Marshall. 2017. *Global Report 2017: Conflict, Governance and State Fragility*. Vienna, VA: Center for Systemic Peace.

Marx, Karl. 1868/1990. *Capital*, Vol. 1. Translated by Ben Fowkes. London: Penguin Classics.

McCleary, Rachel M. and Robert J. Barro. 2006. "Religion and Economy." *Journal of Economic Perspectives* 20(2): 49–72.

McCleary, Rachel M. and Robert J. Barro. 2019. *The Wealth of Religions*. Princeton, NJ: Princeton University Press.

McCloskey, Deirdre N. 2006. *The Bourgeois Virtues: Ethics for an Age of Commerce*. Chicago: University of Chicago Press.

McCloskey, Deirdre N. 2010. *Bourgeois Dignity: Why Economics Can't Explain the Modern World*. Chicago: University of Chicago Press.

McCloskey, Deirdre N. 2016. *Bourgeois Equality: How Ideas, Not Capital or Institutions, Enriched the World*. Chicago: University of Chicago Press.

McCloskey, Donald N. 1976. "English Open Fields as Behavior towards Risk." In *Research in Economic History: An Annual Compilation of Research*, Vol. 1, ed. Paul Uselding. Greenwich, CT: JAI Press, pp. 124–70.

McKendrick, Neil, John Brewer, and J.H. Plumb. 1982. *The Birth of Consumer Society: The Commercialization of Eighteenth-century England*. London: Europa.

McLean, Ian W. 2013. *Why Australia Prospered: The Shifting Sources of Economic Growth*. Princeton, NJ: Princeton University Press.

Mehlum, Halvor, Karl Moene, and Ragnar Torvik. 2006. "Institutions and the Resource Curse." *Economic Journal* 116(508): 1–20.

Meng, Xin, Nancy Qian, and Pierre Yared. 2015. "The Institutional Causes of China's Great Famine, 1959–1961." *Review of Economic Studies* 82(4): 1568–611.

Michaels, Guy and Ferdinand Rauch. 2018. "Resetting the Urban Network: 117–2012." *Economic Journal* 128(608): 378–412.

Michalopoulos, Stelios and Elias Papaioannou. 2016. "The Long-run Effects of the Scramble for Africa." *American Economic Review* 106(7): 1802–48.

Minns, Chris and Patrick Wallis. 2012. "Rules and Reality: Quantifying the Practice of Apprenticeship in Early Modern England." *Economic History Review* 65(2): 556–79.

Mitch, David. 1999. "The Role of Skill and Human Capital in the 'British' Industrial Revolution." In *The British Industrial Revolution: An Economic Perspective*, ed. Joel Mokyr. Boulder, CO: Westview Press, pp. 241–79.

Mokyr, Joel. 1990. *The Lever of Riches*. Oxford: Oxford University Press.

Mokyr, Joel. 1998. "The Second Industrial Revolution, 1870–1914." In *Storia dell'economia Mondiale*, ed. Valerio Castronono. Rome: Laterza, pp. 219–45.

Mokyr, Joel. 2002. *The Gift of Athena: Historical Origins of the Knowledge Economy*. Princeton, NJ: Princeton University Press.

Mokyr, Joel. 2009. *The Enlightened Economy: An Economic History of Britain, 1700–1850*. New Haven, CT: Yale University Press.

Mokyr, Joel. 2016. *A Culture of Growth: The Origins of the Modern Economy*. Princeton, NJ: Princeton University Press.

Mokyr, Joel and John V.C. Nye. 2007. "Distribution Coalitions, the Industrial Revolution, and the Origins of Economic Growth in Britain." *Southern Economic Journal* 74(1): 50–70.

Mokyr, Joel, Assaf Sarid, and Karine van der Beek. 2020. "The Wheels of Change: Technology Adoption, Millwrights, and Persistence in Britain's Industrialization." Working Paper.

Montesquieu, Charles de. 1748/1989. *The Spirit of the Laws*. Translated by Anne M. Cohler, Basia C. Miller, and Harold S. Stone. Cambridge: Cambridge University Press.

More, Thomas. 1516/1997. *Utopia*. New York: Dover.

Morris, Ian. 2005. "Archaeology, Standards of Living, and Greek Economic History." In *The Ancient Economy*, ed. Ian Morris and J.G. Manning. Stanford, CA: Stanford University Press, pp. 91–126.

Mui, Hoh-Cheung and Lorna H. Mui. 1989. *Shops and Shopkeeping in Eighteenth-century England*. Kingston: McGill-Queen's University Press.

Murtazashvili, Jennifer Brick. 2016. *Informal Order and the State in Afghanistan*. New York: Cambridge University Press.

Nath, Pratyay. 2018. "Through the Lens of War: Akbar's Sieges (1567–69) and Mughal Empire-building in Early Modern North India." *South Asia: Journal of South Asian Studies* 41(2): 245–58.

Naumenko, Natalya. 2021. "The Political Economy of Famine: The Ukrainian Famine of 1933." *Journal of Economic History* 81(1): 156–97.

Needham, Joseph. 1995. *Science and Civilisation in China*. Cambridge: Cambridge University Press.

Nef, John U. 1932. *The Rise of the English Coal Industry*. Vols. 1–2. London: Routledge.

Nelson, Richard R. and Edmund S. Phelps. 1966. "Investment in Humans, Technological Diffusion, and Economic Growth." *American Economic Review* 56(1/2): 69–75.

North, Douglass C. 1966. *The Economic Growth of the United States 1790–1860*. New York: W.W. Norton & Company.

North, Douglass C. 1981. *Structure and Change in Economic History*. New York: Norton.

North, Douglass C. 1990. *Institutions, Institutional Change, and Economic Performance*. Cambridge: Cambridge University Press.

North, Douglass C. and Robert Paul Thomas. 1973. *The Rise of the Western World*. Cambridge: Cambridge University Press.

North, Douglass C., John Joseph Wallis, and Barry R. Weingast. 2009. *Violence and Social Orders: A Conceptual Framework for Interpreting Recorded Human History*. New York: Cambridge University Press.

North, Douglass C. and Barry Weingast. 1989. "Constitutions and Commitment: The Evolution of Institutions Governing Public Choice in Seventeenth-Century England." *Journal of Economic History* 49(4): 803–32.

Nunn, Nathan. 2008. "The Long-term Effects of Africa's Slave Trades." *Quarterly Journal of Economics* 123(1): 139–76.

Nunn, Nathan. 2012. "Culture and the Historical Process." *Economic History of Developing Regions* 27(Supplement 1): S108–26.

Nunn, Nathan and Diego Puga. 2012. "Ruggedness: The Blessing of Bad Geography in Africa." *Review of Economics and Statistics* 94(1): 20–36.

Nunn, Nathan and Nancy Qian. 2010. "The Columbian Exchange: A History of Disease, Food, and Ideas." *Journal of Economic Perspectives* 24(2): 163–88.

Nunn, Nathan and Leonard Wantchekon. 2011. "The Slave Trade and the Origins of Mistrust in Africa." *American Economic Review* 101(7): 3221–52.

Ó Gráda, Cormac. 2015. *Eating People Is Wrong and Other Essays*. Princeton, NJ: Princeton University Press.

Ober, Josiah. 2018. *Demopolis: Democracy before Liberalism*. Cambridge: Cambridge University Press.

O'Brien, Patrick. 2000. "Mercantilism and Imperialism in the Rise and Decline of the Dutch and British Economies 1585–1815." *De Economist* 148(4): 469–501.

Ogilvie, Sheilagh. 2003. *A Bitter Living: Women, Markets, and Social Capital in Early Modern Germany*. Oxford: Oxford University Press.

Ogilvie, Sheilagh. 2011. *Institutions and European Trade: Merchant Guilds, 1000–1800*. Cambridge: Cambridge University Press.

Ogilvie, Sheilagh. 2019. *The European Guilds: An Economic Analysis*. Princeton, NJ: Princeton University Press.

O'Rourke, Kevin H. 2007a. "Culture, Conflict and Cooperation: Irish Dairying before the Great War." *Economic Journal* 117(523): 1357–79.

O'Rourke, Kevin H. 2007b. "Property Rights, Politics and Innovation: Creamery Diffusion in Pre-1914 Ireland." *European Review of Economic History* 11(3): 395–417.

O'Rourke, Kevin H. and Jeffrey G. Williamson. 1999. *Globalization and History: The Evolution of a Nineteenth-Century Economy*. Cambridge, MA: MIT Press.

Ostrom, Elinor. 1990. *Governing the Commons: The Evolution of Institutions for Collective Action*. Cambridge: Cambridge University Press.

Oto-Peralías, Daniel and Diego Romero-Ávila. 2014. "The Distribution of Legal Traditions around the World: A Contribution to the Legal-origins Theory." *Journal of Law and Economics* 57(3): 561–628.

Palma, Nuno. Forthcoming. "The Real Effects of Monetary Expansions: Evidence from a Large-scale Historical Experiment." *Review of Economic Studies*.

Palma, Nuno and Jaime Reis. 2019. "From Convergence to Divergence: Portuguese Economic Growth, 1527–1850." *Journal of Economic History* 79(2): 477–506.

Pamuk, Şevket. 2007. "The Black Death and the Origins of the 'Great Divergence' across Europe, 1300–1600." *European Review of Economic History* 11(3): 289–317.

Parente, Stephen L. and Edward C. Prescott. 2002. *Barriers to Riches*. Cambridge, MA: MIT Press.

Parker, Geoffrey. 2014. *Imprudent King: A New Life of Philip II*. New Haven, CT: Yale University Press.

Pascali, Luigi. 2017. "The Wind of Change: Maritime Technology, Trade, and Economic Development." *American Economic Review* 107(9): 2821–54.

Patel, Dev, Justin Sandefur, and Arvind Subramanian. 2021. "The New Era of Unconditional Convergence." *Journal of Development Economics* 152: art. 102687.

Pavlik, Jamie Bologna and Andrew T. Young. 2019. "Did Technology Transfer More Rapidly East–West than North–South?" *European Economic Review* 119: 216–35.

Penn, Thomas. 2011. *The Winter King: Henry VII and the Dawn of Tudor England*. New York: Simon & Schuster.

Perkins, Dwight and John P. Tang. 2017. "East Asian Industrial Pioneers: Japan, Korea, and Taiwan." In *The Spread of Modern Industry to the Periphery since 1871*, ed. Kevin O'Rourke and Jeffrey Williamson. Oxford: Oxford University Press, pp. 169–96.

Pincus, Steven C.A. and James A. Robinson. 2014. "What Really Happened during the Glorious Revolution?" In *Institutions, Property Rights, and Economic Growth: The Legacy of Douglass North*. New York: Cambridge University Press, pp. 192–222.

Pipes, Richard. 1974. *Russia under the Old Regime*. London: Penguin.

Platt, Brian. 2004. *Burning and Building: Schooling and State Formation in Japan, 1750–1890*. Cambridge MA: Harvard University Press.

Platt, Stephen R. 2018. *Imperial Twilight: The Opium War and the End of China's Last Golden Age*. New York: Knopf.

Platteau, Jean-Philippe. 2017. *Islam Instrumentalized*. Cambridge: Cambridge University Press.

Pollack, A.F. and F.W. Maitland. 1895. *The History of England Law, Before the Time of Edward I*, Vol. 1. Cambridge: Cambridge University Press.

Pomeranz, Kenneth. 2000. *The Great Divergence: China, Europe and the Making of the Modern World Economy*. Princeton, NJ: Princeton University Press.

Pomeranz, Kenneth. 2005. "Women's Work and the Economics of Respectability." In *Gender in Motion: Divisions of Labor and Cultural Change in Late Imperial and Modern China*, ed. Bryna Goodman and Wendy Larson. Lanham, MD: Rowman and Littlefield, pp. 239–63.

Postan, M.M. 1973. *Medieval Trade and Finance*. Cambridge: Cambridge University Press.

Pritchett, Lant. 1997. "Divergence, Big Time." *Journal of Economic Perspectives* 11(3): 3–17.

Pritchett, Lant and Lawrence H. Summers. 1996. "Wealthier Is Healthier." *Journal of Human Resources* 31(4): 841–68.

Puga, Diego and Daniel Trefler. 2014. "International Trade and Institutional Change: Medieval Venice's Response to Globalization." *Quarterly Journal of Economics* 129(2): 753–821.

Putnam, Robert D., Robert Leonardi, and Raffaella Y. Nanetti. 1993. *Making Democracy Work: Civic Traditions in Modern Italy*. Princeton, NJ: Princeton University Press.

Rajan, Raghuram G. and Luigi Zingales. 2003. "The Great Reversals: The Politics of Financial Development in the Twentieth Century." *Journal of Financial Economics* 69(1): 5–50.

Ransom, Roger and Richard Sutch. 1988. "Capitalists without Capital: The Burden of Slavery and the Impact of Emancipation." *Agricultural History* 62(3): 133–60.

Redding, Stephen and Anthony J. Venables. 2004. "Economic Geography and International Inequality." *Journal of International Economics* 62(1): 53–82.

Reid, Anthony. 2015. *A History of Southeast Asia: Critical Crossroads*. Oxford: Wiley Blackwell.

Richardson, Gary. 2008. "Brand Names before the Industrial Revolution." NBER Working Paper 13930.

Richerson, Peter J. and Robert Boyd. 2010. "The Evolution of Free Enterprise Values." In *Moral Markets: The Critical Role of Values in the Economy*. Princeton, NJ: Princeton University Press.

Richter, Daniel K. 2011. *Before the Revolution: America's Ancient Pasts*. Cambridge, MA: Belknap Press.

Robinson, James A., Ragnar Torvik, and Thierry Verdier. 2006. "Political Foundations of the Resource Curse." *Journal of Development Economics* 79(2): 447–68.

Rodrik, Dani, Arvind Subramanian, and Francesco Trebbi. 2004. "Institutions Rule: The Primacy of Institutions over Geography and Integration in Economic Development." *Journal of Economic Growth* 9(2): 131–65.

Root, Hilton L. 1991. "The Redistributive Role of Government: Economic Regulation in Old Régime France and England." *Comparative Studies in Society and History* 33(2): 338–69.

Root, Hilton L. 2020. *Network Origins of the Global Economy: East vs. West in a Complex Systems Perspective*. Cambridge: Cambridge University Press.

Rosenbloom, Joshua. 2004. "Path Dependence and the Origins of the American Cotton Textile Industry." In *The Fibre that Changed the World: Cotton Industry in International Perspective*, ed. David Jeremy and Douglas A. Farnie. Oxford: Oxford University Press, pp. 365–91.

Rosenthal, Jean-Laurent. 1992. *The Fruits of Revolution*. Cambridge: Cambridge University Press.

Rosenthal, Jean-Laurent and Roy Bin Wong. 2011. *Before and beyond Divergence*. Cambridge, MA: Harvard University Press.

Roser, Max. 2021a. "Children Born per Woman." *Our World in Data*. Data available at: https://web.archive.org/web/20180916202120if_/https://ourworldindata.org/grapher/children-born-per-woman.

Roser, Max. 2021*b*. "The Rise of Basic Schooling since the 19th Century." *Our World in Data*. Data available at: https://web.archive.org/web/20180921060942mp_/https://ourworldin data.org/primary-and-secondary-education.

Roser, Max. 2021*c*. "The Short History of Global Living Conditions and Why It Matters That We Know It." *Our World in Data*. Data available at: https://ourworldindata.org/a-history-of -global-living-conditions-in-5-charts.

Ross, Michael L. 2015. "What Have We Learned about the Resource Curse?" *Annual Review of Political Science* 18: 239–59.

Rostow, Walt W. 1960. *The Stages of Economic Growth: A Non-Communist Manifesto*. Cambridge: Cambridge University Press.

Rubin, Jared. 2011. "Institutions, the Rise of Commerce and the Persistence of Laws: Interest Restrictions in Islam and Christianity." *Economic Journal* 121(557): 1310–39.

Rubin, Jared. 2017. *Rulers, Religion, and Riches: Why the West Got Rich and the Middle East Did Not*. New York: Cambridge University Press.

Sachs, Jeffrey D. and Pia Malaney. 2002. "The Economic and Social Burden of Malaria." *Nature* 415(6872): 680–5.

Sachs, Jeffrey D. and Andrew M. Warner. 2001. "The Curse of Natural Resources." *European Economic Review* 45(4–6): 827–38.

Saito, Osamu. 2005. "Pre-modern Economic Growth Revisited: Japan and the West." LSE Working Paper No. 16/05.

Saito, Osamu. 2009. "Land, Labour and Market Forces in Tokugawa Japan." *Continuity and Change* 24(Special Issue 01): 169–96.

Salter, Alexander William and Andrew T. Young. 2019. "Polycentric Sovereignty: The Medieval Constitution, Governance Quality, and the Wealth of Nations." *Social Science Quarterly* 100(4): 1241–53.

Scheidel, Walter. 2017. *The Great Leveler: Violence and the History of Inequality from the Stone Age to the Twenty-first Century*. Princeton, NJ: Princeton University Press.

Scheidel, Walter. 2019. *Escape from Rome*. Princeton, NJ: Princeton University Press.

Schulz, Jonathan F. 2020. "Kin Networks and Institutional Development." Working Paper.

Schulz, Jonathan F., Duman Bahrami-Rad, Jonathan P. Beauchamp, and Joseph Henrich. 2019. "The Church, Intensive Kinship, and Global Psychological Variation." *Science* 366(6466).

Sequeira, Sandra, Nathan Nunn, and Nancy Qian. 2020. "Immigrants and the Making of America." *Review of Economic Studies* 87(1): 382–419.

Shiue, Carol H. 2005. "From Political Fragmentation towards a Customs Union: Border Effects of the German Zollverein, 1815 to 1855." *European Review of Economic History* 9(2): 129–62.

Shiue, Carol H. and Wolfgang Keller. 2007. "Markets in China and Europe on the Eve of the Industrial Revolution." *American Economic Review* 97(4): 1189–216.

Shleifer, Andrei, Florencio Lopez de Silanes, and Rafael La Porta. 2008. "The Economic Consequences of Legal Origins." *Journal of Economic Literature* 46(2): 285–332.

Siedentop, Larry. 2014. *Inventing the Individual: The Origins of Western Liberalism*. Cambridge, MA: Harvard University Press.

Smith, Adam. 1776/1976. *An Inquiry into the Nature and Causes of the Wealth of Nations*, ed. R.H. Campbell and A.S. Skinner. Liberty Fund (reproducing Oxford University Press edition). https://www.libertyfund.org/books/an-inquiry-into-the-nature-and-causes-of-the-wealth -of-nations-vol-1/.

Smith, Richard M. 1991. "Demographic Development in Rural England, 1300–48: A Survey." In *Before the Black Death: Studies in the "Crisis" of the Early Fourteenth Century*, ed. Bruce M.S. Campbell. Manchester: Manchester University Press, pp. 25–78.

Sng, Tuan-Hwee. 2014. "Size and Dynastic Decline: The Principal–Agent Problem in Late Imperial China, 1700–1850." *Explorations in Economic History* 54: 107–27.

Sng, Tuan-Hwee and Chiaki Moriguchi. 2014. "Asia's Little Divergence: State Capacity in China and Japan before 1850." *Journal of Economic Growth* 19(4): 439–70.

Sokoloff, Kenneth L. and Stanley L. Engerman. 2000. "Institutions, Factor Endowments, and Paths of Development in the New World." *Journal of Economic Perspectives* 14(3): 217–32.

Solow, Barbara L. 1987. "Capitalism and Slavery in the Exceedingly Long Run." *Journal of Interdisciplinary History* 17(4): 711–37.

Solow, Robert M. 1956. "A Contribution to the Theory of Economic Growth." *Quarterly Journal of Economics* 70(1): 65–94.

Southern, Richard. 1970. *Western Society and the Church in the Middle Ages*. New York: Penguin.

Spolaore, Enrico and Romain Wacziarg. 2021. "Fertility and Modernity." *Economic Journal*. https://doi.org/10.1093/ej/ueab066.

Squicciarini, Mara P. and Nico Voigtländer. 2015. "Human Capital and Industrialization: Evidence from the Age of Enlightenment." *Quarterly Journal of Economics* 130(4): 1825–83.

Stasavage, David. 2002. "Credible Commitment in Early Modern Europe: North and Weingast Revisited." *Journal of Law, Economics, and Organization* 18(1): 155–86.

Stasavage, David. 2003. *Public Debt and the Birth of the Democratic State*. Cambridge: Cambridge University Press.

Stasavage, David. 2011. *States of Credit*. Princeton, NJ: Princeton University Press.

Stasavage, David. 2014. "Was Weber Right? The Role of Urban Autonomy in Europe's Rise." *American Political Science Review* 108(2): 337–54.

Stasavage, David. 2016. "What We Can Learn from the Early History of Sovereign Debt." *Explorations in Economic History* 59: 1–16.

Stasavage, David. 2020. *The Decline and Rise of Democracy: A Global History from Antiquity to Today*. Princeton, NJ: Princeton University Press.

Steckel, Richard H. 2009. "Heights and Human Welfare: Recent Developments and New Directions." *Explorations in Economic History* 46(1): 1–23.

Stewart, Dugald. 1793/1980. "Account of the Life and Writings of Adam Smith LL.D." In Adam Smith, *Essays on Philosophical Subjects*, ed. W.P.D. Wightman and J.C. Bryce. Oxford: Oxford University Press, pp. 269–352.

Styles, John. 2021. "The Rise and Fall of the Spinning Jenny: Domestic Mechanisation in Eighteenth-century Cotton Spinning." *Textile History* 51(2): 195–236.

Sugihara, Kaoru. 2004. "The State and the Industrious Revolution in Tokugawa Japan." LSE Working Paper.

Tabellini, Guido. 2010. "Culture and Institutions: Economic Development in the Regions of Europe." *Journal of the European Economic Association* 8(4): 677–716.

Tawney, R.H. 1936. *Religion and the Rise of Capitalism. A Historical Study*. London: John Murray.

Taylor, Leigh Shaw and E.A. Wrigley. 2014. Occupational Structure and Population Change. In *The Cambridge Economic History of Modern Britain* (new edn.), Vol. 1: *Industrialisation, 1700–1870*, ed. Roderick Floud, Jane Humphries, and Paul Johnson. Cambridge: Cambridge University Press pp. 53–88.

Temin, Peter. 2006. "The Economy of the Early Roman Empire." *Journal of Economic Perspectives* 20(1): 133–51.

Thompson, E.P. 1965. *The Making of the English Working Class*. Harmondsworth: Penguin.

Tilly, Charles. 1975. "Reflections on the History of European State-making." In *The Formation of Nation States in Western Europe*, ed. Charles Tilly. Princeton, NJ: Princeton University Press, pp. 3–84.

Tilly, Charles. 1990. *Coercion, Capital, and European States, AD 990–1990*. Oxford: Blackwell.

Tocqueville, Alexis de. 1958. *Journeys to England and Ireland*. New Haven: Yale University Press.

Troesken, Werner. 2015. *The Pox of Liberty: How the Constitution Left Americans Rich, Free, and Prone to Infection*. Chicago: University of Chicago Press.

Tullock, Gordon. 1967. "The Welfare Costs of Tariffs, Monopolies, and Theft." *Western Economics Journal* 5(3): 224–32.

Turner, Frederick Jackson. 1893. "The Significance of the Frontier in American History." *Proceedings of the State Historical Society of Wisconsin*.

Valencia Caicedo, Felipe. 2018. "The Mission: Human Capital Transmission, Economic Persistence, and Culture in South America." *Quarterly Journal of Economics* 134(1): 507–56.

van Bavel, Bas. 2016. *The Invisible Hand? How Market Economies Have Emerged and Declined since AD 500*. Oxford: Oxford University Press.

van Bavel, Bas, Eltjo Buringh, and Jessica Dijkman. 2018. "Mills, Cranes, and the Great Divergence: The Use of Immovable Capital Goods in Western Europe and the Middle East, Ninth to Sixteenth Centuries." *Economic History Review* 71(1): 31–54.

van Zanden, Jan Luiten. 2009. *The Long Road to the Industrial Revolution: The European Economy in a Global Perspective, 1000–1800*. Leiden: Brill.

van Zanden, Jan Luiten, Eltjo Buringh, and Maarten Bosker. 2012. "The Rise and Decline of European Parliaments, 1188–1789." *Economic History Review* 65(3): 835–61.

van Zanden, Jan Luiten and Maarten Prak. 2006. "Towards an Economic Interpretation of Citizenship: The Dutch Republic between Medieval Communes and Modern Nation-states." *European Review of Economic History* 10(2): 111–45.

van Zanden, Jan Luiten and Bas van Leeuwen. 2012. "Persistent but Not Consistent: The Growth of National Income in Holland, 1347–1807." *Explorations in Economic History* 49(2): 119–30.

Voigtländer, Nico and Hans-Joachim Voth. 2006. "Why England? Demographic Factors, Structural Change and Physical Capital Accumulation during the Industrial Revolution." *Journal of Economic Growth* 11(4): 319–61.

Voigtländer, Nico and Hans-Joachim Voth. 2013a. "How the West 'Invented' Fertility Restriction." *American Economic Review* 103(6): 2227–64.

Voigtländer, Nico and Hans-Joachim Voth. 2013b. "The Three Horsemen of Riches: Plague, War, and Urbanization in Early Modern Europe." *Review of Economic Studies* 80(2): 774–811.

Voth, Hans-Joachim. 2001. "The Longest Years: New Estimates of Labor Input in England, 1760–1830." *Journal of Economic History* 61(4): 1065–82.

Vries, Peer. 2015. *State, Economy and the Great Divergence: Great Britain and China, 1680s–1850s*. London: Bloomsbury Publishing.

Vries, Peer. 2020. *Averting a Great Divergence*. London: Bloomsbury.

Waldinger, Maria. 2017. "The Long-run Effects of Missionary Orders in Mexico." *Journal of Development Economics* 127: 355–78.

Waldinger, Maria. 2019. "The Economic Effects of Long-term Climate Change: Evidence from the Little Ice Age." Working Paper.

Wallis, Patrick. 2008. "Apprenticeship and Training in Premodern England." *Journal of Economic History* 68(3): 832–61.

Ward-Perkins, Bryan. 2005. *The Fall of Rome, and the End of Civilization*. Oxford: Oxford University Press.

Watson, Andrew M. 1983. *Agricultural Innovation in the Early Islamic World: The Diffusion of Crops and Farming Techniques, 700–1100*. Cambridge: Cambridge University Press.

Weatherill, Lorna. 1988. *Consumer Behaviour and Material Culture in Britain, 1660–1700*. London: Routledge.

Weber, Isabella M. 2021. *How China Escaped Shock Therapy: The Market Reform Debate*. London: Routledge.

Weber, Max. 1905/1930. *The Protestant Ethic and the Spirit of Capitalism*. Translated by Talcott Parsons. London: Allen and Unwin.

Weber, Max. 1978. *Economy and Society: An Outline of Interpretive Sociology*, Vol. 1. Berkeley, CA: University of California Press.

Weingast, Barry R. 1997. "The Political Foundations of Democracy and the Rule of Law." *American Political Science Review* 91(2): 245–63.

Whatley, Warren C. 2018. "The Gun–Slave Hypothesis and the 18th Century British Slave Trade." *Explorations in Economic History* 67: 80–104.

Whatley, Warren C. and Rob Gillezeau. 2011. "The Impact of the Transatlantic Slave Trade on Ethnic Stratification in Africa." *American Economic Review* 101(3): 571–6.

White, Lawrence H. 2012. *The Clash of Economic Ideas*. Cambridge: Cambridge University Press.

WHO. 2018. "WHO Global Ambient Air Quality Database." Data available at: https://www.who.int/airpollution/data/cities/en/.

Williams, Eric. 1944. *Capitalism and Slavery*. Chapel Hill, NC: University of North Carolina Press.

Williamson, Jeffrey G. 2006. *Globalization and the Poor Periphery before 1850*. Cambridge, MA: MIT Press.

Williamson, Oliver. 1985. *The Economic Institutions of Capitalism*. New York: The Free Press.

Wilson, Andrew. 2011. "City Sizes and Urbanization in the Roman Empire." In *Settlement, Urbanization, and Population*, ed. Alan Bowman and Andrew Wilson. Oxford: Oxford University Press, pp. 161–95.

Wong, R. Bin. 1997. *China Transformed: Historical Change and the Limits of European Experience*. Ithaca, NY: Cornell University Press.

Wong, R. Bin. 2012. "Taxation and Good Governance in China 1500–1914." In *The Rise of Fiscal States: A Global History, 1500–1914*, ed. Bartolome Yuan-Casaliia, Patrick K. O'Brien, and Francisco Comín Comín. Cambridge: Cambridge University Press, pp. 353–78.

Woodard, Colin. 2011. *American Nations: A History of the Eleven Rival Regional Cultures of North America*. New York: Penguin.

Woodberry, Robert D. 2012. "The Missionary Roots of Liberal Democracy." *American Political Science Review* 106(2): 244–74.

Wooton, David. 2015. *The Invention of Science*. London: Allen Lane.

World Bank. 2019. "World Development Indicators: GDP per Capita (Current US$)." Data available at: https: //data.worldbank.org/indicator/ny.gdp.pcap.cd.

World Bank. 2020*a*. "Total Population Living in Extreme Poverty, by World Region." Data available at: https://ourworldindata.org/grapher/total-population-living-in-extreme-poverty-by-world-region.

World Bank. 2020*b*. "World Development Indicators." Data available at: https://datacatalog.worldbank.org/dataset/world-development-indicators.

World Justice Project. 2020. "Rule of Law Index." https://worldjusticeproject.org/our-work/research-and-data/wjp-rule-law-index-2019/current-historical-data.

Wright, Gavin. 2020. "Slavery and Anglo-American Capitalism Revisited." *Economic History Review* 73(2): 353–83.

Wright, Mary C. 1957. *The Last Stand of Chinese Conservatism: The Tung-Chih Restoration, 1862–1874*. Stanford, CA: Stanford University Press.

Wrigley, E.A. 1989. *Continuality, Chance and Change: The Character of the Industrial Revolution in England*. Cambridge: Cambridge University Press.

Wrigley, E.A. 2010. *Energy and the English Industrial Revolution*. Cambridge: Cambridge University Press.

Wrigley, E.A, R.S. Davies, J.E. Oeppen, and R.S. Schofield. 1997. *English Population History from Family Reconstitution, 1580–1837*. Cambridge: Cambridge University Press.

Wrigley, E.A. and R.S. Schofield. 1981. *The Population History of England, 1541–1871: A Reconstruction*. Cambridge: Cambridge University Press.

Xue, Melanie Meng. 2020. "High-value Work and the Rise of Women: The Cotton Revolution and Gender Equality in China." Working Paper.

Xue, Melanie Meng. 2021. "Autocratic Rule and Social Capital: Evidence from Imperial China." Mimeo.

yü Têng, Ssu. 1943. "Chinese Influence on the Western Examination System: I. Introduction." *Harvard Journal of Asiatic Studies* 7(4): 267–312.

Ziegler, Philip. 1969. *The Black Death*. London: Collins.

Index

Page numbers in *italics* refer to figures and tables.

Acemoglu, D.
  and Johnson, S., Robinson, J.A. 11, 33, 40, 41, 114, *115*, 139
  and Robinson, J.A. 50–1, 52, 187, 208
  and Wolitzky, A. 95–6
Africa
  colonization 108, 114, 116, 117–19, 120, 122–3
  and independence 199–200
  cultural norms 84–5
  geographic factors 20–2
    ruggedness of terrain 11, *12*
  Jewish traders, North Africa 53, 80–2
  slave trades 109–13
  trust 11, 111
agriculture
  Black Death, impact of 93–4, 95–6
  capitalism 95, 153–4
  China 216–17, 218
  climate and geography 25–6
  Dutch Cultivation System, Java, Indonesia 121–2
  England/Britain
    capitalist agriculture 153–4
    crop yields (18th century) *107*
    labor force 177
  gender norms 85, *86*
  India 117, *118*
  and Malthusian model of population 92
  potato, introduction of 107
  Soviet Russia 195–6
  and technology 6, 22–4
Alesina, A., Giuliano, P., and Nunn, N. 85, *86*
Allen, R.C. 8–9, 34, 151, 154, 166, 168–71, 174, 175, 178–9, 192, 206
  and Weisdorf, J.L. 153
Americas/New World and European Empires 104–5, 107, 116
  Atlantic trade route 32–3, 137–8, 139, 140
amoral familism 79–80

Anderson, R.W., Johnson, N.D., and Koyama, M. *26*, 27
Anne of England 88
Appleby, J. 194
apprenticeships 164
Arkwright, R.: water frame 166, *167*, 168
Arrow, K.J. 83
Arteaga, F., Desierto. D, and Koyama M. 140
Ashraf, Q. and Galor, O. 92
Asia
  East Asian Tigers 207–11
  per capita GDP *199*
  trade routes and colonization 104–5
Athenian democracy 50, 56, 59
Atlantic economy and Industrial Revolution, Britain 156–8
Atlantic trade 32–3, 137–8, 139
  slave 108, 109, *110*, 158–60
Australia 189
autocracy and democracy 48–9

Bai, Y. and Kung, J. 124, 133
Bailey, M. 95
Balla, E. and Johnson, N. 155
Banerjee, A. and Iyer, L. 117, *118*
Banfield, E.C. 79–80
Barro, R. and McCleary, R. 73
Bates, R.H. 200
Becker, G.S.
  and Lewis, H.G. 100
Becker, S.O.
  and Boeckh, K., Hainz, C., Woessmann, L. 84
  and Hornung, E., Woessmann, L. 73–4, 182
  and Woessmann, L. 73, 74
Beckert, S. 160, 161
Belgian Congo 114, 116
Benedictow, O. 92
Berg, M. 158, 179

Berman, H. 46, 76
Bernhofen, D.
    and Brown, J. 205
    and Eberhardt, M, Li, J., Morgan S. 134 213
birth rates/fertility *see* demographic
    transition; European Marriage
    Pattern (EMP); Malthusian model
Black Death 6, 92–6, 99, 103, 135–6, 152, 153
Blake, W. 179
Blaydes, L. and Chaney, E. 78, *79*
Boettke, P. 196
Bogart, D. 146, 151
    and Alvarez-Palau, E.J., Dunn, O., Satchell,
        M., Taylor, L.S. 29, 32
    and Richardson, G. 42, 146
    and Satchell, M., Alvarez-Palau, E.J., You,
        X., Taylor, L.S. 29, 30–1
Bolt, J. and van Zanden, J., *112, 115*
Botticini, M. and Eckstein, Z. 74
Brandt, L., Ma, D., and Rawski, T.G. 14, 214,
    216, 218–19
Brenner, R. 95, 154
Britain/England 1, *2*, 14, 15–16, 223, 224
    Black Death, impact of 94, 95, *97*
    bourgeois pursuit of profit 69–70
    Civil Wars 144
    common law 46–7
    and Dutch Republic/Netherlands 75–6,
        152–3, 162–3, 164
    European Marriage Pattern (EMP) *98*,
        99–100
    and France 32, *33*, 42, 46, 94, 95, 122
    and Japan, per capita GDP (1280–1850) *203*
    monarchy and Parliament 56–8, 60–1,
        143–7
    natural resources and industrialization
        33–5
    property rights 41–2
    state formation, capital and coercive
        hybrid model of 62
    total GDP, population, and GDP per
        capita (1270–1870) 149, *150*
    transport infrastructure 29, 30–2, 146,
        151
    see also Industrial Revolution, Britain
British colonization 106, *107*, 108, 120,
    122–3
    Hong Kong 214
    transatlantic slave trade 108, *109*, 158–60
    see also India, British Raj
Broadberry, S. 190
    and Custodis, J., Gupta, B. 200, *203*,
        211–12
    and Guan, H., Li, D. *203*, 211–12
    and Wallis, J. 7
Bruhn, M. and Gallego, F. 116

Cagé, J. and Rueda, V., 123
Calvinism 71–3, 141, 194
Campbell, B. 93–4
Cantoni, D. Dittmar, J. and Yuchtman, N. 75
capital-intensive paths to state formation
    61–2
capitalism
    agriculture 95, 153–4
    primitive accumulation and colonization
        106
    Protestant work ethic and 71–3, 194
Caribbean islands 108, 116, 156, 158–9, *208*
Carmichael, S.G., de Pleijt, A., van Zanden,
        J.L., and de Moor, T. 100, 101
Cartwright, E. 174
catch-up growth 186–7, 198–202, 223
    China 218
    East Asian Tigers 208–9
    Japan 204
Catholicism
    Jesuit missions, South America 123, *124*
    marriage policies 80, *81*, 134–5
    medieval Europe 134–5
Central Europe 95–6, 100
Chaney, E. 19, 78
Charles I of England 144
Charles I of Spain (Charles V of the Holy
        Roman Empire) 33, 139, 141, 155
China 211–20, 223–4
    adoption of industrial technologies 188
    Eurasian steppe and state formation
        132–4
    fertility restrictions 101
    gender norms and cotton textile
        production 85–7
    Grand Canal and economic development
        29, 213
    vs. Europe
        clan-based vs. individualistic cultures
            82, 215–16
        science and technology 70–1
    war 62–3
Christianity *see* Catholicism; Protestantism
Cipolla, C.M. 52
cities
    Industrial Revolution, Britain/England
        156–8
    Roman and medieval Britain and France
        32, *33*
city-states 62
    Italy 62, 80–2, 135–6, 137
    and territorial states, interest rates *63*
clan-/kin-based cultures 80–2, 215–16
Clark, G. 8, 40, 72, *90*, 91, *97*, 153
    and Cummins, N. 185
    and Jacks, D. 35

Clegg, J.J. 192
climate change 5, 225
  historical variations 25–7
climate and geography 19, 25–6
coal/coal mining 33–5, 168–9, 170
Code of Hammurabi 44–5
coercive-intensive paths to state formation
  61–2
Cohn, S. 94
colonization 104–5, *107*, 125
  benefits for colonizers 105–9
  delayed industrialization 198–202
  legal systems 46–7
  resource grab 113–19
  silver linings for colonized 119–24
Columbus, C. 104
Commercial Revolution 26, 52–4, 56, 134–5
  guilds 54–6, 101, 164
communism
  China 216–20, 223–4
  Soviet Russia 195–7, 223
  vs. market-based institutions, North and
    South Korea 40, 41
Confucianism 68, 71, 82, 211, 215, 219
Congo
  Belgian 114, 116
  Kuba Kingdom 84–5
Consumer Revolution, Britain 151–3, 158
consumption baskets, historical estimation
  of income 8–9
continents, vertical and horizontal
  alignment of 22–4
convergence
  political institutional development 187–8
  see also catch-up growth
Coşgel, M., Miceli, T. and Rubin, J. 78, 187
cotton textile production and trade
  Britain 160–1, 165–6, *167*, 168, 171
    import ban (1721) 146
  China 85–7
  India 200
  Japan 206
  US 190–2
Cox, G.W. 42
craft guilds 54–5
Crafts, N. 174, 176–7
Crompton, S.: spinning mule 166, *167*
Crosby, A.W. 22–3
culture
  adoption of industrial technologies 188
  Africa, impact of slave trade 111–13
  definitions, differences and effects of
    66–8
  and European take-off 68–71
  and institutions 38–9, 41, 67, 224
  long-term persistence of 79–87

religion and economic growth 71–9
US 194

da Gama, V. 104
Darity, W. 160
"Dark Ages" 26, 134
Davis, D.R. and Weinstein, D.E. 19–20
de la Croix, D., Doepke, M., and Mokyr, J. 55
de Vries, J. 152, 158
  and van der Woude, A. 147, 152–3,
    162–3
death/mortality rates
  and birth rates, Malthusian model 90–2
  colonial settlers 114, *115*
  impact of Black Death 92–4, 96
  infant 21, 88
Dell, M. 116
  and Olken, B.A. 121–2
democracy
  Athenian 50, 56, 59
  and autocracy 48–9
  cultural beliefs and norms 67
  education and Protestant missionaries
    123
demographic transition 101–2, 183–5
Deng Xiaoping 217, 219
Denmark: butter industry 189
Dennison, T. and Ogilvie, S. 100–1
Derenoncourt, E. 159
Desierto, D. and Koyama, M. 45
Desmet, K. and Parente, S. 162
Diamond, J. 19, 22, 23, 32, 132
Dias, B. 104
Dippel, C. 117
disease
  Africa 21, 114
  among rich (18th century) 88
  animal–human interactions 23–4
  Black Death 6, 92–6, 99, 135, 152, 153
Dittmar, J.
  and Meisenzahl, R. 74
  and Yuchtman, N. 75
Donaldson, D. 32, 120–1
  and Hornbeck, R. 31, 193
Drelichman, M. and Voth, H.-J. 60, 140
Dutch Cultivation System, Java, Indonesia
  121–2
Dutch Republic/Netherlands 140–3, 147–8,
    152–3, 162–3, 164
  Protestantism 75–6
Dutch Revolt 141

East Asian Tigers 207–11
East India Company (British) 108, 142, 200
East India Company (Dutch) 147
economic freedom and rule of law 39–40

economic growth 3–8
  uneven diffusion of modern 185–90
  see also catch-up growth
economic and political institutions
    49–52
education
  China 215, 219
  colonial investment/legacy 116–17, 122
  Islamic vs. secular and scientific 78
  Japan 204, 205–6
  and missionaries 123–4
  and Protestantism 73–4
  Second Industrial Revolution 182–3
  and unified growth theory 102, 103
  US 193
  see also human capital investment
Edward I of England 57–8, 143
Eltis, D. and Engerman, S. 159–60
Engels, F. 178–9
Engerman, S. and Sokoloff, K. 193
England see Britain/England
Enlightenment: Republic of Letters 171–4
Epstein, S.R. 55
equal rights 49–52
ethnic factionalism/partition and
    colonization 111–13, 119
Eurasian steppe and state formation 130,
    132–3
Europe 129–31
  and Atlantic trade 32–3, 137–8, 139
  divergence within 137–40
  geography and institutional development
    131–4
  medieval period 134–7
  parliaments and rise of limited
    government 56–8, 59, 140–7
  post-Roman invasions and political
    fragmentation 133–4
  see also colonization
European and Islamic rulers, duration of
    rule 78, 79
European Marriage Pattern (EMP) 97–101, 138
European take-off and culture 68–71
extractive institutions
  colonial 113–17, 121–2
  and inclusive institutions 50–1
extreme poverty see poverty/extreme poverty

famine
  China 216, 217
  pre-Black Death 93–4
  Soviet Russia 196
Feinstein, C.H. 8, 177
Fernández, R. and Fogli, A. 85
Fernández-Villaverde, J., 46
  and Koyama, M., Lin, Y., Sng, T.-H. 132

fertility/birth rates see demographic
    transition; European Marriage
    Pattern (EMP); Malthusian model
Finley, M., 69
fiscal capacity 58–64
Florence, Italy 50, 62, 94, 136
Floud, R. 9
Fogel, R.W. 9, 31
Foreman-Peck, J. 100
"fractured land" hypothesis 132
France
  birth rate 184–5
  and England 32, 33, 42, 46, 94, 95, 122
  legal system 46, 47
  parlements 58
  property rights 42, 43
Frankema, E.H.P. 122
  and van Waijenburg, M. 120
Franklin, B. 71, 194
Friedman, B.M. 5
Fukuyama, F. 134–5, 218

Galbraith, J.K. 201
Galor, O. 97, 98, 102, 182, 185–6
GDP measurement 4, 5–6, 7, 8–9
gender norms 85–7
Gennaioli, N. and Voth, J.-H. 64
geography 19–20, 35–6
  East Asian Tigers 209
  Eurasian steppe 132–3
  and industrialization 32–5
  and institutional development 131–4
  and modern development 20–2
  topography and climate 24–7
  and transport infrastructure 27–32
Germany
  catch-up growth 181, 186–7
  European Marriage Pattern (EMP) 97, 101
  Hansa guild 55
  legal system 46, 47
  Protestantism 71, 73, 75–6
Glahn, R. von 213
globalization, first era of 189–90
Goldin, C. 193
  and Katz, L. 182, 193
Glorious Revolution (1688) 61, 144–5, 146
"Golden Age of Islam" (7–10th centuries)
    76–7
Goldstone, J.A. 6, 147
Gorbachev, M. 196
Great Divergence debate 14, 34–5, 106–7
Great Enrichment 129
Great Leap Forward, China 216–17
Gregory, P. 195–6
Greif, A. 38–9, 40–1, 53–4, 67, 80–2, 83
  and Milgrom, P., Weingast, B.R. 55

Greif, A. (*cont.*)
  and Rubin, J. 45, 143–4
  and Tabellini, G. 82
growth reversals 7
  former colonies 11, *13*, 114, 116
guilds 54–6, 101, 143, 164
Guinnane, T.W. 184
Gulick, S. 68
Gupta, B. 108, 200–1

Habsburg monarchy 84, 138, 139–40, 141
Haggard, S. 210, 211
Hajnal, J. 97, 98
Hargreaves, J.: spinning jenny 165–166, 168
Harley, C.K. 161, 194
Harper, K. 25, 103
Hayek, F.A. 66
height
  historical estimation of wealth 9
  and length of continents 22–3
Heldring, L., Robinson, J.A., and Vollmer, S.
    154
Henrich, J. 66, 80, 102, 135
Henry II of England 143, 144
Henry III of England 57
Henry V of England 2
Henry VII of England 143, 144
Henry VIII of England 75, 143, 144
Henry, Prince of Portugal 104
Hobsbawm, E.J. 160, 179
Hoffman, P.T. 62
Hong Kong
  as British colony 210, 214
  see also East Asian Tigers
Hornbeck, R. and Rotemberg, M. 32, 193
household formation and European
    Marriage Pattern (EMP) 96–101
Huillery, E. 122
human capital investment
  demographic transition in Britain/
    England 185, *186*
  East Asian Tigers 211
  and European Marriage Pattern (EMP)
    100
  Imperial China 215
  Japan 204–6
  and Second Industrial Revolution 180–3
  and unified growth theory 101–2, 103
  US 194
  see also education

immigration, US 194, *195*
inclusive and extractive political
    institutions 50–2
India 200–2
  British Raj 201

economy 108, 201
  and Princely States 117
  railroads 32, 120–1
  taxation institutions 117, *118*
extreme poverty *202*
independence and economic planning 201
protectionist policy 209–10
war 63
individualism
  US 194
  vs. kin-based cultures 79–82, 215–16
Industrial Revolution, Britain 9, 14, 129,
    149–51, 174–5, 224
  and agrarian capitalism 95
  capitalist agriculture 153–4
  consumer revolution 151–3, 158
  cotton textiles 160–1, 165–6, *167*, 168, 171
  demography 99–100
  enlightened economy 171–4
  and fruits of 176–80
  geography 20, 33–5
  innovative economy 165–6, *167*
  market size 161–2
  mercantilism and Empire 156–8
  political institutions 154–5
  skilled mechanical workers 163–5
  state capacity 162–3
  transatlantic slave trade 108, 109, *110*,
    158–60
  and unified growth theory 102
  wages and innovation 168–71
  see also Second Industrial Revolution
industrialization
  and climate change 5, 225
  and geography 32–5
  and Protestantism 73–4
  see also catch-up growth; modern
    economy, rise of
"industrious revolution" 152–3
infant mortality 21, 88, 100
infanticide, East Asia 101
inheritances laws
  Europe 99
  Islamic 77
Inikori, J.E. 108, 159–60
innovation *see* technological innovation
institutions 11, 37, 64–5, 130–1, 187–90, 223–4
  colonial 113–17, 121–2, 199–200
  and culture 38–9, 41, 67, 223–4
  definitions and frameworks 38–41
  economic and political 47–52
  and European Marriage Pattern (EMP) 100–1
  geography and development of 131–4
  guilds 54–6, 101, 164
  individualistic vs. kin-based cultures 82
  legal systems 43–7

parliaments and limited government 56–8, *59*, 140–7
property rights 41–3
war and state finances 58–64
see also Commercial Revolution; political institutions
intellectual elites 171–4
intellectual property rights 155
Irwin, D. 194
Islam, influence of 72, 76–9
Italy
  city-states 62, 80–2, 135–6, 137
  merchants 53–4, 62
  North–South cultural divide 79–82
Iyer, S. 117
Iyigun, M., Nunn, N., Qian, N. 27

James I of England 144
James II of England 144
Japan 202–6, 220, 224
  Eurocentric perspective on culture 68
  fertility restrictions 101
  geography 19–20, 25
Java, Indonesia: Dutch Cultivation System 121–2
Jedwab, R.
  and Johnson, N., Koyama, M. 94–5
  and Moradi, A. 121
Jesuit missions, South America 123, *124*
Jews 27, 45, 57, 74
  traders in North Africa 53, 80–2
John of England 2, 56–7
Johnson, N. and Koyama, M. 45, 147, 161
Jones, E. 132

Kamen, H. 96
Karaman, K. and Pamuk, S. 61
Kaufmann, D., Kraay, A., Mastruzzi, M. 41, *42*
Kelly, M.
  and Mokyr, J., Ó Gráda, C. 156, 162–4, 177
  and Ó Gráda, C. 156, 166, 171
kin-/clan-based cultures 79–82, 134–5, 215–16
Ko, C., Koyama, M, and Sng, T.-H. 133
Kohli, A. 200
Koyama, M. 152
  and Moriguchi, C., Sng, T.-H. 203–5, 213
Kuba Kingdom, Congo 84–5
Kuran, T. 47, 77, 108, 131
  and Rubin, J. 37

La Porta, R., de Silanes, F.L., Shleifer, A., Vishny, R.W. 46
labor
  Britain/England
    agriculture 153–4, 177
    Black Death, impact of 94, 95–6

Industrial Revolution 163–5, 174, 178–9
  education 182
  European Marriage Pattern (EMP) 98–9
  forced 114, 116, 158, 160
  "industrious revolution" 152–3
  slave trade and 158–60, 191–2
  women 85–7, 99, 101, 138, 205
  see also wages
Lamoraux, N. 43
Lampe, M. and Sharp, P. 189
Landes, D.S. 70, 71
Lankina, T. and Getachew, L. 123
legal systems 37, 43–7
  see also Islam
Lemire, B. 152
Lenin, V. 196
Leopold II of Belgium 116
life expectancy 88, *89*
  as measure of living standards 9
Little Ice Age 26–7
Low Countries 24–5, 62, 139, 141
Lowes, S.
  and Montero, E. 116
  and Nunn, N., Robinson, J., Weigel, J. 84
Luther, M. 73

Ma, D. 206
  and Rubin, J. 155
Macartney, G. 70
Macaulay, T. 179–80
McCloskey, D.N. 69, 129, 134, 153, 160
Maddison, A. 8
Magna Carta 56–7
Majewski, J. 191–2
malaria 21, 114
Malthus, T. 88–9, 96–7, 179, 184
Malthusian model 89–92, 96–7, 101–2, 178, 185, 216
  and Black Death 92–6
Mann, C. 24
manufacturing *see* Industrial Revolution, Britain; modern economy, rise of
Mao Zedong 216–17, 219
market access 31–2, 136, 193
market economy 151–2, 213, 216
market exchange 151
markets
  and competition 38, 215, 223
  expansion of 28
  and geography 24
  and growth 223
  and immigration 194
  and innovation 162, 223
  integration of 29, 121, 156, 162, 213
  size, Britain: Industrial Revolution 161–2, 191

marriage 80, *81*, 135, 183, 184
  see also European Marriage Pattern (EMP)
Marshall, M.G. and Elzinga-Marshall, G. 48
Marx, K. 106, 154
  and Engels, F. 178–9
McLean, I. 189
measurement of wealth 1–2, 4, 5–6, 7, 8–10
medieval period 134–7
  see also Commercial Revolution
mercantilism and Empire, Britain:
          Industrial Revolution 156–8
merchant guilds 55–6
Michalopoulos, S. and Papaioannou, E.
          117–19
Middle East 137
  Arab Spring 67
  capital investment 42–3
  European colonization 108
  Islam, influence of 76–9
Mill, J.S. 179
mining
  coal 168–9, 170
  precious metals 114, 116, 139
missionaries 70, 122–4
modern economy, rise of 9, 129–30
  and colonialism 106
  demographic transition 101–2, 183–5
  East Asian Tigers 207–11
  European Marriage Pattern (EMP) 99–100
  Industrial Revolution and fruits of 176–80
  Japan 202–6
  Second Industrial Revolution 180–3
  Soviet Russia 195–7
  uneven diffusion of modern economic
          growth 185–90
  US 190–4, *195*
Mokyr, J. 35, 155, 160, 171–4, 175, 180, 181,
          182, 192, 215
  and Nye, J.V.C. 146
  and Sarid, A., van der Beek, K. 163
monarchy
  disease and life expectancy 88
  England 143–6
  Habsburg 84, 138, 139, 140, 141
  and parliaments 56–8, 60–1, 143–7
Montesquieu, C. de 19, 25, 134
mortality *see* death/mortality rates
mountains 132
  coasts, and climate 24–7
  ruggedness of terrain 11, *12*, 25

Native Americans 117
natural experiments 41, 83–4
natural resources *see* resources
natural state and open-access order systems
          51–2, 57, 187

Needham, J. 70, 214
Nef, J.U. 33–4
Nehru, J. 201
Nelson, R.R. and Phelps, E.S. 182
Netherlands *see* Dutch Republic/
          Netherlands
Newcomen, T.: steam engine 168–9
Nigeria 199–200
  and South Korea, per capita GDP *207*
norms
  cultural beliefs and 38–9, 41, 66–7
  gender 85–7
  persistence 79–87
  trust 82–5
North, D.C. 38, 139–40, 180, 190–1, 193
  and Thomas, R.P. 38
  and Wallis, J.J., Weingast, B.R. 51, 52, 57,
          187
  and Weingast, B.R. 145
North-South cultural divide, Italy 79–82
Nunn, N. *110*, 111, *112*, *113*
  and Puga, D. 11, *12*, 25
  and Qian, N. 27, 107
  and Wantchekon, L. 11, 111

Ober, J., 50
Ogilvie, S. 55–6, 101
open-access order and natural state systems
          51–2, 187
Ottoman Empire 37, 78, 84, 105, 155, 187,
          188

Pamuk, S. 94
parliaments
  and limited government 56–8, *59*, 140–7
  and Protestantism 75
Pascali, L. 189
patent system, Britain 155
Pavlik, J.B. and Young, A.T. 24
Peel, R. 70, 168
Philip II of Spain 33, 60, 139, 141, 155
plagues *see* Black Death
Platt, B. 204
Platt, S.R. 70
political fragmentation
  and cultural unity, Europe 173, 214
  and topography 130, 132, 133–4
political institutions 47–9
  Britain: Industrial Revolution 154–5
  China 214–15, 217–20
  East Asian Tigers 210–11
  and catch-up economic growth 187–8
  and economic institutions 49–52
  Soviet 196–7
  US 192–3
  see also parliaments

political legitimacy
  China 214, 219
  Islamic societies 77–9
  Protestant societies 75–6, 141, 143–5
Pomeranz, K. 14, 34–5, 85–7, 213
population 88–9, 102–3, 138
  Black Death 92–6
  change and transition to modern
    economic growth 101–2, 183–5
  China 215–16
  East Asian Tigers 211
  England 149, 150, 156, 157, 178, 179, 183–4,
    186
  household formation and European
    Marriage Pattern (EMP) 96–101
  pre-industrial Malthusian pressure 89–92
  US 190, 194, 195
Portugal: colonialism 104, 106, 107, 108, 109
poverty/extreme poverty 198, 201–2, 222
  Africa 111, 112
  China 212, 216
  decline of 2–3, 4, 15
  India 201–2
  and pre-industrial population pressure
    89–92
primitive accumulation and colonization
  106
printing presses 78, 123, 136–7, 187
property rights 41–3, 46, 139–40, 145–6, 201,
  204
  intellectual 155
protectionist policies
  India 201, 209–10
  US 193–4
Protestantism
  education 73–4
  missionaries 123, 124
  as source of political legitimacy 75–6
  Spanish Habsburgs and Dutch Revolt 141
  work ethic and capitalism 71–3, 194
Prussia 61, 73–4, 182
public goods and colonization 120–2

Qianlong Emperor of China 70, 71

railroads
  Britain 29
  British India 32, 120–1
  US 31–2, 193
religion 71–9
  missionaries 122–4
  see also Catholicism; Islam; Protestantism
rents 51
  craft guilds 54, 55
  elites 136, 146, 196, 201
  monopoly 57, 140

Republic of Letters, Europe 171–4
resources
  and colonization 106–7, 113–19
  and industrialization 33–5
  resource curse 132, 140
"reversal of fortunes": former colonies 11,
  13, 114, 116
Ricardo, D. 179
Richardson, G. 54
Richerson, P.J. and Boyd, R. 66
Roman Climatic Optimum 25–6
Roman Empire 103, 109
  elites 69, 105, 224
  and post-Roman invasions 133
  transport infrastructure, impacts of 27–9,
    32, 33
Roman law 46
Rosenthal, J.-L. 43
  and Wong, R.B. 62–3
rubber extraction, Belgian Congo 114, 116
Rubin, J. 72, 75–6, 77–8
ruggedness of terrain 11, 12, 25
  see also mountains
rule of law 39–40, 41, 42, 54, 57, 65, 218
  autocracies vs. democracies 49
  vs. rule by law 45
Russia 61, 84
  Soviet 195–7, 223

Sā'id, Abū-Qāsim 19, 25
Sachs, J.
  and Maloney, P. 21
  and Warner, A. 132
Saito, O. 204
Scheidel, W. 29, 64, 134
science and technology
  China vs. Europe 70–1
  Dutch Republic 147–8
  Republic of Letters 171–4
  Second Industrial Revolution 180–3
  see also technological innovation
Second Industrial Revolution 180–3
serfdom, feudal system and Black Death
  95–6
Shiue, C. 161
  and Keller, W. 133, 213
Singapore see East Asian Tigers
skilled mechanical workers, Britain:
  Industrial Revolution 163–5, 174
slave armies, Middle East 78
slave trades 109–13
  and slave labor 158–60, 191–2
Smith, A. 28–9, 140, 162, 213, 223
Solow, B.L. 158–9, 160
Solow model of economic growth 185–6
South American colonies see Portugal; Spain

South Korea
  and Bolivia 39–40
  and Nigeria 207
  and North Korea 40–1
  see also East Asian Tigers
Southey, R. 179
Soviet Russia 195–7, 223
Spain
  decline of 139–40
  Dutch Revolt 141
  parliaments 56, 59
  Philip II 60
  South American colonies 33, 104, 106,
    107, 114, 118, 138, 140
spinning jenny 165–6, 168
spinning mule 166, 167
Spolaore, E. and Wacziarg, R. 184–5
Stalin, J. 196
Stasavage, D. 59, 62, 63, 135
state finances and war 58–64
state formation
  China 132–3
  paths to 61–2
steam engine 168–70
steamships 188–9
sugar 121–2
  and other luxury goods 108, 158–9
sustained economic growth 6–8, 9, 69, 129,
    138, 149, 179, 223, 224

Taiwan see East Asian Tigers
tariffs, US 193–4
taxes/revenues 57–8, 59–62, 141
  Britain 163
  China, Qing dynasty 213
  European colonies 116–17
  Japan 204–5
technological innovation
  and agriculture 6, 22–4
  climate change mitigation 225
  Industrial Revolution 155, 165–71, 174,
    178–9
  Middle Ages 136–7
  Second Industrial Revolution 180–3
  transportation 30–2
  uneven diffusion of modern economic
    growth and 185–90
  unified growth theory 102
  US 192–3
  war 62, 188
  see also science and technology
Thompson, E.P. 179
Tilly, C. 61–2
transatlantic trade see Atlantic trade
transport infrastructure 27–32, 33, 188–9
  US 31–2, 192–3

trust
  Africa 11, 111
  cultural differences 79–82
  persistence of 82–5

unified growth theory 102, 103
urban and rural effects of war 62–3
urbanization 8, 107
  Black Death, impact of 96
  and industrialization, Britain 156–8
  reversal of fortunes in former
    colonies 13
  Western Eurasia 76–7
US 1, 7, 31–2, 50
  Native Americans 117
  regional subcultures 66–7
  rise of modern economy 190–4, 195

Valencia Caicedo, F. 123–4
van Bavel, B. 43
  and Buringh, E., Dijkman, J. 42–3
van Zanden, J.L. 164
  and Buringh E., Bosker, M. 56, 61
  and Prak, M. 135
Venice 24–5, 62, 136
Voigtländer, N. and Voth, H.-J. 96, 99–100
Voltaire 172, 214
Voth, H.-J. 153
Vries, P. 163, 204–6

wages
  Black Death, impact of 94–5, 96, 97,
    152
  European Marriage Pattern (EMP) 138
  Industrial Revolution, Britain 168–71
  and prices, historical estimation of
    wealth 8–9
  real, and GDP per capita income 177–9,
    203
Wallis, P. 164
war
  and climate 27
  English Civil Wars 144
  and industrial technologies 188
  Napoleonic 178, 188
  and state finances 58–64
  and wages 96
  Wars of the Roses 143
  World War II 19–20, 206, 211
water frame 166, 167, 168
water transport 24–5
  steamships 188–9
Watt, J.: steam engine 169, 170, 179
Weber, M. 71–3, 76, 194
Whatley, W.C. and Gillezeau, R. 111, 113
White, L. 201

William of Orange 141
   and Mary 144–5
Williams, E. 108, 158, 159
Williamson, O. 43
Wong, B. 214
Woodberry, R. 123
Wooten, D. 168
World Bank *199, 202, 207, 208, 212*
World Bank Governance Index (WBGI) 41, *42*

Wrigley, E.A. 34
   and Davies, R.S., Oeppen, J.E., Schofield,
     R.S. *98*
   and Schofield, R.S. *183, 186*
Wright, G. 192
Wright, M. 215

Xi Jinping 219
Xue, M.M. 85–7, 214–15